Answers
TO THE BIGGEST QUESTIONS ABOUT
Sanatan

Amishi Seth is as an author, playwright and screenwriter. With over 50 successful projects under her belt, her work spans across published books, plays, animated series and films. She has contributed to some of India's most beloved children's franchises, including *Chota Bheem* and *Krishna Balram*, while also collaborating with prestigious organizations, such as *The Times of India*, Raell Padamsee's ACE Productions, Birla Edutech and ADAPT (formerly the Spastics Society of India). Additionally, Amishi is the author of three children's books: *The Goofies Go on a Holiday* (2015), *The Goofies Tear Down Their House* (2019) and *The Strawberry Farm* (2019). As a spiritualist, she has also given numerous lectures on Sanatan scriptures and the history of India, and regularly explores these topics on her YouTube channel in a popular series called 'Pep Thoughts'.

Answers
TO THE BIGGEST
QUESTIONS ABOUT
Sanatan

Amishi Seth

RUPA

Published by
Rupa Publications India Pvt. Ltd 2025
161-B/4, Gulmohar House,
Yusuf Sarai Community Centre,
New Delhi 110049

Sales centres:
Bengaluru Chennai
Hyderabad Kolkata Mumbai

Copyright © Amishi Seth 2025

The views and opinions expressed in this book are the author's own and
the facts are as reported by her which have been verified to the
extent possible, and the publishers are not in
any way liable for the same.

All rights reserved.
No part of this publication may be reproduced, transmitted,
or stored in a retrieval system, in any form or by any means,
electronic, mechanical, photocopying, recording or otherwise,
without the prior permission of the publisher.

P-ISBN: 978-93-6156-325-6
E-ISBN: 978-93-6156-740-7

First impression 2025

10 9 8 7 6 5 4 3 2 1

The moral right of the author has been asserted.

Printed in India

This book is sold subject to the condition that it shall not, by way
of trade or otherwise, be lent, resold, hired out, or otherwise circulated,
without the publisher's prior consent, in any form of binding or cover
other than that in which it is published.

For the believer:

*The God we love exists in every speck of Creation.
Therefore, to love God is to love all of Creation.*

For the non-believer:

*We are all connected by the same Cosmic Consciousness that
pervades the universe. Therefore, we cannot hurt or help
another without hurting or helping ourselves.*

Contents

Preface   *xi*

Section I
From the Epics and the Purans

1. Why Did Lord Ram Abandon Mother Sita?   3
2. Why Did the Pandavs Cheat in the Kurukshetra War?   12
3. Ram or Ravan—Who Was the Better Man?   17
4. How Could the All-knowing Lord Shiva Not Recognize His Son?   22
5. Why Did Mother Sita Undergo the Demeaning Agnipariksha?   29
6. What Was Lord Krishna's Ras Leela?   36
7. Was Vibhishan Right in Abandoning His Brother, Ravan?   43
8. Duryodhan or Yudhishthir—Who Was the Real Villain?   49
9. Why Is the Bungling Indra King of the Gods?   66
10. Why Is Dev Rishi Narad So Respected and Adored?   72
11. Was Karn a Victim of the Caste System?   84
12. How Could Hanuman Swallow the Sun?   87
13. Was it Fair for Ahilya to Be Cursed?   92
14. Was it Misogynistic for Draupadi to Have Five Husbands?   96

Section II
From Sanatan Culture

15. Why Does Sanatan Dharm Have So Many Gods and Goddesses? How to Know Which One to Worship? ... 105
16. Why Do Sanatan Gods Behave like Humans? ... 113
17. What Is the Shivling? ... 118
18. How Can Sanatan Dharm Have Gods like Ganesh, Hanuman and Narasimha? ... 123
19. What Was the Status of Women in Ancient Bharat? ... 125
20. What Was the Caste-system in Ancient Bharat? ... 138
21. Why Do Brahmins Seem to Be Given More Importance in Sanatan Dharm? ... 145
22. Does Science Have its Origins in Sanatan Dharm? ... 149
23. What Are Yagyas? ... 190
24. What Do Rituals in Sanatan Dharm Mean? ... 198
25. When God Is Everywhere, Why Should One Visit a Temple? ... 206
26. What Were Prosperity and Society like in Ancient Bharat? ... 209
27. Is God Serious and Punishing or Happy and Fun-loving? ... 216
28. Why Do Sanatanis Fast? ... 220
29. Why Do Sanatani Gods Ride Animals? ... 224
30. If We Are God, Why Do We Not Feel like God? ... 227
31. Why Doesn't Sanatan Dharm Give Ready-made Answers? ... 229

32.	Does Sanatan Dharm Focus on Afterlife?	233
33.	Why Would Hinduism Be Under Attack?	236
34.	Is it Necessary to Wear One's Cultural Symbols?	242
35.	Is Sanatan 'Itihas' History or Fantasy?	249
36.	Why Do Hindus Often Name Their Children after Gods?	256
37.	Did the British Give Bharatiyas the Idea of One India?	260

Section III
Basics

38.	Basic Concepts of Sanatan Dharm	265

Glossary — 280
References — 295
Bibliography — 323

Preface

Nothing, not even that which is written in the Vedas must be accepted unless one is thoroughly convinced of it through logic, debate, discussion or experience.

—Teaching in the various Upanishads

Conceived in the spirit of the Upanishads, *Answers to the Biggest Questions about Sanatan* attempts to address many morally debatable instances in the Ramayan, Mahabharat, Purans, and Sanatan Dharm in general, through logical investigation. While quoting such instances, and other matters of philosophical and spiritual interest, I have referred to authentic translations in English and Hindi of the following scriptures originally written in Sanskrit—Maharishi Valmiki's Ramayan, Krishna Dvaipayan Ved Vyas's Mahabharat, the Purans and Upanishads, among others.

At times, Sanatan/Hinduism is considered a regressive blend of magic and wars. Therefore, the idea behind writing this book was to make people, particularly the youth, appreciate the sophistication of intellectual, scientific, social and spiritual thought in ancient Bharat.

Multiple invaders and colonizers robbed Bharat of its true identity and transformed Bharatiyas into mere 'apers' of the West. Philosophical, religious and scientific treatises written in Sanskrit were gradually wiped out from the collective consciousness of mainstream Bharatiya society. Sanatan *itihas*, the practical and profound Sanatan culture, and its scientific and spiritual contributions to the world were obfuscated. Since Bharatiyas were no longer aware of what their ancestors had accomplished, they no longer took pride in their nation and what it once stood for.

'Mythology' was a convenient term used by the colonizers, particularly the British, to dismantle the cultural construct of their colonies and divest the colonized of the pride that they once took in their own *sanskriti*. This was done to manipulate the masses into physical and intellectual slavery.

When the Turko-Afghan invader Bakhtiyar Khilji burnt down the library at Nalanda, over nine million books across 108 subjects were destroyed—such was the breadth of knowledge and wisdom of the ancient Bharatiyas. Archaeological surveys reveal that students across Asia learnt Sanskrit to prepare for entrance exams to universities like Nalanda, Takshashila, Vikramashila, Odantapura, Pushpagiri and Sharada Peeth, to name a few. The advances made by scholars in ancient India in science, technology, psychology, philosophy, economics and the life sciences were remarkable even by today's standards. Some of these achievements have been discussed in this book.

The intention is not to convert or influence anyone but only to enlighten the reader about Sanatan. Every chapter, based on historical fact and not written from the lens of a follower of the faith, addresses a controversy/question, and is complete in itself. Hence, the reader may begin with any chapter. However, all the chapters offer deep insights into the themes of Sanatan. Therefore, reading the entire book will help the reader gain an in-depth understanding of Sanatan as a logical, rational mega-concept.

Sanatan is neither glorification of the victorious, nor is it biased or dogmatic. For instance, while the Ramayan mentions the atrocities committed by Ravan, it does not shy away from describing Ravan as a great scholar and devotee of Lord Shiva. So, while on the one hand, devotees burn effigies of Ravan during Dusshera, they also sing the 'Shiv Tandav Stotram' composed by him in praise of Lord Shiva.

Preface

In this book, the word 'India' has been largely replaced by the word 'Bharat'. This is because before the arrival of the invaders, Bharatvarsha existed for millennia as one of the most advanced civilizations of the world. The word 'Bharatvarsha' is still used before any *anushthan*—a practice that began in ancient Bharat—to identify the address and family of the *yajman*.

Hinduism Is about Dharm; It Is Not a Religion

Hinduism is not a religion. When the original name for the Hindu way of life—Sanatan Dharm—was in use, Hinduism was *a way of life*; it was not a 'religion'. In Sanskrit, the word 'Dharm' means 'the right action' or 'the right way of living'—one that creates joy and fulfilment for an individual, his/her family, country and the world, irrespective of his/her professional and personal role in society. Therefore, the word 'Dharm' is devoid of any religious connotation.

The events in the Ramayan, Mahabharat and the Purans are dramatic and entertaining. No wonder then, that these have been adapted so often as novels, plays, films and on television. However, this book is not about dramatic narratives but about logical discussions on the issues covered.

As an author, novelist, playwright, screenwriter and director, I am aware that a dramatic adaptation of any work necessitates some creative license to make the material entertaining and cost-effective. Over time, the cumulative effect of such creative licenses ends up diluting or distorting the original narrative.

Consider this: Duryodhan insisted on the game of dice because he was deeply hurt and insulted when Draupadi mocked him for being a blind man's son when he tripped and fell in the Palace of Illusions. This made Duryodhan want to avenge himself. However, the Ved Vyas Mahabharat clearly states that when Duryodhan fell in the Palace of Illusions, Draupadi had done nothing offending. Duryodhan himself admitted to Dhritarashtra that he was jealous of the Pandavs' wealth and wanted to snatch it from them. For Duryodhan, the humiliating experience of his tour of the Palace of Illusions was only an agonizing reminder of the extraordinary wealth that the Pandavs had and that he did not. Hence, the game of dice had nothing to do with honour or Draupadi; it was a nefarious plot to usurp the wealth of the Pandavs.

The reader will find many such popular myths busted in this book.

The events mentioned in this book are in no particular order—the idea is not to present the epics chronologically, but rather to analyse the controversies generated by particular events in the Ramayan, Mahabharat and the Purans.

I have spelled the names of prominent figures, terminologies, etc. the way they are meant to be pronounced. Thus, the reader will find that 'Pandavas' is written as Pandavs, 'Karna' as Karn, 'Rama' as Ram, etc.

Finally, Sanatan is an ocean of wisdom and knowledge. It is impossible for a single individual to understand it, let alone express it in its totality. Therefore, to write this book, I sought refuge in the basic tenets and philosophy of Sanatan which are simple and all-encompassing, and which have kept it alive as one of the most vibrant, scientific and progressive cultures in the world. I hope that the reader will find the analyses in this book convincing and worth emulating in the affairs of contemporary life: Sanatan is not only practical and relevant but necessary in these times for world peace and prosperity.

I surrender this book to the formless Brahman, the Universal Consciousness that pervades the entire cosmos. May the Supreme Divine Consciousness reside in this material and in its reader as Truth, Love and Understanding.

Jai Bharat
Jai Shri Ram
Aum Namah Shivaya

SECTION I

FROM THE EPICS AND THE PURANS

1

Why Did Lord Ram Abandon Mother Sita?

Leave Sita at Valmiki's ashram.

For all the ideals that the Ramayan has epitomized for humanity since eons past, one incident in the epic continues to anger generations—Mother Sita, the pregnant queen, having to leave Ayodhya for the forest. Many say that the 'Uttar Ramayan' is not even a part of the original Valmiki Ramayan. But the 'Uttar Ramayan' was indeed written by Valmiki, who mentioned this incident in the 'Bal Kand' of the Valmiki Ramayan.[1]

The question most frequently asked is, how could the 'ideal king' Ram be so unjust to a woman who He knew to be innocent? By allowing Mother Sita to leave Ayodhya, didn't Lord Ram pave the way for further degradation of women? In the name of protecting Dharm, didn't both Ram and Sita actually end up promoting Adharm? Shouldn't they have done something to rid their society of bigoted ideals instead of succumbing to them?

Such a question, while valid, merits a deeper analysis of the situation. If one considers the following aspects of the Ramayan, one will appreciate that painful and unfair as it was, Sita's relegation to the forest was perhaps the best way in which the matter could have been resolved to uphold Dharm, the welfare of society, and to compel the subjects to reflect on their attitude towards women. Hopefully, by the end of this chapter, the reader will be convinced.

Treta Yug

At the time of the Ramayan, societal norms were different from what they are today. Under similar circumstances today, neither would anyone object to Sita being the queen of Ayodhya, nor would the ideal couple Ram and Sita have taken such a drastic decision. This is because, today, i.e. in 'Kali Yug' (also 'Kalyug'), abduction of women, unfairness, corruption, moral bankruptcy are so commonplace that they hardly provoke outrage. The moral and ethical standards of the 'Treta Yug' were far higher than those of Kali Yug. In Sanatan scriptures, this difference is called *yug dharm*—standards of ethics and morality change according to the *yug* or epoch.

Background

There were whispers in the entire kingdom questioning Mother Sita's chastity because She had spent 10 months in another man's home.[2] But it was not just Sita who was being judged here. People even thought of Lord Ram as a weak king smitten by a woman who was no longer fit to be their queen.[3] They were worried that their king and queen leading an amoral life would set a terrible precedent in society, endangering the dignity of all families in the kingdom.[4]

When Lord Ram found out about the demeaning opinions that the subjects had about Mother Sita, He could not bring Himself to even tell Mother Sita about it. The man who had walked away from His impending coronation to live like a nomad for 14 years in the forest with a smile[5] was consumed by grief.[6] But then, sending Sita away seemed the only way to resolve the issue.

Alternatives

Lord Ram and Mother Sita could have ignored what people said or thought about them.

In the Treta Yug, administration and monarchy were based on the principle of duty. This duty was called *rajdharm*. It stipulated that from the moment the king and queen donned the crown, they had no dreams, happiness, joys, sorrows, or ambitions of their own. Their lives would now be dedicated only to *rajdharm*, the most important aspect of which was to be *ideals of the highest moral standards* in society. This duty was uncompromisable because the way they were *perceived* in terms of their morality would have a direct impact on the moral and ethical fabric of their kingdom.

When leaders appear to falter, their followers falter too. When the young in the family think that the head of the family is unreliable, they accept no accountability for their own actions; when subordinates know that their boss accepts bribes, they give themselves the license to be corrupt; when the polity realizes that politicians have no integrity, it allows itself to compromise on ethics. If immorality is perceived to percolate from the top, it spreads like a virus across all strata of society. Therefore, not only must leaders *be* ethical, they must be *perceived* as ethical too. Also, when a king or queen's credibility is in question, there is general distrust of their decisions and actions. In such circumstances, the kingdom runs the risk of plunging into disarray. As Lord Ram told His brothers, He would have sacrificed His own life, or even the lives of His brothers, to honour the will of His people.[7]

Mother Sita was chaste and innocent but many in the kingdom did not think so; that was enough to taint the image of the royal family, and by extension, of society in general.

That the royal couple did not appear to embody the ethical and spiritual standards expected of them was not acceptable to the people of Ayodhya. *Rajdharm* required that the king and queen respect their view. Think of this as a democracy within monarchy and people's opinion as their mandate. Therefore, Lord Ram and Mother Sita could *not* have ignored what their subjects thought of them without breaking their vow to fulfil their *rajdharm* at all times.

People could have been educated on what had actually transpired with Ravan and in Lanka.

Imagine initiating a mass gathering or a national interview with the king and queen to discuss the chastity of the queen, or having officers of the kingdom converse with the subjects to discuss the queen's chastity! Most would agree that this would have been demeaning not only for the royal family, but for the queen herself and for the image of the kingdom.

Also, nowhere does the Valmiki Ramayan state that any subject of Ayodhya had openly confronted the royal family with their misgivings. Had any of the subjects gone to the court, there could have been scope for clarification. But without an open discussion on what exactly happened during the 14 years of exile, a perception once created in the minds of the people, even if wrong, could not be erased.

Lord Ram could have left with Mother Sita, thus ensuring that She did not have to face the injustice alone.

Doing this would have further strengthened people's opinion that Lord Ram was a weak man who had placed His wife above His kingdom and His subjects in violation of His pledge to follow *rajdharm*. If the king violated His own pledge, what integrity could be expected from His officers and subjects? Also, Ram leaving with Sita would have done little to alter people's mistaken perception of Her.

The decision was unjust not only for Mother Sita but for Lord Ram as well, for He too was compelled to give up His beloved wife and the possibility of a happy family life.

Mother Sita could have undergone another agnipariksha and the people would have got proof of Her chastity.

Anyone reading this would be mortified even at the thought of this alternative. Could anything have been more demeaning for Her?

Hence Mother Sita leaving alone for the forest was the only dignified way in which the situation could be tackled. She left the palace in the middle of the night, with none of the subjects around to see Her leave or stop Her so that no one could doubt Her determination.[8]

Aftermath

Lord Ram stayed back in Ayodhya and followed *rajdharm*, dedicating His life to the welfare of His subjects, winning their love, trust and adoration. But even as He followed His *rajdharm*, He did not flinch from supporting His wife before His subjects.

Even though Lord Ram had no heir, He did not get married again.[9] When the *ashwamedh yagya*, one of the most sanctified practices of the Vedic Age, was organized in Ayodhya, Ram had a life-size statue of Sita sculpted in gold to be placed beside Him as He performed the sacred rites of the *yagya* in glaring view of His subjects.[10] In doing so, Ram sent a clear message to His people—as king, He had respected their wish; as a man and a husband, He believed in and loved His wife; to Him, only Sita deserved to be the rightful queen of Ayodhya.

The credibility that Lord Ram earned with His establishment of what is hailed even today as Ram Rajya (also Ramrajya)—the ideal form of governance—made people understand that if such a Dharmic king and His family held Mother Sita in such high regard, She must have been chaste and innocent.

By that time, Maharishi Valmiki had sent Luv and Kush to go around Ayodhya and sing to Her people the story of the Ramayan.[11] When people heard of all that had transpired during the 14 years of exile, they realized the terrible sacrifice their beloved king and queen had to make because of their narrow-mindedness.[12]

That Lord Ram and Mother Sita chose to not explain and made such a supreme sacrifice for the sake of their subjects only added to their god-like stature. By remaining silent, Ram and Sita put an end to all debate. They made people realize their folly on their own. Realization took time, but when it dawned, it stayed.

Why Did Mother Sita Choose to Leave Ayodhya?

After Luv and Kush's recital of the Ramayan, Lord Ram and the people of Ayodhya realized that Luv and Kush were Ram and Sita's sons.[13] Hence, Sita was asked to take an oath of chastity one last time.[14] She did not protest. She simply took the oath saying, 'If I have been loyal to my husband, may Mother Earth, my mother, accept me back.'[15] Immediately the ground split open and a throne appeared.[16] Bhu Devi (Mother Earth) was seated on the throne and She took Sita with Her into the netherworld.[17] This was Sita's silent assertion.[18] Why She did this can be answered with the following question: *Should a woman, or any person for that matter, allow themselves to be treated like an object that can be discarded just because people don't like it anymore, and be brought back just because people decide it should not have been discarded in the first place?*

Mother Sita was the queen, an example to all of womankind. If She accepted such fickle and disrespectful treatment as the queen, what hope would the ordinary women of Her kingdom have had for a life of dignity? Her decision to go back to Her mother—in defiance of Her husband, Her sons and Her people—left an indelible impression on the collective consciousness of the people of Bharat.

That Lord Ram and Mother Sita have been the subject of love and devotion throughout Bharat and that we still question the injustice they both had to endure, is proof that the people of Ayodhya, and by extension, the people of Bharat have accepted and corrected their mistakes. What else explains the fact that the people of the very land that once misjudged Mother Sita understand and revere Draupadi who chose to have five husbands and was almost disrobed in the court of Hastinapur (See also, Chapter 14: 'Was it Misogyny for Draupadi to Have Five Husbands?')?

By sacrificing their personal happiness, Lord Ram and Mother Sita restored open-mindedness, honour and dignity for all women for all time to come.

Mother Sita and Feminism

Mother Sita never gave in to what She thought was wrong. When Lord Ram asked Her to stay back in Ayodhya while He went into exile for 14 years, She asserted Her right, duty and desire to accompany Him.[19] When He tried to instruct Her about looking after His parents and maintaining cordial ties with Bharat, She became indignant and brushed aside His advice, saying, 'My parents have taught me my duties, I do not need those instructions from you.'[20] When Ram tried to scare Her by citing the many dangers in the forest to dissuade Her from accompanying Him,[21] She even taunted Him, saying, 'Did my father perceive in you a man or a woman?'

During their exile, when Lord Ram agreed to protect the *rishi*s from the *rakshasa*s,[22] Mother Sita debated with Him about the ethics of His stand. Her perspective was that by killing demons who had caused them no direct harm, the Dharmic warrior in Ram was in danger of getting corrupted through compulsive killing.[23] Ram convinced Her that even though they were living like *sanyasi*s, He was still a Kshatriya and could not deny protection to those who sought it from Him. Once convinced, Sita supported Him wholeheartedly.[24]

When Lord Ram ordered Lakshman to not leave Mother Sita's side in the forest, She ensured that Lakshman came to Lord Ram's rescue when She thought that the latter was in trouble as He went after the Golden Deer. Of course, all of this was a well-orchestrated drama by Lord Vishnu and Goddess Lakshmi[25] (See also, Chapter 5: 'Why Did Mother Sita Undergo the Demeaning Agnipariksha?').

When Hanuman asked Mother Sita to accompany Him back to Lord Ram, She refused, choosing to stay back in Lanka, because annihilating Ravan and his army was a matter of duty and honour for Lord Ram.[26]

When Lord Ram spoke offensively to Mother Sita after defeating Ravan, She did not spare Him and ordered Lakshman to build a pyre for Her. The *agnipravesh* was Her decision.

When Lakshman told Mother Sita of Lord Ram's decision to abandon Her, She accepted it for She understood Lord Ram's reasons.[27] She brought up Her sons as a single mother and later, in interest of Her self-respect and Her rights as a woman, She gave up Lord Ram and the kingdom after handing Her sons over to Him.

Mother Sita was strong, independent and assertive. She lived like an equal partner and was perfectly capable of handling the tough, rustic life of the forest and the ordeal at Lanka.

2

Why Did the Pandavs Cheat in the Kurukshetra War?

But Keshav! This is against the rules of War!

Arjun, this is to protect Dharm.

In the Kurukshetra War, the Kauravs killed only one warrior of the Pandav forces—Arjun's son, Abhimanyu—by violating the rules of war. The Pandavs on the other hand killed every commander of the Kaurav forces through deceit, be it Bheeshm, Dronacharya, Karn, or Duryodhan himself. But why?

When the Pandavs were 'good' and followed Dharm, they had to suffer untold miseries, but when they resorted to Adharm, they won the war. Thus, it may be concluded that success cannot be attained through fair means alone. The war itself, a *dharmyuddh*—a war between right and wrong, good and evil—needed the so-called 'good side' to resort to Adharm at times for Dharm to finally win—a paradox inherent to Dharm.

The war, by extension the universe, made no distinction in the suffering it doled out to both sides. None of the Pandavs' sons survived the war. Parikshit, Arjun's grandson, too was brought back to life by Lord Krishna after being murdered in his mother's womb. Millions of warriors were slain and even the good side suffered unimaginable grief and misery. And all this destruction took place in the name of Dharm, which is supposed to create happiness and joy for all? Even the presence of Krishna, Lord of the Universe, on the Pandavs' side could not spare them intense sorrow.

So, what is the point in being on the side of Dharm? Are these stories just feeble attempts to induce a semblance of solace and propriety into life which is otherwise a mélange of random, often chaotic events designed to make people suffer?

No doubt, such questions are valid but their resolution requires us to define good and evil; Dharm and Adharm. There are different levels of Dharm and Adharm. These concepts do not exist as stand-alone rules of life but rather as 'what is best' in the situation. The 'greater good' or the 'great evil' is one that impacts society as a whole. Good and evil are not so much about the 'action', but rather about the 'intention' behind the action.

The Kurukshetra War was not about the Pandavs fulfilling their personal ambition of becoming the rulers of their rightful kingdom of Hastinapur. It was about defeating forces that could attempt to disrobe a woman in the very court that was built as a temple of justice for all. This was a war against the forces of corruption and selfish ambition (See also, Chapter 8: 'Duryodhan or Yudhishthir—Who Was the Real Villain?').

A layman insulting a woman was a punishable act. But a prince, a king, a Kshatriya doing so was unpardonable. A prince, a king or an officer of the administration was duty-bound to protect the rights and dignity of everyone in the kingdom. They also had the power, strength and resources to impact the entire society. That they would use the same resources to promote Adharm was a curse to society. Hence, they had to be stopped—and destroyed—if need be. Their very conduct would set a terrible example for their subjects and plunge society into chaos.

Some interpretations of the Mahabharat suggest that Duryodhan was a good king. But how could a man who could use a pathetic ruse like gambling to change the imperial construct of the entire country, who could attempt to have his own sister-in-law disrobed in court, who was so consumed with jealousy and anger that he would stop at nothing to fulfil his personal ambition, ever be a good ruler? Such a ruler would be a living licence to his officers and subjects to be selfish, arrogant, corrupt and debased. He, and every force that supported him, had to be destroyed.

Yudhishthir too had to be held accountable. With his weakness for gambling, he was the one who had wagered his brothers and his wife. His brothers too could have chosen to disobey him and protect their wife, but they did not. Ordinarily, the Pandavs would not have deserved any sympathy but for the fact that before the Kurukshetra War, they had already spent 13 years in exile. Had they wanted, they could have avoided this as their allies were seething and hungry for war. The Pandavs had repeatedly sought forgiveness from Draupadi and had vowed to never allow a repeat of such circumstances. Hence, though they could never be absolved of the crime they had already committed, they were better placed to ensure that the women in their kingdom were protected and that no woman would ever have to undergo an ordeal like Draupadi's (See Chapter 8).

Duryodhan on the other hand, had no remorse about what he had done. He had led a life of luxury and power while the Pandavs punished themselves through their exile.

In spite of his personal weakness for gambling, Yudhishthir had genuinely accepted the invitation for a *game*. However, for Duryodhan this was not a game, it was *war*.

Left to themselves, the Pandavs would have never cheated in the war. But the Kauravs came to the battlefield with unfair advantages. Bheeshm had the boon of picking the time of his death which he could use to fight the forces of corruption and degradation. Instead, he chose to strengthen these. There were no 'fair' means to defeat him.[1] Karn could have used his prowess to help the cause of Dharm, but he did not. He had to be stopped[2] (See also, Chapter 11: 'Was Karn a Victim of the Caste System?'). Dronacharya was the *guru* to the princes, and hence the *guru* to the entire kingdom. He could have behaved like a torchbearer of Dharm rather than a loyal servant to an unfair, weak king. Duryodhan could not be killed unless, as cursed by Rishi Maitreyi, the same thigh that he had beaten to insult the great *rishi* would be broken and cause his death in war.[3] Therefore, to kill Duryodhan, breaking his thigh was essential or else, paradoxical as it may seem, the curse would have made Duryodhan invincible.

On a deeper analysis of the Mahabharat, one would see that Bheeshm, Dronacharya, and Karn were more to blame than even Duryodhan because they *knew* they were supporting evil and did not stop doing so even at the cost of the greater collective good. Duryodhan openly declared that he hated the Pandavs. Bheeshm, Dronacharya and Karn supported the Pandavs inwardly, yet feigned loyalty to Duryodhan. Not only did they use their powers to promote evil, given their status and rank in society, they also violated the pledge of their duties. The Pandavs, on the other hand, fought a collective battle on behalf of society as a whole, setting aside their personal prejudices and morality to reestablish Dharm in society.

An instance from the Kurukshetra War depicts how Lord Krishna upheld the higher purpose of this war as more important than the limited ideals of individual ethics.

Lord Krishna had taken a vow to not lift a weapon in the war, but Arjun's lack of will forced Krishna to do so. After receiving the sermon of the Bhagvad Gita, though Arjun agreed to fight, he could not bring himself to kill Bheeshm. Krishna sensed his hesitation and was outraged. He reminded Arjun that Bheeshm was fighting to protect Adharm.

He threatened Arjun that if he was not willing to fulfil his duty as a warrior, then Krishna Himself would kill Bheeshm. An infuriated Krishna then brought forth His deadly 'Sudarshan Chakra', leapt off the chariot and charged at Bheeshm with it. An ashamed and petrified Arjun rushed to Krishna, fell at His feet and begged Him not to break His vow of not wielding a weapon; he promised Krishna that he would now fight with total detachment and a sense of duty.[4] Later, Arjun defeated the mighty Bheeshm. Krishna proved through personal example that the protection of Dharm for societal good was a goal far higher than personal integrity.

The Kurukshetra War can be summed up thus—it is easy to follow the 'right' when there is no risk of personal pain or sacrifice. However, this is just a disguised form of selfishness, because the moment one perceives a personal risk, one would either shy away from taking a stand or follow Adharm blatantly. The Pandavs had to suffer the loss of their sons—a risk they were aware of well before the war. Yet, they chose to fight because their duty as Kshatriyas and warriors to fight the forces of evil was far more important than their personal and familial happiness. Imagine the millions who would have benefitted from their Dharmic rule, ensuring security, prosperity, dignity and honesty for all? That alone was worth the price of the Kurukshetra War.

3

Ram or Ravan—Who Was the Better Man?

> *...when I ventured to bring Sita as your wife...*
> *that cruel Lakshman disfigured me.*

Lately, an attempt has been made to interpret the Ramayan from Ravan's perspective: Ravan's actions were justified as avenging his sister Surpanakha's humiliation. Another argument advanced is that Ravan's sense of virtue did not allow him to violate Sita despite having her in his custody. If only one had read the Valmiki Ramayan, there would be no doubt about what a demon Ravan truly was (See also, Chapter 1: 'Why Did Lord Ram Abandon Mother Sita?').

Ravan and His Exploits

Mother Sita was not the first woman whom Ravan had abducted. She was, however, the last.[1] A known rapist and molester,[2] Ravan had a harem of 1,000 wives and more women in his gynaeceum.[3] He had kidnapped, violated and raped the wives, mothers and daughters of *rishi*s,[4] *rakshasa*s, *gandharv*s, *dev*s, *siddha*s and *kinnar*s, among others, by the hundreds, including Rambha, an *apsara* and the daughter-in-law of his half-brother, Kuber.[5] Once, when he raped an *apsara* called Punjikasthala, she went to Lord Brahma seeking justice.[6] At the time, Brahma could not kill Ravan because of a boon—that Ravan could not be killed by a being other than human. So Brahma cursed Ravan—if he ever violated a woman again, his head would explode into a thousand pieces. It was because of this curse that Ravan did not dare to force himself on Mother Sita.[7]

Such was the depravity of the *rakshas* clan that in the court, Mahaparsva, Ravan's minister, advised him to violate Mother Sita repeatedly.[8] However, after praising the minister for his advice, Ravan cited Brahma's curse to explain why he could not do so.[9]

Blinded by his thirst for power and control over all three worlds,[10] the 'great, avenging brother' Ravan had murdered Surpanakha's husband Vidyutjihv, son of the chief Kalaka, of the Kalaka Danav race.

The Valmiki Ramayan clearly states the atrocious and offensive things that Ravan said to Mother Sita when he abducted Her and while She was in his custody in Lanka.[11] Lewd language is a form of sexual abuse, not to mention the dubious strategies he adopted to trick Sita into accepting him. These ploys included presenting the fake head of Lord Ram to Her, making false announcements of Lord Ram and Lakshman's deaths, getting ogresses to brainwash and threaten Sita into accepting Ravan, and subjecting Her to other torturous illusions.[12]

Although Ravan had a huge kingdom, his focus on perverted activities and carnal gratification was slowly eating away at the administrative systems of his kingdom, making these weak and inefficient.[13] His employees were underpaid and he had no idea what was happening in his kingdom; all he wanted around him were women and ministers who flattered him.[14]

Ravan had unleashed untold atrocities on the peace-loving *rishi*s. He would desecrate their *havan*s, rape their women, and murder them and their families.[15] To put an end to their sufferings, the *rishi*s beseeched Lord Vishnu to incarnate

Himself as an ordinary mortal and kill him[16]. Vishnu had to incarnate as an ordinary mortal because Ravan had a boon that no *devata, gandharv, asur, rakshas, nag, kinnar* or ghost could kill him.[17] Ordinary humans were excluded from the boon because Ravan considered them too insignificant to pose any threat to him.

Surpanakha's Encounter with Lord Ram and Lakshman

Surpanakha was gallivanting in the forest when she first caught a glimpse of Lord Ram in his hut.[18] The moment she laid eyes on him, she was consumed with lust. She approached Him, asking Him to leave Mother Sita and marry her instead and lead a life of eternal pleasure with her.[19] That Surpanakha was motivated by lust and not love becomes obvious because when Ram turned down her proposition and directed her instead to approach Lakshman—who was just as handsome—she immediately went after the latter with the same proposition.[20]

While making such an offer is not unethical if it is based on mutual consent, in this instance, there was no consent either from Lord Ram or Lakshman. Lord Ram clearly told her of His loyalty towards Mother Sita,[21] and Lakshman told her of his vow to be in constant service of his brother and sister-in-law.[22] However, despite such unequivocal refusal from both brothers, Surpanakha did not stand down. Instead, she announced her intention to devour Sita and even attacked Her, as Sita was the reason the brothers had had the *audacity to reject her*.[23] Needless to say, there was not an iota of maturity in Surpanakha's conduct.

When she attacked Mother Sita, what were Lord Ram and Lakshman supposed to do? Let her kill Sita because Surpanakha was a woman? Or were they supposed to protect Sita? Therefore, outraged at Surpanakha's impudence, Lakshman chopped off her ears and nose on Ram's command. Thus, it was Surpanakha's immaturity and lust that set off a tragic chain of events.[24]

Surpanakha's Lie to Ravan

An injured Surpanakha told Ravan that in all three worlds, she had never seen a woman as beautiful as Sita and that it was *when she went to bring Sita for Ravan that Lakshman chopped off her nose and ears*.[25] She made no mention of her advances towards Lord Ram and Lakshman. Surpanakha and Akampana, one of Ravan's spies, described Sita's physical beauty to him in great detail, stating that such a gorgeous woman belonged only in Ravan's harem, and encouraged him to abduct Her and make Her his wife. Subsequently, Ravan decided to abduct Her as he had abducted hundreds of other women.[26] Clearly, Ravan did not steal Sita to avenge the supposed 'injustice' done to his sister; he kidnapped Her to feed his lust.[27] And can a man who steals another man's wife—even for *supposed* revenge—ever be an honorable, respectable being?

Honesty of Narratives

The Ramayan mentions in no uncertain terms that Ravan was a scholar in all the arts. He knew all the four Vedas and perhaps no one in the world was as knowledgeable or accomplished as him. But even Lord Shiva—whom Ravan was devoted to—had warned him while gifting him his sword called 'Chandrahas' that the weapon would protect him only as long as he tread the path of Dharm.[28]

As mentioned earlier, Sanatanis respect Ravan's scholarship

and chant the 'Shiv Tandav Stotram' composed by him in praise of Lord Shiva.[29] But Sanatanis also burn his effigy on Dussehra to signify that no amount of scholarship, learning and wealth can supplant Dharm, and a pervert like Ravan deserved to be destroyed.

4

How Could the All-knowing Lord Shiva Not Recognize His Son?

Bring my son back to life... Now!

Lord Ganesh is perhaps the most adored of all Sanatan gods. His delightful form makes Him cute and huggable while giving Him an undeniable aura of power, intelligence, compassion and wisdom. The story of how Ganesh got this form, however, has confounded generations of Bharatiyas.

Narratives and Time Cycles

According to the Brahma Vaivart Puran and the Shiva Puran, Lord Ganesh lost His original 'human' head because Shani cast His cursed glance on Him, and it was Lord Vishnu who put the elephant head on Ganesh. However, the elephant too was brought back to life by Vishnu at the same time.[1]

In another version, mentioned in both the Shiva Puran and the Ganesh Puran, Lord Shiva is the one who severed the boy's head. These versions are not contradictory; Lord Brahma tells Narad Muni in the Shiva Puran that these episodes are from different time cycles.[2]

Sanatan scriptures elaborate on the cyclical nature of time. The second-highest unit of such a cycle is the *kalpa*, which is 4.32 billion years. The four *yug*s keep repeating themselves throughout the *kalpa* a thousand times over (See also, Chapter 22: 'Does Science Have Its Origins in Sanatan?').

All major events of the universe keep repeating themselves in each *kalpa*, with minor variations based on how events pan out and what lesson is required in a particular *yug* of a particular *kalpa*. For instance, Rishi Markandeya—who was blessed with immortality by Lord Shiva—has witnessed the creation and dissolution of the cosmos 16 times.[3] The immortal Kakabhushundi has already seen the Ramayan recur 11 times.

The episode of Lord Shiva severing Lord Ganesh's head is from the present *kalpa*—Svetvaraha—that we live in. The Matsya Puran and Kurma Puran list the names of 30 *kalpas*.

What Happened in the Current Svet Kalpa?

The episode is not as simple as Lord Shiva being stopped by Vinayak while Parvati was bathing, and an enraged Shiva beheading the boy, unaware that He was His own son. The actual episode was more complicated.

The Shiva Puran and Ganesh Puran mention that Goddess Parvati had two friends, Jaya and Vijaya, who advised Her to create a *gan* (also called *ganas*, *gans* were Shiva's attendants and devotees who lived in Mount Kailash with Him and His family). Later, Vinayak also came to be called 'Ganapati', head of the *gans*, who would exclusively obey Her, as all the other *gans* gave precedence to Shiva's orders.[4] Once, in spite of Her having instructed Nandi to not allow anyone in, Shiva had entered Her chambers while a helpless Nandi stood guard at the gate. It was then that Parvati decided to create Her own *gan*.[5] She sculpted a form from the scrubs of Her body and infused it with life. She blessed the boy with many boons, and giving Him a staff, instructed Him to keep watch.

Later, Lord Shiva arrived and Vinayak stopped Him at the entrance of His own house.[6] Shiva told the boy who He was, that the house the boy was guarding belonged to Him and that He was Parvati's husband. However, even as Shiva was explaining, Ganesh attacked Him with His staff. Shiva got angry and tried to reason with the boy again, but Ganesh struck Him again.[7] Though enraged, Shiva remained outside the house and sent His *gan*s to enquire about the boy.[8] But instead of merely enquiring, the *gan*s, arrogant because of the importance they regularly received from Shiva, ended up threatening Vinayak with dire consequences if He did not make way for Shiva.[9] While the *gan*s were pompous, Ganesh was no less haughty about the boons bestowed on Him by His mother and threatened the *gan*s.[10] The *gan*s then went back to Shiva who incited them to fight as He did not want to be laughed at for being denied entry into His own house by His own wife.[11] The *gan*s rallied around and a war ensued with Ganesh on one side and crores of *gan*s on the other. Even the *dev*s arrived there.[12] Shiva sent Brahma to Ganesh to try and reason with the boy and stop the war.[13] But the moment He saw Brahma, Ganesh launched an attack on Him too, ignoring His call for a truce.[14] The *dev*s jumped into the fray but none was any match for Ganesh, as He was protected by the Adi Shakti—the source of all power and energy in the universe.[15] The *gan*s and *dev*s started running helter-skelter in fright. Many prayed to Shiva to protect them. Since Shiva and Vishnu could not deny protection to those seeking it, they had no option but to arrive there and fight Ganesh even if it meant Shiva fighting His own son. *Apsara*s and *rishi*s gathered there to witness this mega-war, the likes of which they had never seen before.[16]

Meanwhile, Goddess Parvati felt that asking Ganesha to stand down would be insulting to Her, as by attacking Ganesh, the *gan*s were really attack Her since Ganesh was Her creation.[17] She and Her friends were also extremely annoyed at the impatience of the *gan*s. 'Couldn't they have waited for just a few more minutes?' She, therefore, sent help to Ganesh in the form of two of Her *shakti*s.[18] Even Lord Vishnu and Lord Shiva were no match for them and were repeatedly defeated.[19] Finally, as Vishnu distracted Ganesh, Shiva used His *trishul* and decapitated the boy.[20] Shiva was aggrieved at losing His son but when Parvati learnt of this, She was furious and sent forth billions of her *shakti*s to devour the universe.[21] Out of desperation, the *rishi*s went to pacify Her, placating Her with their prayers for succour.[22] Finally, Parvati calmed down and commanded them, 'The only way to restore order in the universe is to bring Ganesh back to life.'[23] To do that, Shiva send the *dev*s to the north, asking them to bring back the head of the first creature they saw.[24] The creature they saw was an elephant,[25] whose head was then duly placed on Ganesh's body and thus Shiva brought Ganesh back to life.[26]

Clash of Egos

What sense does the above episode make? How could the great Lord Shiva, Parvati and Ganapati be a party to it? If we analyse the above episode, we realize that this entire drama was nothing but a clash of egos.[27] Shiva was so egoistic that He cared more about His reputation than a simple wish of His wife. Parvati was so conceited that She did nothing to stop the war between the *gans*—who were also *Her* loyal devotees—and Ganesh just because She wanted to have the upper hand. The *gans* and *dev*s too were haughty about their powers while Ganesh was supercilious about the powers given by His mother.

Isn't this exactly how things happen in our daily lives? Insignificant events often spiral out of control, ruining our lives and those of our loved ones only because of our unrelenting egos. This episode is a classic example that regardless of who one is, those who are arrogant meet with the only end reserved for them—humiliation and eventual destruction.

In this episode, Lord Shiva was defeated in the battle and had to resort to distracting Ganesh to win over Him. Goddess Parvati lost Her son. The *dev*s and *gan*s were routed by a mere boy. Ganesh lost His head (for the Divine, life and death are not as significant as they are for humans because the Divine is the very source of both).

This battle could have been avoided if Lord Shiva had been more patient; Goddess Parvati had ended the fight and explained Her reasons for creating Ganesh to Shiva; the *gan*s and *dev*s had shown more respect to Parvati and not fought with Her son; Ganesh had simply prayed to Shiva about His need to obey His mother instead of challenging the *gan*s to a fight and attacking Shiva, Brahma and Vishnu.

The matter was resolved only when everyone gave up their egos and arrived at a compromise *after* the realization of their mistakes and taking into account the sensitivities of the others involved. Lord Shiva lovingly made this *gan* created by His wife, 'The Chief of all His *Gan*s' hence the name Ganapati.[28] Parvati happily accepted Her son even though He no longer looked the same as She had created Him—He now had an elephant head.[29] The *gan*s and *dev*s respectfully and happily accepted Lord Ganesh—their enemy till a few moments ago—as their chief.[30] Ganesh reverentially apologized to everyone for His arrogance.[31]

Arrogance breeds unnecessary and completely avoidable chaos, discord and destruction. An inflated ego is the greatest obstacle to happiness, growth and fulfilment, both in material and spiritual life. Who better than Lord Ganesh, remover of obstacles, along with Lord Shiva and Goddess Parvati to teach this lesson to the world?

It is foolish to think that Lord Shiva, Goddess Parvati and

Lord Ganesh fell prey to ego.[32] The three of them are aspects of the Supreme Consciousness or Brahman, also called the Paramatma. Shiva, Parvati and Ganesh pervade every speck of Creation and are also beyond it. They are beyond time, space and circumstance, so how could they and their decisions be bound by one simple, senseless circumstance? This episode was designed to teach humans, *dev*s and *gan*s an important lesson—the first step for anyone hoping to attain happiness, success and fulfilment in any endeavour, is to shed their ego. The act of teaching through personal example is called *leela*, play-acting by God (See also, Chapter 16: 'Why Do Sanatan Gods Behave like Humans?'). All the *devata*s knew that Shiva's insistence on having the boy removed was only His *leela*.[33] Ganesh too admitted that the way He had behaved was the way most humans would have behaved.[34]

Is Ganesh the Elephant or the Son that Goddess Parvati Created?

Vinayak or Ganapati (also known as Ganesh) is neither. Sanatan philosophy clarifies that each being is merely an indweller of the body they are born in. The mind and intellect are faculties that are given to the being to use in a particular lifetime. In reality, every being is the *atma* or a part of the Paramatma who only uses the body they live in and the mind and intelligence they are given. To use an analogy, every drop of the ocean is the ocean in itself. If it is placed in a pail or a bottle, the drop only gets separated from the ocean and inhabits the container in which it is filled.

Likewise, every *atma* is a drop in the ocean of the Paramatma, and it only inhabits the body in which it must lead a life. A realized soul understands and experiences this Truth. Such a soul knows that it is neither the body or mind, nor the intellect or ego. It is the Paramatma, and Ganesh—being the 'God of Gods'—is complete in His experience of being the Paramatma. He could inhabit any body, yet His divine faculties would always remain intact.

Of the myriad symbolisms attributed to Lord Ganesh's peculiar form, the one frequently overlooked is that in the ultimate analysis, any being is inherently beyond a mind and body; a being is pure, Divine Energy—omnipresent, omniscient and omnipotent. The name 'Mahaganapati' refers to this aspect of Ganapati as the ultimate godhead, the source of all that there is, with or without a tangible form. Ganesh would have remained God of Gods, with a human head, an elephant head or in any other form. The name 'Vinayak' too means 'one without a *nayak*', i.e. one who has no master and who Himself is the Universal Absolute.

5

Why Did Mother Sita Undergo the Demeaning Agnipariksha?

Lakshman, light the pyre.

For generations, Mother Sita's *agniparikhsa* has been regarded as a blot on the idealism that the Ramayan has epitomized. Scholars and devotees alike have struggled to align this mortifying demand for *agnipariksha* with the ideal character of Lord Ram. Many believe that the *agnipariksha* is nothing but a distortion of the actual story, and that it likely never happened.

While the Brahma Vaivart Puran and other versions of the Ramayan, including Tulsidas's *Ramcharitmanas*, offer an engrossing explanation for the *agnipariksha*, the Valmiki Ramayan clarifies that Lord Ram did not demand the *agnipariksha*. But He spoke so harshly to Mother Sita that She Herself ordered Lakshman to set up the pyre. That being said, there has been mass outrage at this episode which is perceived as one of utter humiliation and injustice to Mother Sita and all of womankind. But on connecting the dots from what is written in the Valmiki Ramayan about this episode, the sense of indignation could *possibly* be put to rest.

At the very outset, had similar events unfolded in this day and age, there would have been no concept, expectation and acceptance of an *agnipariksha*. But the Ramayan happened in the Treta Yug—a *yug* in which humanity was connected to all aspects of nature and could interact with celestial beings, the sun, the moon, the ocean, and more, as though they were just as alive and accessible as other humans in their surroundings.

Episode in the Valmiki Ramayan

First, this was an *agnipravesh* (entry into the fire) and *not* an *agnipariksha* (trial by fire). Mother Sita chose to enter the fire; She was *not* asked to do so, and Lord Ram was opposed by one and all at the time.

According to the Valmiki Ramayan, after Ravan was vanquished in the war, since Lord Ram could not enter a city as an ascetic, He asked Vibhishan to bring Mother Sita out of Lanka[1] in complete honour and glory. As She approached, Ram was filled with relief and joy, but also *misery*.[2] He was relieved to see Sita after 10 months, joyous to behold the love of His life, and miserable, as He clearly stated, for fear of public opinion which, as a king, He would have to respect.[3] He told Her, 'Your sight to me is as disagreeable as light to a man with poor eyesight.'[4] In this verse itself, Ram admitted that He was the one with poor eyesight and that She was light. He asked Her to go wherever She liked, with whomever She liked.[5]

What Lord Ram said sounded cruel; no self-respecting woman would take such sordid insults lightly and Mother Sita certainly did not. Terribly hurt, She neither begged nor pleaded with Him. Instead, She confronted Him for His hypocrisy in that assembly of thousands of *vanar*s and demons.[6] She publicly admonished Him, His lack of trust, and for blatantly insulting Her in front of so many people.[7] She reminded Him how Her non-uterine birth from Mother Earth and Her adoption by the great King Janak placed Her at a spiritual stature higher than even Ram.[8] She was openly contemptuous of Ram for punishing Her for a crime committed by a demon.[9] She called Ram ignorant and feeble and then ordered Lakshman to light the pyre.[10]

Lakshman too was livid with Lord Ram and was about to lash out at Him,[11] but on seeing the expression on Ram's face, He understood the latter's hidden intention. Thus, Lakshman controlled Himself and assembled the pyre.[12] The demons and *vanar*s assembled there were beside themselves with grief at this torment that Mother Sita was about to endure.[13] *Rishi*s, *gandharv*s and gods arrived in the sky in their aircrafts.[14] Even Lord Shiva and Lord Brahma made an appearance as Mother Sita fearlessly, *unhesitatingly* plunged into the fire.[15] Seeing this, Lord Ram was filled with anguish and sorrow.[16]

Many people consider this an attempt by Mother Sita to kill Herself. Nothing is further from the truth. Before entering the pyre, She called upon Agni Dev (the God of Fire) and other gods, commanding Him to protect Her from the flames as She did *not* deserve this unfair treatment. She asserted that since She was unblemished, She expected to remain untouched by the fire.[17]

The gods assembled in the sky asked Lord Ram how He—being the Lord of Lords—could behave like an ordinary mortal and allow Sita to descend into the fire.[18] But neither they nor Lakshman stopped Ram or Sita. Why that was so, is explained later in this chapter.[19] During the *agnipravesh*, Agni Dev himself appeared before the assembly with Sita—who was unscathed by the blazing flames. He did not plead with Ram but rather commanded Him to take Sita back and treat Her with utmost honour and respect as none of what had happened had been Mother Sita's fault.[20]

Lord Ram admitted joyfully and tearfully that Mother Sita and He were one, and as inseparable as the sun and its light. He always knew that She could never be tempted or taken in by Ravan's *maya*, and that She had indeed suffered grave injustice at the hands of a revolting demon.[21]

This episode clearly shows that in being unfair to Mother Sita, Lord Ram stood alone. None assembled at the *agnipravesh*, be that Lakshman, the *vanar*s, demons, gods, *rishi*s, Lord Brahma or Lord Shiva, agreed with Lord Ram. Sita Herself had not taken kindly to the way Ram had spoken to Her and had confronted Him openly as any self-respecting, strong woman would. Even before He allowed Sita to enter the pyre, Ram had described Himself as a man with diseased eyesight. Why then did He allow Her to plunge into the fire?

The prime witnesses of the *agnipravesh* were Lakshman, the *vanar*s and the celestials[22] — the same beings who had seen Lord Ram grieve unabashedly for His wife, shed tears in Her memory and do everything within His power to avenge the injustice done to Her.

The *vanar*s had lived with and fought alongside Lord Ram long enough to know how much He loved and adored Mother Sita. They had seen enough of His compassion and wisdom to know that He could never have misunderstood nor judged Sita. Then how could the man who had spent 14 years in an unfair exile only to honour the unjust demand of his stepmother,[23] the man who had touched the feet of Ahilya,[24] (See also, Chapter 13: 'Was it Fair for Ahilya to Be Cursed?') the woman who had knowingly cheated on Her husband and been redeemed,[25] the man who had punished Vali for forcefully holding on to Sugreeva's wife Ruma and reinstated her as the queen of Kishkindha,[26] *how could such a man ever hurt any woman, much less His own wife whom He loved so deeply?*

The *vanar*s and celestials knew that there *had* to be a deeper reason for this uncharacteristic display of misogyny by Lord Ram. Lakshman had understood it by the expression on His face and complied.

For all gathered at the *agnipravesh*, witnessing Mother Sita emerge unscathed from the fire, watching Agni Dev become powerless before Her divine aura, would have created the *only* logical perception possible—though abducted by a demon, Sita, was powerful enough to protect Her dignity and self-respect even when She was forced to live in the enemy's den where She was subjected to untold debauchery and trauma,[27] purely on the strength of Her own character and conviction.

Mother Sita was not a damsel in distress waiting to be rescued. She had rescued Herself the moment Ravan had abducted Her.[28] It was a matter of allowing Lord Ram to gather His forces to annihilate the entire demon clan. And Sita had proven this fact much before the war. When Hanuman had come to Lanka looking for Her, He had offered to take Her back to Ram but She had refused to accompany Hanuman, choosing to stay back in Lanka instead, for She wanted Her husband to fulfil His duty of restoring Dharm in the world.[29] She had also sent Ram messages about combat strategies in the impending war.[30] The *agnipravesh* ordained Mother Sita as a goddess—equal to Ram in power and potency—in the hearts of His devotees. Centuries later, everybody still blames Ram of failing Sita; but there is no blemish whatsoever on Sita.

According to the Valmiki Ramayan, Lord Ram admitted later that He had orchestrated this drama only to ensure that Sita would never be misunderstood and that Her honour would always remain intact in the world. He knew that the fire would not be able to touch Her.[31]

Agnipravesh in the Brahma Vaivart Puran and the Ramcharitmanas

Lord Ram was Lord Vishnu in human form and Mother Sita was an incarnation of Vishnu's consort, Goddess Lakshmi.[32] According to the Brahma Vaivart Puran and *Ramcharitmanas*, one day, when Lakshman was out in the forest to gather food, the Divine couple summoned Agni Dev, and Mother Sita handed over the core of Her Divine powers to Him for safekeeping since He was the only god capable of handling the Divine potency of Goddess Lakshmi. Once that had been surrendered to Agni Dev, what remained was only a shadow of Her Divine aura—the Chhaya Sita. Ravan had abducted this Chhaya Sita, and the *agnipravesh* was a way for the Chhaya Sita to return to the fire and for the real Sita to emerge back from the fire.[33] Although many argue that this version is a desperate attempt to defend the indefensible, if one gives it due consideration, it makes sense.

Mother Sita's Divine essence needed to be removed from the drama that unfolded, for had She held on to Her celestial powers, Ravan would have been blown to smithereens had he so much as looked at Her lustfully. The war would have ended before it even began. But the battle was necessary to fulfil certain pre-destined conditions.

First, Lord Ram's Divine mission was to wipe out not only Ravan but the entire *rakshas* clan, including everyone who had committed atrocities against the *rishis*, women and ordinary mortals.[34]

Second, Vibhishan, a Dharmic ruler, had to be instated as the leader of the *rakshas* clan so that those remaining, and their future generations, could be redeemed and directed towards the path of Dharmic living. Merely killing Ravan would not have accomplished this as there were many in line—as egotistical and ruthless as Ravan—who would have been rightful heirs to the throne before Vibhishan could have laid claim to it.

Third, on separate instances, Lord Vishnu had been cursed that one day, He too would experience the pain of losing the love of His life, and that He would have to win Her back with the help of the *vanars*. This curse had to be fulfilled. (Even the mightiest Sanatan gods accepted retribution for their karma in spite of having the power to negate all karmic ill-effects and exist beyond its laws. This they did to set an example to mankind.)

Fourth, the world needed a spectacle to convince mankind that Dharm was a power more colossal than the mightiest monarchy, status, scholarship and material wealth. No matter how cruelly used, these would be futile against the Divine Strength of morality and true spirituality.

Fifth, the war was necessary, and while Mother Sita (Goddess Lakshmi) could have ended it well before it even began—because no matter how lofty the ideal, a goddess could not have allowed even the mere thought of violating a woman go unpunished—She had to will Herself to let go of Her Divine potency. However, once the mission was accomplished, She entered the fire to retrieve Her Divine essence. Thus, this entire drama was orchestrated by Ram and Sita together.

Whether one goes by the Valmiki Ramayan or the Brahma Vaivart Puran and the *Ramcharitmanas*, arguably, the *agnipravesh* ended up as a testament to and not a test of Mother Sita's Divine strength, thereby establishing Her as much the hero of Ramayan as Lord Ram.

Maharishi Valmiki had given three names to this epic—'Ramayanam' (Ram's Journey), 'Sitayah Charitam Mahat' (Sita's Sublime Legend) and 'Poulastya Vadham' (Ravan's Killing). Somehow, only one stuck.[35]

6

What Was Lord Krishna's Ras Leela?

Look around you and within you;
show me one place where he is not.

Ras Leela, one of the most popular concepts in the Puranic tradition, has often been misconstrued as a purely sensual relationship between the *gopi*s—Radha in particular—and Lord Krishna. Such an interpretation is both erroneous and myopic.

Spiritual and Emotional Life of the Gopis and Other Inhabitants of Gokul

First, Lord Krishna stayed in Gokul and Vrindavan only till the age of 14, after which He went to Mathura. All the *gopi*s were much older than Him; they were happily married and most of them were even mothers. They had witnessed the miracles He had performed in His childhood—killing the dreaded ogress Putana as a breast-feeding baby; subjugating dozens of mighty *asur*s sent by Kansa; defeating the fearsome serpent Kaliya inside the Madhu Lake, releasing the *gandharv*s Nalakubera and Managriva from their curse; lifting Mount Govardhan, among other such instances—that proclaimed his Divinity to the world.

Whether Lord Krishna was a five-year-old child or a 14-year-old youth, the people of Gokul always turned to Him for help when they were attacked by demons or threatened by impending calamities. Of course, they knew that their darling Krishna was none other than God Himself. How then, could the *gopi*s be anything but devoted to Him? For years, they had pined for Him. Collectively, they had kept the sacred Katyayani *vrata*, praying to Goddess Katyayani for Krishna to accept their love.

How the Gopis' Love Created A Miracle

The love the *gopi*s felt for Lord Krishna is most popularly captured in the paintings of the Ras Leela which depict multiple Krishnas, each paired with a different *gopi*, dancing with each of them in the same setting at the same time. What was it about the *gopi*s that made Krishna miraculously appear in multiple places simultaneously? After all, God's miracles are not so much about God's power, but rather the power of the devotees who force God to perform miracles with the intensity of their devotion.

Having Lord Krishna all to herself shows the depth of love each *gopi* had for Him. This can be understood by the reader through a simple experiment. Think of someone you love, pour out all your love with as much intensity as you can muster into the thought of that person till you see them before you, feel their touch, feel their breath, and then hold on to that presence for a prolonged period. You will be able to appreciate the enormous amount of love and energy needed to manifest this kind of presence of the person you love, with you. Such is the intensity with which every *gopi* must have loved Krishna to experience Him dancing only with her step-for-step, beat-for-beat, breath-for-breath. What a transcendental experience the Ras Leela must have been for every *gopi*! The Bhagavat Puran says that even the *dev*s would assemble in Vrindavan's sky to witness this thrilling phenomenon!

By being with Lord Krishna, the *gopi*s were not with 'another man' but rather with the Supreme Divinity that contained the entire cosmos within itself. They were bewitched not by the physical form of Krishna but rather by the Divine Essence that His form embodied. Therefore, manifesting Krishna with them was second nature to the *gopi*s. They experienced Him not just in Nandigram as they danced with Him, but every moment of every day, in everything they saw or did. Tamil poet-saint Subramania Bharati speaks of the *gopi*s' constant communion with Krishna in his famous song 'Kakkai Siraginile Nandalala', which recounts actual incidents from the Bhagavat Puran.

> Whenever I see a crow, Nandalala
> Its black form reminds me of your dark complexion
> Wherever I look, Nandalala
> The green (of leaves and grass) reminds me of your green blue complexion
> Whatever sound I hear
> To me is the music of your flute
> If I burn my finger while lighting the lamp
> I feel your affectionate touch since I see you in the flame.

The instances the song refers to are drawn from the Bhagavat Puran, after Lord Krishna had left Vrindavan for Mathura. He sent Uddhav—one of His closest devotees—to enquire about His foster parents, Nanda and Yashoda, His childhood friends and the *gopi*s.

While in Vrindavan, Uddhav witnessed the following: the *gopi*s would gather at Nanda's residence every evening at the twilight hour to light their lamps from the one in his house. On that particular evening, a *gopi* entered Nanda's house to light her lamp. She was taking too long, so the other *gopi*s were getting impatient. Yashoda came out from the inner chambers and saw this *gopi* standing before the flame, transfixed. Her fingers were scalding in the flame but she seemed unaware of that. Yashoda panicked and pulled the *gopi*'s charred fingers out of the fire and tried her best to wake her up, but she could not. She then called out to the others, and together, they lay the *gopi* down so that she could rest. With great difficulty, they finally brought her back to consciousness. When she came to, the *gopi* told the others that she had seen Krishna's mesmerizing form in the flame and in the ecstasy of seeing Him, she had not realized that her fingers were burning. She had not experienced any pain whatsoever! This happened months—possibly *years*—after Krishna had left Vrindavan, never to return.

In the Bhagvad Gita (Chapter 11, Verse 5) while giving Arjun the *darshan* of His 'Virat Roop', Krishna directs him thus:[1]

*pashya mein partha rupani shata shotha sahastrashaha
naanaa vidhani divyaani naanaa varnaakritini cha*

(O [Arjun]! See my heavenly forms by hundreds and thousands, of different kinds, and of various shades and shapes. It is I who has taken the various forms of everything you see in Creation.)

The *gopi*s had already experienced what Lord Krishna declared to Arjun. Arjun needed to witness the Virat Roop to understand that everything in the Universe was nothing but Krishna Himself; but the *gopi*s could perceive Krishna in everything around them in every moment of their lives.

As Uddhav walked through the streets and forests of Vrindavan, he witnessed so many *gopi*s entranced before stones, trees, shrubs, mountains, rivers and grass, calling out Krishna's name, feeling His pulsating presence everywhere they went, in everything they did.

While detailing the nine forms of *bhakti*, Sanatan scriptures talk of the *gopi*s as examples of its highest form, called Atma Nivedanam, a form of devotion so transcendental that the devotee loses all sense of self and is eternally absorbed in her lord. All the *gopi*s thought about was Krishna, all they spoke about was Krishna, and everything they did was an offering to Krishna. This, even as the *gopi*s performed every worldly duty for their families. How then can such a sublime form of devotion be mistaken for mundane seduction or sensuousness?

One may ask that if the *gopi*s experienced Krishna no matter where they were, or what they did, what was the need for them to congregate at Nandigram to see Him, be by His side, and dance with Him? The answer lies in another, similar, question: Why do devotees, with the faith that their chosen form of god is omnipresent, omniscient and omnipotent, still visit them in their respective temples?

The *gopi*s were far more spiritually advanced than even the most powerful *rishi*s of the time. Once, Lord Krishna is belived to have developed a terrible headache. He announced that only the dust from feet of a true devotee could cure Him. Messengers were dispatched from Dwarka all over Bharat, to His greatest devotees, including powerful *rishi*s in penance, great kings and friends. None of them could offer the required cure... They all pleaded—how could they, mere mortals, dare to give dust from their feet to their mighty Lord? They begged to be spared such sacrilege. To them, their *ordinariness* before the Lord was more important than the Lord Himself. But the moment a messenger reached Vrindavan and informed the *gopi*s of Krishna's suffering, they immediately offered the dust from their feet to relieve their beloved Krishna from His agony. Thus, Krishna was cured.[2]

This incident shows the greatness of the *gopi*s' simple love for Lord Krishna—it was beyond intellectual chatter and the *appropriate* ways of the world. They had long crossed the boundaries posed by dualities like human and god, *paap* and *punya*, and their consciousness had merged with that of Krishna's. It is this spiritual union that is (mis)represented as mere sexuality, while in reality, the Ras Leela is the ecstatic union of the *jivatma* with the Paramatma, and the dissolution of Prakriti into Purusha.

Why Does Radha Get More Importance than the Other Gopis?

Radha is not mentioned in the Bhagavat Puran. However, there are elaborate references to Radha in the Brahma Vaivart Puran. Radha assumes greater importance than the other *gopi*s because She was the earthly manifestation of the Divine Radha—the Divine Feminine—who had incarnated in the 'Dwapar Yug' along with Her cosmic counterpart, Sri Krishna.[3]

Why Has Ras Leela's Sensual Interpretation Been Accepted?

Firstly, the myopic view of the Ras Leela as a purely sensual bond has also been reinforced by theatrical and literary works which ignore or undermine its spiritual essence. But they too cannot be faulted beyond a point. After all, when a devotee's individual consciousness merges with the Universal Consciousness, i.e. she attains the state of 'Moksh' or Liberation, and the bliss that the devotee experiences cannot be depicted or described, how can a finite mind even begin to perceive the experience of infinity, much less express it appropriately? How can language—restricted by motifs of the mundane—even try to convey the sublime? Hence, the artist tries to articulate the exhilaration of the union of the *jivatma* and Paramatma by using familiar themes of visualization and reference. When the performer offers the relatable to explain the indescribable, it becomes the duty of the audience witnessing the performance, or reading the material, to look beyond the surface of the narrative and seek its essence, unravel its layers of meaning and be awakened into its truth.

Secondly, the open-mindedness about the way Ras Leela is interpreted and presented comes from a philosophy deeply rooted in the Hindu psyche. A Hindu believes that 'Moksh' is the ultimate goal of every living being. When the devotee attains 'Moksh', all ideas and differences of right and wrong—*paap* and *punya*—are dissolved into the absolution of wholeness and bliss. Such a devotee, so soaked in divine ecstasy, could never even think of hurting or harming anyone. In fact, the heart of such a devotee would be capable of only feeling love towards all of Creation.

Therefore, to the Hindu, the Ras Leela, however presented, is above all an expression of the dissolution of the individual soul into the Divine Soul; he regards anyone who has been able to attain this state as freed from the shackles of the worldly codes of conduct. The Hindu views such a realized soul as always worthy of reverence.

7

Was Vibhishan Right in Abandoning His Brother, Ravan?

Even in the most difficult circumstances,
May I always do the right thing!

The character of Vibhishan in the Ramayan has sparked intense debate—was it right of Vibhishan to betray his brother, Ravan, his clan and his entire family, and side with Lord Ram? Not only did he support Ram, he also gave away the intricate secrets of the *rakshas* warriors without which it might have been impossible for Ram's army to defeat Ravan. This was because the *rakshasa*s had illusionary powers designed to confuse and trick their opponents, and only an insider would have the details on how to overcome these deadly traps. Vibhishan caused his entire clan to be massacred.

Kumbhakarn, on the other hand, had the good sense to point out to Ravan his grave crime in abducting another man's wife; he implored Ravan to let go of Mother Sita and seek forgiveness.[1] However, when Ravan did not relent, Kumbhakarn stood by his elder brother, for is this not what family is all about? People who will be there for you through thick and thin, who will stand by you no matter what?

So, who was right and who followed Dharm—Vibhishan or Kumbhakarn?

Relationship between Dharm and Existence

Sanatan philosophy has always been rooted in a deep connection between Man and the Creator to the extent that every individual is verily God himself. Every being is the Paramatma shrouded in the veil of *maya*. The moment this veil is lifted, the *atma* realizes its true self and experiences itself as Paramatma. So, if every individual is God, then by extension, every individual is also deeply connected to nature and the cosmos, which is also a manifestation of the Paramatma. If one were to look at life and loyalties from this perspective, every individual belongs as much to the rest of the world as to their family, for each being is first the Paramatma, then the *atma*, and only after that, a son, daughter, brother, sister, and so on. Also, since Sanatan philosophy believes in reincarnation, these roles too change from one lifetime to another.

According to Sanatan, the purpose of life is to attain liberation from the cycle of birth and death. From this point of view, all relationships are karmic accounts that need to be settled by assuming a particular role in relation to the other in a particular lifetime. Hence, while the truth about a person being God is eternal, irrespective of the number of lifetimes it takes them to realize and experience it, every relationship, no matter how close, is temporary and restricted to a limited time, or at best, to one complete lifetime.

How does this translate into the here-and-now of everyday life? The answer lies in two words—duty and ethics. Since every individual is connected to the universe/world/nature, their first duty and ethics should be the greater good of the larger world, before finally concentrating on their individual level. The diagram below represents this journey:

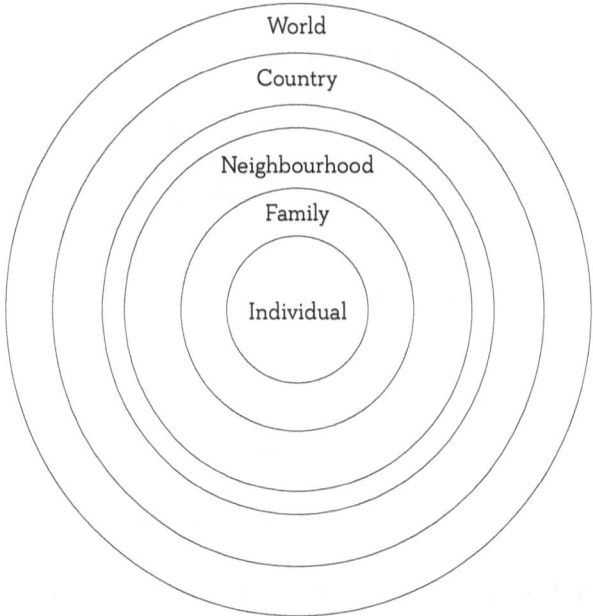

The more expansive an individual's view, the more they are in tune with their true selves as the *atma* and the omnipresent Paramatma. The boundaries of the circles are governed by the values of justice, integrity and universal well-being. So, while it is not Dharmic for any country to attack another only in the pursuit of power and wealth, for the country attacked, it is their Dharm to fight the war to protect its people and maintain the universal values of freedom and peace. The same understanding can be applied to any of the circles in the above diagram.

Character and Values of Vibhishan and Ravan

The Valmiki Ramayan and the Ved Vyas Mahabharat, both mention that due to his jealousy of Kuber, Ravan did *tapasya* for a 1,000 years.[2] His brothers too joined him but for other reasons. When Lord Brahma asked Vibhishan to ask for a boon, all Vibhishan asked for was, 'Even under the most trying circumstances, may I never do anything wrong and may I have the knowledge of the Brahmastra...'[3] So pleased was Brahma with Vibhishan's plea that in addition to what Vibhishan wanted, he also granted him the boon of immortality, since a man who always wanted to do the right thing could never hurt or harm any living creature on Earth.[4]

On the other hand, Ravan asked for immortality.[5] However, knowing the bend of his mind, Lord Brahma refused to grant him that boon.[6] Hence, Ravan tried to trick Lord Brahma by saying, 'May I never be defeated by the *gandharv*s, *dev*s, *yaksha*s, *kinnar*s, *nag*s, *asur*s, ghosts, and spirits.'[7] Ravan did not include humans in the boon for he regarded them as too weak to pose any threat to him. Lord Brahma granted Ravan the boon—none except a human could kill Ravan.

The first thing Ravan did after receiving the boon was to usurp Lanka, his brother-in-law Kuber's kingdom, even as Kuber invited Ravan to share his wealth and live in brotherly co-existence.[8] Once, when Kuber sent him brotherly advice to give up his evil ways, Ravan killed his messenger and attacked Kuber as punishment for the audacity of advising him.[9] Ravan was a megalomaniac, a rapist and a tormentor of the *rishi*s. The *devata*s and *rishi*s collectively prayed to Lord Vishnu to intervene and destroy Ravan because his existence was detrimental to the peace and well-being of not just millions of people but to the expansive and harmonious way of life which the *rishi*s and their followers lived by.[10]

Vibhishan had repeatedly tried to reason with Ravan, pointing out that Ravan's crime of abducting Mother Sita would lead to a massacre of the *rakshas* clan, but his well-meaning advice was always met with contempt and scorn. Far from considering Vibhishan's entreaties, Ravan and his ministers would discuss even meaner strategies to demoralize Lord Ram and his army.[11] There was no redemption possible for Ravan.

Hence, as an *atma* or as the citizen of the world, it was not just Vibhishan's duty but that of every Dharmic person as well to help destroy Ravan (See also Chapter 1: 'Why Did Lord Ram Abandon Mother Sita'; Chapter 3: 'Ram or Ravan—Who Was the Better Man?', and Chapter 5: 'Why Did Mother Sita Undergo the Demeaning Agnipariksha?').

How Could Kumbhakarn Have Influenced Ravan?

The mighty *rakshas*, Kumbhakarn was stuck in the second circle of familial ties. Among Ravan's most powerful warriors, Kumbhakarn was an accomplished scholar and an expert in matters of Dharm.[12] But of what use was this power and scholarship when he overlooked the protection of the weak and oppressed? He was nothing but a hapless servant in the hands of the oppressor. Instead of helping his clan and his kingdom tread the path of Dharm, he used his prowess to further evil. Had Kumbhakarn stood up against Ravan even before Mother Sita was abducted, perhaps the need for this war would not have arisen in the first place. And had at least some of Ravan's warriors revolted against him and forced him to follow Dharm, this entire massacre could have been averted.

What does this tell us? Since only a few have the courage to stand up for Dharm, it does not make those few wrong, and the majority right. Education, scholarship, skill, talent, knowledge are not just useless, but acutely dangerous when used to further or even to uphold evil.

If Vibhishan was wrong in abandoning his family and siding with Lord Ram, for the sake of Dharm, by extension of that logic, every soldier who guards the border has abandoned his family and is Adharmic, every doctor, every health and sanitation worker who fought COVID-19 had put their family in jeopardy, and was hence Adharmic, and every lawyer who protects a rapist, a murderer to earn a plush life for the family, or every politician who loots the country to fulfil his own ambitions or to provide for the family is Dharmic.

Why Was Vibhishan's Help Needed?

According to the boon that Lord Brahma had granted Ravan, only a human could kill him. Hence Vishnu had to incarnate himself as a mortal and lead an ordinary life. So, as a human being, while Lord Ram could be a warrior par excellence, an ideal king, the 'Maryada Purushottam' (best among honourable men), He could not have behaved like the omniscient Vishnu. Ram needed help as any human does, from family and friends.

Even from a philosophical perspective, life gives every person an opportunity in big or small ways, to pick a side. The side we pick defines who we have chosen to become; the side we pick determines the course that we chart out for ourselves and those around us, since all our choices, though individual, are collective in consequence. This massive war was the time for the *rakshasa*s to pick a side. Only Vibhishan picked the right one.

8

Duryodhan or Yudhishthir—Who Was the Real Villain?

I want what the Pandavs have, else I shall end my life.

Many argue that Yudhishthir was largely responsible for what happened in the course of the game of dice, including the dastardly manner in which Draupadi was insulted, because he decided to wager his wife. Duryodhan was unfairly made the scapegoat for a crime committed by Yudhishthir, and did not deserve to be killed. Moreover, Duryodhan was an astute and able king and history may have been unjust to him because history is written by the victors—in this case the Pandavs, especially Yudhishthir.

The Mahabharat was not written or commissioned by the Pandavs but rather by Maharishi Ved Vyas, the grandfather of both the Pandavs and the Kauravs. More importantly, Ved Vyas was a powerful sage who possessed complete knowledge of the past, present and future. He was the great *guru* who had classified and documented the Vedas into their four forms and branches, and also the historian who had documented episodes from the beginning of time in the 18 Purans.

Moreover, Maharishi Ved Vyas 'saw' the Mahabharat through *divya drishti*—like a movie flashing before his inner eye—just like Maharishi Valmiki had seen the Ramayan. Ved Vyas was asked to document the Mahabharat by Narad Muni, and Valmiki was asked to document the Ramayan by Lord Brahma. Both great *rishi*s were blessed with an insight into the innermost thoughts and motivations of the various beings involved in the epics that they recorded.

The Mahabharat was written by the all-knowing Lord Ganesh, while Maharishi Ved Vyas only narrated the episodes as they flashed before him. The cave from which Ved Vyas narrated the Mahabharat and the one in which Lord Ganesh wrote it, still exists in Managaon, Bharat's last village before the northern border, near the popular pilgrimage site, Badrinath.

The fact that Yudhishthir's title 'Dharmraj' has been repeatedly questioned since the time of the Mahabharat, shows that his reputation suffered after wagering his wife. That said, when it is clear Yudhishthir was wrong even if just that once, why did Lord Krishna support him in the Kurukshetra War? Also, what makes Yudhishthir and the Pandavs, not Duryodhan and the Kauravs, the true upholders of Dharm?

To answer these questions, it is important to compare the deeds of Duryodhan and Yudhishthir during three phases of their lives—before the game of dice, during the game of dice, and after the game of dice.

Duryodhan

Before the Game of Dice

The moment Duryodhan was born, the kingdom of Hastinapur was struck by a series of deadly omens. Duryodhan's first cry sounded like the braying of a donkey. He was joined by donkeys braying throughout the kingdom. The sky was filled with carnivorous and scavenging birds—like vultures and crows—screeching menacingly; jackals howled, thunder and lightning struck, and a terrible storm broke out ravaging the entire kingdom, while the animals became restless and began wailing.[1]

Dhritarashtra consulted astrologers and they agreed that these portents were brought about by the newborn baby. They predicted that the child would be the personification of negativity and no matter how well he was taught, he would only imbibe greed and jealousy. Eventually, the child would cause the ruin of his entire clan.

On hearing this, Vidur and the rest of the Brahmins pleaded with Dhritarashtra to get rid of this first-born child as 99 more sons would soon emerge from their 'incubation vessels' where they were being tended to for more than two years. But Dhritarashtra would have none of it.

As a teenager, Duryodhan planned to murder all the Pandavs several times. On one such occasion, he targeted Bhim. He first befriended all the Pandavs and organized a grand picnic and feast in their honour. Then he secretly poisoned Bhim, threw his body into the River Ganga. When Bhim returned safely, Duryodhan strangled Bhim's charioteer. After this, on several other occasions, he tried to poison Bhim and kill all the Pandavs, but Duryodhan's half-brother Yuyutsu, Vidur's spies, and the loyal servants of the palace would alert the Pandavs about Duryodhan's deadly schemes and save their lives.[2]

When Duryodhan attacked Panchal (as *guru dakshina* for Dronacharya) with his 99 brothers and the entire army of Hastinapur, he was routed.[3]

When Yudhishthir—the eldest prince and the best pupil of Guru Dronacharya—became the crown prince, Duryodhan once again pretended to honour the Pandavs, and conspired to have them—along with their aged mother, Kunti—burnt alive in Lakshagriha, the 'Palace of Lacquer', at Varnavrat.[4] Everyone in the kingdom was sure that the ruthless murder of the Pandavs had been a conspiracy hatched by Dhritarashtra and his sons.[5] When it was revealed that the Pandavs were alive and had married Draupadi, thus forging an alliance with a powerful king like Drupad, Duryodhan strategized with Karn and Dhritarashtra to try and destroy the Pandavs again.[6] Among the strategies were, (a) sending Karn to bring the Pandavs back to Hastinapur, and once they arrived, murdering them using different tactics and methods; (b) enticing the Pandavs with women so that Draupadi left them; (c) planting a *purohit* among the Pandavs to create dispute among the brothers; and (d) planting Brahmins to convince the Pandavs to remain in Panchal and to never return to Hastinapur since Hastinapur was 'dangerous' for them!

Finally, for fear of the newfound power of the Pandavs, given their alliance with the influential kingdom of Panchal and its friends and allies, the Pandavs were given half the kingdom—the half that was a forested wasteland, dense, attacked by demons and infested with snakes. That part of the kingdom was called Khandavaprastha.[7]

However, far from being punished for his crimes, Duryodhan enjoyed a bounteous kingdom managed by stalwarts like Bheeshm, Vidur and Dronacharya. When Duryodhan saw the amount of wealth and adoration that Yudhishthir and the rest of the Pandavs had earned, he was consumed with jealousy. He came back to Hastinapur and went into depression.[8]

'I cannot tolerate that the Pandavs have more wealth than I do,' is what Duryodhan told Dhritarashtra when he returned from Yudhishthir's *rajasuya yagya*. Dhritarashtra repeatedly pleaded with him, 'The Pandavs have earned all this wealth and status with their own effort and intelligence. It is wrong of you to covet it. Earn your own wealth. You have the same education as the Pandavs. The Pandavs started with nothing else but you have the wealth of our kingdom, stalwarts and warriors like Bheeshm, Dronacharya, Karn who will do anything for you. You are capable of doing your own *rajasuya yagya.*' But Duryodhan's one-pointed reply to all his father's entreaties was, 'I do not want to earn my own wealth; I want what the Pandavs have.'

Duryodhan also repeatedly intimidated Dhritarashtra with tales about the invincibility of Arjun and Bhim in a proper war, and thus coerced his father into granting permission for the game of dice, using emotional blackmail as the ultimate ruse, 'If I do not get what the Pandavs have, I shall kill myself.[9]

Yudhishthir

Before the Game of Dice

Yudhishthir was the son of Yam, God of Death, (also called Dharm) for Yam spares no one, friend or foe, when the time for death is nigh, and hence, is absolutely fair. The moment Yudhishthir was born, the following words reverberated across the sky, 'This great man will be the foremost among virtuous and pious men. This eldest son of Pandu will be known as Yudhishthir. He will be a mighty and truth-abiding king on Earth. He will be praised, celebrated and reputed in all the three worlds. He will be a noble, fiery and glorious king.'[10]

Yudhishthir did not complain to Dhritarashtra about Duryodhan's various attempts to murder the Pandavs because Vidur stopped him from doing so. Vidur knew that Dhritarashtra would never punish his son and the complaints could put the lives of the Pandavs in greater jeopardy.[11]

Yudhishthir was the wisest among Dronacharya's pupils and had shown signs of being a just, farsighted and compassionate administrator from an early age. The people of Hastinapur loved him and wanted him to be the next king.[12]

While Duryodhan was defeated even with an entire army by King Drupad during the battle of Panchal, Yudhishthir and his brothers vanquished King Drupad purely through their own military and strategic abilities.[13]

Yudhishthir agreed to all five brothers marrying Draupadi only because Maharishi Ved Vyas had already told them that Draupadi and the Pandavs were destined to be husbands and wife since their previous lives to fulfil a greater plan of the *devata*s; and not because Kunti had unknowingly asked the brothers to 'divide' the *bhiksha* they had received[14] (See also, Chapter 14: 'Was it Misogynistic for Draupadi to Have Five Husbands?').

For Yudhishthir, the interest of the entire Kuru clan was of utmost importance. Hence, instead of immediately going to war with his uncle, he happily accepted the wasteland of Khandavaprastha, and took it up as a challenge with his brothers, to turn it into a thriving kingdom called Indraprastha.

Yudhishthir's rule in Indraprastha was characterized by foresight and justice. The benevolent policies that he employed even with other kingdoms won him the loyalty of not just the officers in his administration but also those of other kingdoms. Hence, he became known as 'Ajatshatru'—one without enemies. He knew how to maintain a balance between the four 'Purusharthas'; 'Dharm', upholding righteousness; 'Arth', earning wealth; 'Kaam', fulfilling the dreams and desires of his subjects; and 'Moksh', working with a spiritual bend of mind.[15]

Yudhishthir was an innately spiritual being rather than an ambitious king. He was aware of the needs and desires of his people and relentlessly worked towards fulfilling them, making generous use of his treasury for the good of all.

Yudhisthir's subjects loved their king and were his *bhakt*s as were people from other kingdoms. He always had a calm, smiling and pleasant demeanour. He never uttered a lie or condescending or insensitive words. He duly consulted relevant people in taking decisions, ensuring the well-being of everyone concerned, thus bringing stability and prosperity to his own kingdom and to other kingdoms as well.

There was no corruption in the administration. The people of the kingdom did not utter falsehoods even among themselves. All *varna*s flourished and the kingdom had abundant food and wealth. The positive atmosphere in the kingdom, the strict adherence to Dharm—both by the people and the administration—the foresight, and commitment to the people's welfare ensured timely rains, almost no natural disasters, diseases, or pandemics. The kingdom was impenetrable and safe, women were protected and secure. No crime was tolerated and the Pandavs were forever dedicated to implementing innovative schemes for the welfare of their subjects. The treasury had immeasurable wealth.

Rajasuya Yagya

Yudhishthir had become very powerful and wealthy, and was perceived to be so benevolent that he deserved to do the *rajasuya yagya* and become the 'Chakravarti Samrat'—King of Kings. Yudhishthir didn't want to perform the *rajasuya yagya* since he did not believe in any display of power, but Narad Muni carried a message from Yudhisthir's late father Pandu that he wanted him to perform the *yagya*. Therefore, Yudhishthir agreed to perform the ritual to honour his father's and brothers' wishes.[16]

Even after becoming the 'Chakravarti Samrat', Yudhishthir wanted to mend ties with Duryodhan. Hence, to give Duryodhan respect and importance during the *rajasuya yagya*, he granted him the honour of accepting gifts—brought by kings and people from kingdoms all over the world—on his behalf. It is here that Duryodhan witnessed the respect that Yudhishthir and the Pandavs commanded—and the wealth they had amassed—and was consequently consumed by jealousy.[17]

On one of the days of the *yagya*, after the rites for the day had been completed, Shishupal was rightfully killed by Lord Krishna. After the *yagya* was over, as Maharishi Ved Vyas was about to leave Indraprastha, Yudhishthir asked him, 'Will the killing of Shishupal in the days of such a powerful *yagya*, lead to any untoward consequences?' To this, Ved Vyas replied, 'When a fight or killing happens during the *rajasuya yagya*, it creates a war so massive that it wipes out most of the Kshatriya community within 13 years. Such a war will now happen. Since this was your *yagya*, you, Yudhishthir, will be the medium of the war. The unforgivable crimes committed by Duryodhan will be the cause of the war, and the mighty Arjun and Bhim will be its executors.' With that, Ved Vyas left.[18]

So disturbed was Yudhishthir at hearing what Maharishi Ved Vyas had to say that he wanted to end his life so that the 'medium' of the war itself could be annihilated and a deadly war could be prevented. But after he was stopped by his brothers, Yudhishthir took a vow that, thereafter, leave alone fighting, he would not so much as speak unkindly to anyone—least of all to the Kauravs—and would give them anything they asked for so that the lives of half the Kshatriya community could be saved.[19]

Barely a few days after the *yagya*, Vidur arrived in Indraprastha bearing an invitation from Dritarashtra for a game of dice. Vidur clearly informed Yudhishthir of Duryodhan's intentions to usurp all his wealth. Yudhishthir did not want to gamble, regardless of who he was playing against. But he still accepted the invitation because, in those days, no king could refuse the invitation from another king for a game of dice. As the Chakravarti Samrat, Yudhishthir could not violate that norm. Moreover, this invitation was from Yudhisthir's uncle Dhritarashtra. He had taken a vow to not refuse the Kauravs and to do his best to maintain friendly ties with them.[20]

In the Grand Hall where the game of dice was to be

played, Yudhishthir confronted Duryodhan and Shakuni on their intentions and warned them. He also tried to convince them that gambling by its very nature was unbecoming of those who were wise, capable and hard-working. But of course, Duryodhan and Shakuni would have none of it.[21] It was only when they actually sat down to play, and Yudhishthir graciously announced that he would let Duryodhan cast the first die, that Duryodhan revealed Shakuni would play on his behalf. Yudhishthir could have chosen to walk out, as the invitation was from Dritarashtra, not Shakuni, but he had never imagined how far the game would go.[22]

Duryodhan

During the Game of Dice

Duryodhan had deliberately pretended that he would be the one gambling with Yudhishthir until the very last moment because he knew that if he had revealed that Shakuni would play on his behalf, Bheeshm would never have permitted the game. This was because Shakuni was a master mathematician who knew how to apply mathematical secrets of concepts like probability in games of chance. Shakuni was invincible in the science and art of gambling. By not announcing Shakuni's involvement until just before the first die was cast, Duryodhan put Yudhishthir in a quandary.[23]

After losing his kingdom, his brothers, and himself, Yudhishthir wanted to walk out of the game but it was Duryodhan and Shakuni who took advantage of a broken man and enticed him, 'Bet Draupadi and if you win this bout, we shall free you too.'[24] Duryodhan had asked for this game because he wanted all the wealth that belonged to the Pandavs. He got the wealth; he even won the Pandavs themselves and made them his servants. Hence, he should have celebrated his victory and put the Pandavs and Draupadi to work in his palace for the rest of their lives. What was the need to have Draupadi dragged into court, and order for her to be disrobed in front of hundreds of kings and other men? What can possibly justify such perversion on the part of Duryodhan, Shakuni, Karn and Dushasan *after* winning the game? Worse still, what twisted sense of Dharm prevented Bheeshm, Dronacharya or any other man in the court from killing Duryodhan on the spot?

Yudhishthir

During the Game of Dice

There is no justification for Yudhishthir *choosing* to wager his kingdom, his brothers, himself and his wife in the gamble. But he wagered himself before he wagered his wife. He did not even think about wagering Draupadi until Shakuni enticed him with an opportunity to win himself back in the last bout. In his destitution, Yudhishthir fell prey to temptation. A man like Yudhishthir, who had never done anything morally wrong in his life, choosing such crassness was unthinkable. But this had already been predicted by Ved Vyas, as mentioned before. And that prophecy was now being played out in open court.

Despite the prophecy, the plight of the Pandavs *can* be blamed solely on Yudhishthir and the madness that descends on anyone who indulges in prolonged gambling. The loser continues playing in the desperate hope of winning back what is lost, and the winner plays driven by the greed for more. The brothers, especially Bhim, were livid with Yudhishthir, as were dozens of other kings in the assembly.[25]

However, had Yudhishthir won any of the rounds, he would have graciously returned everything that Duryodhan had lost and would have never taken the game so far. The very Pandavs who had spared Jayadrath's life because he was the husband of Duryodhan's sister Dushala, would have never thought of treating Duryodhan's sister or wife the way Draupadi was treated.[26] But yes, after this, Yudhishthir lost his stature as 'Dharmraj', and rightfully so.

Duryodhan

After the Game of Dice

After the game was stopped and Draupadi humiliated, suddenly the kingdom of Hastinapur was plagued by the same terrible omens that had accompanied Duryodhan's birth.[27] Terrified by these signs of impending doom, Dhritarashtra returned everything to the Pandavs,[28] but Duryodhan felt no compunction whatsoever. Once again, he blackmailed Dhritarashtra: 'Wherever I look, I see Arjun and Bhim who are thirsting for my blood... Their images and vows haunt me whether I am awake or asleep... I could never win against them in a war, but I know they will never spare me after what I did to Draupadi. If you want to see me alive, call them for another game of dice...'[29]

After the second game of dice, the Pandavs were sent into exile. Duryodhan was so scared that they would be recalled to Hastinapur and their kingdom returned to them that he declared he would starve himself to death, drink poison, hang himself, injure himself fatally or jump into a blazing fire if he ever saw the Pandavs happy and successful again. His depression was eased by Shakuni who promised him that the Pandavs were so principled and ethical that they would never think of returning before the 13 years were over, even if Dhritarashtra and the other elders begged them to come back.[30] So, Duryodhan, Shakuni and Karn were aware of how righteous the Pandavas were, yet they deliberately made them suffer to satiate their greed and jealousy!

Even then, Duryodhan wanted to murder the Pandavs. Maharishi Ved Vyas stopped Duryodhan, Karn, Dushasan and Shakuni from marching into the forest and fighting the Pandavs.[31] Rishi Maitreya came to Hastinapur to reason with Duryodhan and Dhritarashtra but Duryodhan insulted the *rishi* so unabashedly that he pronounced a curse on him— Duryodhan's defiance would lead to a devastating war and the very thigh he beat with such impertinence in the presence of the *rishi* would be shattered by Bhim with his mace.[32]

Duryodhan, Shakuni, Karn, Dushasan and others went to the forest of Dwaitavan only to show off the wealth they had unfairly won from the Pandavs and derive the sadistic pleasure by mocking the Pandavs for their destitution. As Karn said, 'Watching one's enemies miserable is the highest form of happiness, and Draupadi will feel even more humiliated and unhappy than when she was insulted in the court when she sees Duryodhan's wives adorned in silks and jewels...'[33] Need anything more be said about the heartless and perverted mindset of Duryodhan and his accomplices?

To add to it, Duryodhan lost a battle to the *gandharv*s in Dwaitavan. Badly injured, Karn escaped from the battlefield while the *gandharv*s captured Duryodhan, Dushasan, and all the other Kauravs and their wives. At that time, Duryodhan cried out to the Pandavs for help, calling out to Yudhishthir, Arjun, Bhim, Nakul and Sahdev to save him and the reputation of their clan![34]

Duryodhan also deliberately tricked Rishi Durvasa into visiting the Pandavs in the forest with his 10,000 disciples at a time when he knew that they would have no food to offer them. He wanted Rishi Durvasa to be enraged with the Pandavs and curse them.[35]

Duryodhan had no appreciation for the fact that Draupadi

and the Pandavs had left his brother-in-law Jayadrath alive even after he had abducted Draupadi, just because he was Duryodhan's sister Dushala's husband. Far from being grateful or remorseful, Duryodhan and Jayadrath planned revenge on the Pandavs because they had rightfully punished Jayadrath for his actions.

Duryodhan spent the 13 years of the Pandavs' exile forging alliances—many of them through trickery and dubious means—for the war. He had no intention whatsoever of honouring his own conditions of the gamble.[36] Even after the Pandavs had completed their exile and fulfilled the conditions of the game of dice, Duryodhan refused to return the kingdom.[37]

Yudhisthir

After the Game of Dice

All the subjects of Hastinapur wanted to follow Yudhishthir to the forests. They said, 'Our families, our homes, our wealth is no longer safe in a kingdom which the evil Duryodhan wants to rule with the malicious advice of crooked men like Shakuni, Karn and Dushasan. Duryodhan has no regard for propriety and no respect for elders. He wants to usurp the wealth that belongs to others, is arrogant, ruthless and has given up his own pious brothers... How can we as subjects ever remain safe or prosperous under his rule?'

They lamented and pleaded, 'Just as the fragrance of scented flowers perfumes the clothes, air, water, and whatever comes in contact with it, the righteousness of good men benefits all those who come in contact with them. Similarly, the evil of vicious men destroys those who interact with them. We do not wish to be destroyed by remaining in a kingdom ruled by Duryodhan. We want to stay in the company of you Pandavs who are humble, accomplished, truthful, civilized, brave, resourceful and courteous... We will go with you.'[38]

Yudhishthir had a hard time convincing them to return, and was finally able to send them back on the pretext of looking after their mother Kunti who had stayed back in Hastinapur.[39]

Even as a hapless forest-dweller, Yudhishthir behaved like a king, providing for the nearly 10,000 Brahmins who had followed the Pandavs into the forest. For this, he did a *tapasya* of Surya Dev and received the 'Akshay Patra' from him, which produced endless amounts of food, right till Draupadi finished eating her meal.[40]

Throughout the 13 years of exile, Yudhishthir was continuously blamed and admonished by Draupadi and his brothers:[41]

- 'The kingdom protected by Arjun, which even Lord Indra could not have won from us, was snatched away from us in front of our eyes because of your carelessness.'
- 'Hope you have not become so detached from the world that you have lost all courage... You only know the concepts of Dharm but you understand none of them.'
- 'You are not fit to be a Kshatriya.'
- 'We brothers will never be able to forgive ourselves for not protecting Draupadi and for not tearing Duryodhan, Dushasan, Shakuni and Karn to pieces, there and then.'

These are just some of the things that Bhim, Draupadi and the other brothers said to Yudhishthir throughout their exile, all of which he accepted with deep remorse. He repeatedly admitted that it was indeed his fault that Draupadi and his brothers had suffered such a tragic fate.[42]

When Lord Krishna and Draupadi's brother

Dhrishtadyumna visited the Pandavs in the forest, seething and ready to go to war with the Kauravs, Yudhishthir pleaded with them to wait 13 years—till the conditions of the lost wager were fulfilled—as he wanted to fulfil his end of the bargain.[43] Also, the Pandavs needed time to gather allies and sophisticated weapons as they were sure that Duryodhan would spare no money or effort in consolidating his might against them.[44] Yudhishthir even learnt the mathematical secrets of gambling from Rishi Brihadashva so that the norm necessitating a king to accept an invitation for gambling would never again render Yudhishthir vulnerable to Shakuni's expertise in the game of dice.[45]

Yudhishthir also urged his brothers to free Duryodhan, his 99 brothers, and their wives from the clutches of the *gandharv*s as he did not want 'outsiders' to subdue his clan. He wanted to protect the women of his family. This, even when he knew that Duryodhan and his entourage were only there to mock the Pandavs for their destitution, and after they had humiliated Draupadi in open court.[46]

In the twelfth year of the Pandavs' exile, a deer ran off with the implements of a Brahmin who then sought help of the Pandavs. Although they managed to track the deer down several times, it always managed to give them the slip. After a long chase, the exhausted and thirsty Pandavs discovered a pond. The *yaksha* who ruled the pond warned the brothers that if they dared to drink the water without answering his questions, they would die. While the rest of the Pandavs ignored the *yaksha* in their sense of bravado and succumbed to death, Yudhishthir did not. He quickly deduced that some Divine Being had caused the death of his brothers and when asked, agreed to answer all questions with humility.

Each of those questions and their replies given by Yudhishthir are profound life lessons. But what is most important is the boon Yudhishthir asked for. The *yaksha* turned out to be none other than Yudhisthir's father, Lord Yam. To test him further, He asked him to pick any one of his brothers who could be brought back to life. Yudhishthir asked for Nakul's life to be restored. He reasoned that, since he was Kunti's son, at least one son of Madri should live on. Moved by Yudhisthir's sense of fairness, Yamraj brought all the Pandavs back to life. He also asked this eldest Pandav to seek a boon. Yudhishthir asked for the Brahmin's implements to be returned. Moved again, Yam asked him to seek yet another boon and Yudhishthir said, 'The thirteenth year of our exile is approaching. In this year, we have to live incognito according to the conditions of the game of dice. Hence, grant me the boon that none of us will be recognized during this year.'

Yamraj granted this boon, saying that even if the Pandavs roamed the world in their current forms, no one would be able to recognize them throughout the thirteenth year of exile. Then He asked Yudhishthir to seek one more boon. He could have asked for anything. Instead, he said, 'Grant me the boon that I may be able to win over greed, attachment and anger, and that I may always find joy in charity, *tapasya* and Truth.'

Could there be any greater testament to the purity of Yudhishthir's heart? He was fair, generous, compassionate, practical and always committed to doing the right thing, while Duryodhan was the epitome of jealousy, greed, crime and selfishness.[47]

Why Did Lord Krishna Side with Yudhishthir and the Pandavs?

Hours after being crowned Chakravarti Samrat, Yudhishthir was willing to end his life because he did not want to be a medium of death, destruction and war. He was okay to being Chakravarti Samrat and living like a vagabond in the forest so long as he knew he was following Dharm under both circumstances. While he gave up the luxuries and comforts of his kingship, he did not give up the responsibilities of a king in providing for the 10,000 Brahmins who had followed the Pandavs from Hastinapur. In fulfilling the conditions of a wager for exile, even the temptations of an early war and victory could not entice him. But once those conditions were fulfilled, Yudhishthir did not flinch from going to war with his own uncle, cousins and *guru*, because by then, the Pandavs had fulfilled their end of the bargain. Thus the war had become 'the only right thing to do'.

Which man would be so focused on 'doing the right thing' without falling prey to anger, greed or vengeance, regardless of whether he was treated fairly or unfairly by the elders in his family? Which man would be able to maintain his mental and emotional balance after becoming the Chakravarti Samrat and subsequently losing it all to become a hapless pauper wandering in forests for 13 years? Which man would remain reasonable while being weighed down by the guilt of the grave wrong he had committed—for which he was being chastised every single day by his loved ones?

Only an extraordinary man like Yudhishthir.

Yudhishthir committed *one* unforgiveable mistake, but Duryodhan planned and executed a series of crimes—deceit, murder, perversion and revenge born only out of hatred, greed and jealousy. Isn't it ironic that those who detest Yudhishthir for his one mistake choose to sympathize with Duryodhan, whose life is replete with numerous crimes, mostly against the Pandavas who had only wished him well and, therefore, deserved none of it?

9

Why Is the Bungling Indra King of the Gods?

Indra, great in his power and might,
and like Parjanya rich in rain...

Indra, 'King of the Gods', 'Ruler of Heaven', the god who is known to do whatever it takes—ethical or unethical—to protect His realm and position, is perhaps the most controversial character of the Sanatan ethos. Several episodes of the Ramayan, Mahabharat and Purans document many infamous escapades of this powerful 'God of Thunder, Lightning and Rain'. Indra is the one who tried to seduce Ahilya, the wife of Rishi Gautam, by taking on the form of her husband[1] (See also, Chapter 13: 'Was it Fair for Ahilya to Be Cursed?'). Indra tricked Karn into giving up the *kavach* and *kundal* that rendered him invincible, to protect His own son Arjun.[2] He tried to unfairly punish the people of Gokul for not showing Him the reverence He expected of them, by causing torrential rains.[3]

Puranic tales recount instances when Indra sent His *apsaras*—or tried other dubious strategies—to distract *tapasvi*s from their *tapasya* for fear that it would make the *rishi*s more powerful than Him, thereby endangering His position as King of the Gods.

Lord Indra has often been helpless before evils like arrogance, insecurity, selfishness, jealousy and lust, yet He remains King of the Gods! The Trinity—Brahma, Vishnu and Shiva—seems to overlook His many missteps, even as they punish the *rakshasa*s for their crimes. This raises several questions: Shouldn't the King of the Gods epitomize unimpeachable ethics and virtue? Why does verse after verse in the scriptures, predominantly in the exalted text of the Rig Veda, praise Indra?

Indra: An Office, Not a Person

First, Indra is an office, not a person (See also, Chapter 14: 'Was it Misogynistic for Draupadi to Have Five Husbands?'). The person holding the position of Indra does so for one *manvantar*, a unit in the Hindu cyclic calculation of time which spans 306,720,000 years; 14 *manvantar*s make one *kalpa*.[4] The Indra of the current *manvantar* that we are living in is Purandhar. Needless to say, in each cycle of a *manvantar*, the person holding the position of Indra is different.

Therefore, since the persons occupying the office of Indra are many, the aforementioned crimes cannot be attributed to any one person, because in different *kalpa*s, the same instances tend to be repeated with minor variations, depending on how circumstances pan out and what lessons need to be taught to humanity in that particular *kalpa* (See also Chapter 4: 'How Could the All-Knowing Lord Shiva not Recognize His Own Son?').

As a concept though, Indra has both a physical as well as a spiritual connotation. To understand both, it is important to understand some key concepts of Sanatan.

Moksh

'Moksh' is the state of being in which the person is in complete oneness with his innate Divinity, and hence, with the universe. Such a soul is immune to the joys and sorrows of life, exists in a state of undisturbed peace and bliss, and is capable of feeling only love towards all of Creation, completely untainted by ego, greed and selfishness. Such a soul may retire into seclusion. *If* they decide to stay in society, they will dedicate themselves to humanitarian and philanthropic causes. On death, such a soul will never have to be born again. However, it may choose to incarnate in any realm of existence to serve the beings residing there, but is not bound to do so.

Attaining such liberation is the ultimate goal of all life according to Sanatan.

Devs

In Sanatan Dharm, *dev*s are deities or ministers in charge of various responsibilities that are essential to keep the cosmos running. For instance, Varun Dev is responsible for keeping the amount of water on Earth in check. He decides the boundary beyond which the ocean will not spill onto land, ensures that the rains created by Indra are absorbed by the rivers and that all rivers—along with their tributaries—ultimately merge with the ocean. Surya Dev is in charge of providing the right amount of heat energy to sustain life on Earth. Vayu Dev maintains the flow of air and ensures the appropriate balance of gases in the air to keep it breathable.

Lord Indra is responsible for cloud formation, thunder, lightning and precipitation while also leading the *dev*s and utilizing their powers to maintain the delicate balance of the elements on Earth as well as in the cosmos.

Loks

According to the Atharva Veda, the cosmos consists of 14 *lok*s, or dimensions of existence—from the highest degree of spiritual evolution to the lowest:

1. Satya Lok or Brahma Lok
2. Tap Lok
3. Jan Lok
4. Mahar Lok
5. Swar Lok (Swarg or Heaven)
6. Bhuvar Lok
7. Bhu Lok (Earth)
8. Atal Lok
9. Vital Lok
10. Sutal Lok
11. Talatal Lok
12. Mahatal Lok
13. Rasatal Lok
14. Patal Lok

The inhabitants of 'Satya Lok'—the highest *lok*—are souls who have attained the state of 'Moksh'. They have no physical body and exist as subtle energy in an eternal state of 'Nirvana'. Therefore, they are neither bound by duty nor by desire.

As one moves downward, beings become increasingly more materialistic, and hence, more bound to the material world. One can see that 'Swar Lok'—or heaven—is *not* the highest *lok*. This means, beings of this world, though more powerful and spiritual than the ones which exist on 'Bhu Lok'—Earth—are still bound by certain materialistic attachments.

This applies to Lord Indra as well. Indra is bound to the material world by virtue of His duties to keep the various elements of the cosmos in balance, by ensuring that the other gods manage their individual responsibilities and charges well. Need one still emphasize the importance of the office of Indra in the cosmos? That is why the Rig Veda extols Indra, granting Him a stature similar to the Trinity, as He is directly responsible for preserving the delicate balance of elements to keep the universe alive and viable. But unlike Brahma, Vishnu and Shiva—who are beyond time and the *lok*s—Indra is still subject to materialism and negativity. Therefore, Indra is not immune to emotions like insecurity, jealousy, lust, arrogance, selfishness and the like.

However, Lord Indra has an enormous virtuous side. Unlike the *asur*s who have repeatedly tried to conquer all the worlds to establish their supremacy over them, Indra has never been known to attack their *lok*s just to establish His own power over them. Indra and the *devata*s strictly adhere to—and uphold—the order of things as envisaged by Brahma, Vishnu and Shiva. Indra's notorious escapades have been restricted to safeguarding His own position or kingdom rather than usurping that of any other being. So, the *dev*s and Indra are far more deserving of help from the Trinity than the *asur*s who have also been given repeated warnings and ample opportunities to mend their ways, whether it was Tarakasur, Ravan or Hiranyakashipu, among others.

While Indra may have indulged in dubious deeds, according to the scriptures, He was always corrected or punished by the *rishi*s or by the Trinity. Rishi Gautam put a terrible curse on Indra for the crime He committed against Ahilya.[5] Lord Krishna destroyed Indra's ego by lifting Mount Govardhan and protecting the *audacious* villagers of Gokul. In fact, Indra and His *dev*s were banished from heaven several times in many Puranic episodes as punishment for their misdeeds.[6]

So, while the scriptures extol these gods for their power and importance in keeping the cosmos going, they also unabashedly recount instances where they fell short of meeting the demands of Dharm, and the punishment they received for their corrupt deeds.

Spiritual Connotation of Indra

Spiritually speaking, a bungling Indra is essential to promote and explain the true meaning of spirituality to mankind. Sanatan is the only philosophy and way of life that has never sought heaven as a reward for a life well lived. Sanatan seeks only Moksh or eternal liberation and bliss.

While heaven is the reward for a life well lived, Moksh is beyond the desire for reward. A life in heaven is temporary; the experience of Moksh is permanent. A seeker of heaven may be dogmatic; a seeker of Moksh is spiritual.

Hence, Moksh is the higher goal. And if heaven cannot provide Moksh, the genuine seeker has no use even for the superlatively pleasant, comfortable and powerful life in this realm.

Had the *dev*s not been susceptible to attachments and their associated vices, the pleasantness of heaven might have been mistaken as the ultimate goal of human life, and seekers might have ignored the high principle of Moksh. Thus, even in their vices, the *dev*s—Indra in particular—serve as stark reminders of the true purpose of existence. In the ultimate analysis, Moksh, Nirvana, Bodhisattva, Liberation or Divinity is all that matters.

10

Why Is Dev Rishi Narad So Respected and Adored?

Such an effulgent being, wandering in the worlds,
came there with the speed of his mind.

The name 'Narad Muni' immediately brings to mind the image of a gossipy saint, fuelling a fire here, fanning an ember there, nudging unsuspecting subjects into thinking and acting in ways they wouldn't have without his *innocent push*. Narad Muni has created plot points and unexpected twists and turns in many a tale!

One wonders why this gossipy *muni* enjoys such tremendous credibility and reverence among the beings of all the 14 *lok*s mentioned in Sanatan? Why do the *dev*s, *asur*s, *gandharv*s, *nag*s, humans, and even Lord Brahma, Lord Vishnu and Lord Shiva adore, respect and love him?

This chapter attempts to answer these questions. I hope the reader is as awed as I was when I first came across a chapter in the Ved Vyas Mahabharat which completely changed my impression about Narad Muni.

The occasion is one of the times that Narad Muni visits the Pandavs in Indraprastha to teach Yudhishthir the art and science of administration through a series of questions.[1] There are more than 100 such questions in the chapter. However, I have taken only those most relevant to modern times, clubbing a few together and altering the order of some to ensure a fluid read. Apart from these cosmetic adjustments, every word of what follows is what Narad Muni said, as documented in Chapter 5 of the 'Sabha Parv' in the Ved Vyas Mahabharat:[2]

1. 'Yudhishthir, I hope you awaken on time, dress immaculately, hold court with your wise and accomplished ministers and duly attend to and respectfully satisfy all those who come to you with various requests every single day.'
2. 'Oh! The best among winners, are all four *varna*s (Brahmins, Kshatriyas, Vaishyas and Shudras) in your kingdom prosperous and happy? I hope you use the eight methods of augmenting your wealth and treasury.'

Eight methods of augmenting one's wealth and treasury:	
1.	Increase in agricultural produce
2.	Protection of business and industry
3.	Construction of forts and their security
4.	Construction of bridges and their security
5.	Restraint of elephants
6.	Control over mines of gold, gems and other minerals
7.	Taxation
8.	Creation of new habitable cities and villages in hitherto desolate districts

3. 'Are you aware of the farmers and labourers of your kingdom? Do you take interest in their affairs? I hope there is no distrust between you and them. Also, I hope you provide them with continuous employment. Remember that great progress and prosperity of a kingdom depends only on their loving and sincere support. It is only when their needs are taken care of over extended periods of time that they trust the king and become loyal and affectionate towards him.'
4. 'Have you built artificial lakes in different regions of your kingdom? Hope agriculture is not solely dependent on

rainfall (and there are sufficient irrigation facilities available to farmers).'
5. 'Hope the crop and seeds of your farmers are always protected. Do you support every farmer in your kingdom by giving them loans at only one per cent interest?'
6. 'Do good people engage in activities like farming, business and industry, and protection of cows, sincerely and efficiently? It is only when a kingdom depends on these activities for its income that it can progress smoothly and peacefully.'
7. 'In every village of each district in your kingdom, do you have an intelligent, diligent, valiant and fair *panch* who promotes the welfare of your subjects by efficiently executing programmes and tasks designed to benefit your people?'
8. 'Do you protect your cities, and are your villages also protected by numerous valiant soldiers? Do your border villages have the same facilities and resources as your other villages? Also do all the districts, cities and villages pay you their taxes on time?'
9. 'Do your police keep patrolling central as well as remote cities in your kingdom, protecting your subjects from thieves and dacoits?'
10. 'Do the traders and businessmen of your kingdom, and those of others, bring quality goods for sale? Do you honour and respect them? I hope your officers collect the right amount of tax from them and do not swindle them.'
11. 'Do you systematically provide enough raw material to your workers for the four months of the monsoon season so that work can proceed without a hitch?'
12. 'I hope that you identify projects in which the initial investment is less but the returns are manifold, and then you waste no time in beginning them. I also hope that

you don't create obstacles for anyone who is involved in creating wealth this way.'
13. 'Hope you do not hurt righteousness and wealth by:
    a. Ignoring righteousness in your greed for wealth
    b. Ignoring wealth by using it only in the affairs of Dharm (*yagya*, charity, rituals, etc.)
    c. Blowing up your wealth and destroying your righteousness by over-indulging your senses in various temptations and attractions'
14. 'O Sinless King! Do you use the six qualities of a king in order to regularly and thoroughly inspect the seven strategic systems of your kingdom as well as the 15 departments in your kingdom and 18 departments in your enemies' kingdoms through three spies per department?'

The six qualities of a king are:	
1.	Ability to analyze
2.	Ability to think and communicate logically
3.	Knowledge of history
4.	Foresight for the future
5.	Excellence in strategizing
6.	Fearless enthusiasm with commitment
The seven strategic strengths of a kingdom are:	
1.	*Sama:* Enlisting support through explanation, logic, etc.
2.	*Dama:* Charity or promise of reward
3.	*Danda:* Punishment
4.	*Bheda:* Spies and intelligence infrastructure
5.	Healthcare
6.	Vedic *mantras*
7.	Use of specific rituals to gain power and support from different types of beings and forms of energy in nature

The 18 departments/officers of the enemies' kingdoms that need to be spied upon are:	
1.	Ministers
2.	*Purohit* (spiritual advisor to the king)
3.	King-to-be
4.	General
5.	Palace guards
6.	Accountant
7.	Chief of palace staff
8.	Jailer
9.	Treasurer
10.	Chief of security
11.	Police
12.	Record keeper
13.	Construction supervisor
14.	Speaker of the court/court counsellor
15.	Officer executing sentences of the convicted
16.	Border security commander
17.	Forest officer
18.	Heads of forts

(Apart from the first three, the other 15 officers/departments of one's own kingdom should also be inspected from time to time.)

15. 'Are the women in your kingdom completely secure and happy?'
16. 'The best among the descendants of Bharat, I hope the seven *prakriti*s of your kingdom, including the ministers, are not in cahoots with your enemies? And I hope that

the wealthy among your subjects keep away from vices and addictions and love you wholeheartedly.'

The seven *prakritis* are:	
1.	King
2.	Ministers
3.	Friends and allies
4.	Treasury
5.	Idea of nation
6.	Forts and army
7.	General public

17. 'Do you keep information about what your friends, enemies and even those who are neither your friends nor your enemies aspire to do, and when they wish to do it?'
18. 'You do keep giving due gifts of jewels and money to the chief warriors in your enemy camps surreptitiously, don't you?'
19. 'Have you kept as your ministers only those who are as trustworthy as you yourself are, those who are pure-hearted, experienced, excellent communicators, accomplished and have deep affection for you? Because Bharat! The basis of a king's success is right advice, its secrecy and efficient execution.'
20. 'Any secret discussion remains a secret only if it is restricted to two or four pairs of ears. The moment it reaches six pairs of ears, it no longer remains a secret. Therefore, I hope that on any vital or complex matter, you neither reflect all alone nor discuss it with too many people. I hope your clandestine plans do not reach your enemies.'
21. 'Do you get work related to farming, etc. done by sincere, generous, non-greedy, non-corrupt, experienced, tried

22. 'Do you have only those as teachers who are righteous, knowledgeable and scholars of the various *shastras*?'
23. 'Are all your forts well equipped at all times with wealth and resources like food, water, weapons, machines, architects, doctors, masons and soldiers, especially expert archers?'
24. 'Are your *purohit*s humble, well-bred, scholars in various subjects, sincere, pure-hearted and skilled in debating?'
25. 'King! Are you as strict as Yamraj (God of Death) towards punishment-worthy criminals and as pleasant as Dharmraj (God of Righteousness) towards the pious? I also hope that your officers administer your kingdom with fairness and justice.'
26. 'Hope no thief caught by your corrupt guards in the act of thievery is let go just so that they get a share in the loot.'
27. 'Hope you do not burden your subjects with excess taxes. Hope your subjects are not made to suffer at the hands of your officers, the princes, the princesses and the queens.'
28. 'Is your military commander full of enthusiasm? Is he loyal, patient, intelligent, heroic, selfless and efficient? Are the heads of the various divisions of your army and soldiers fearless, non-corrupt and valiant? Do you treat them with due respect and honour?'
29. 'I hope when any of your employees displays extraordinary efficiency or effort in successfully fulfilling a task, you duly honour and reward them.'
30. 'King! Do you come to know of the benevolence displayed by your subjects? And when you come to know of it, do you honour and express gratitude to that benefactor in your court, in the presence of your exalted courtiers?'

31. 'O King! I hope you look after and protect the families of all those who happily risk their lives or undergo great troubles for you.'
32. 'Son of Kunti! Do you look after the one who has sought refuge in you either out of fear, or because of losing all his wealth or having lost to you in battle, as you would look after your son?'
33. 'Do people of the entire world look at you as a fair king who is as trustworthy for them as their own parents?'
34. 'Kuntinandan! Hope you do not attack your enemies out of lust, greed, arrogance or jealousy. I hope you attack only after solidifying the foundations of your own kingdom. Once you vanquish an enemy, I hope you protect them thoroughly and wholeheartedly.'
35. 'Kuntinandan! Before you attack your enemies, do you try the means of *Sama, Dama, Danda* and *Bheda* in the proper manner?' (Successful use of these four tactics is said to prevent war.)
36. 'Hope you never disregard famine or the season of harvest in your enemy's territory and only fight them on the battlefield (hope you do not destroy their fields or trouble their subjects).'
37. 'Your Highness! I hope your food-related items, various garments, perfumes and other personal items are watched over only by trustworthy guards.'
38. 'Hope your granaries, treasury, vehicles, main gates, weaponry, sources of income and other resources are looked after only by non-corrupt, dedicated and diligent men who keep only your best interests at heart and are devoted to you.'
39. 'I hope your employees do not propose to you indulgence in addictions like alcohol, gambling, lust and other vices which waste your time and destroy your wealth.'

40. 'Are you able to manage all your expenses with only one-fourth, half or three-fourths of your income?'
41. 'Do all your accountants and documenters present the records of your income and expenditure to you every morning?'
42. 'I hope you have appointed only intelligent, sincere, knowledgeable, straightforward and devout Brahmins for your *agnihotra*s. I hope you treat them with respect.'
43. 'Do you keep your body healthy by taking prescribed medicines and observing dietary restrictions? And do you de-stress your mind, look after your mental health by associating with experienced and wise men?'
44. 'Do you constantly keep studying, and practising principles in the various *sutra*s like:

    - *Ashwa Sutra:* Principles related to horses
    - *Rath Sutra:* Principles related to vehicles
    - *Dhanurveda Sutra:* Principles related to warfare
    - *Yantra Sutra:* Principles of machines and modernization
    - *Nagarik Sutra:* Principles of public affairs'

45. 'Hope you stay away from the following the 14 administrative flaws because their presence can ruin even well-established empires. They are:

    1. Atheism
    2. Falsehood
    3. Anger
    4. Carelessness
    5. Not associating with the wise and saintly
    6. Laziness
    7. Delay or procrastination in commencing decided projects
    8. Red-tapism

    9. Indulging the five senses
    10. Failure to organize auspicious festivities
    11. Discussions held with foolish ministers who have zero understanding of *Arthashastra* (economics)
    12. Not consulting experts on relevant subjects
    13. Not being able to maintain secrecy on sensitive issues
    14. Attacking all enemies at once'

46. 'Is your mind always engrossed in righteous activities as elucidated in the Vedas? Do you follow Vedic rites with as much dedication as your ancestors did? Do you organize and participate in *yagya*s after restraining your senses and with perfect concentration?'
47. 'Yudhisthir, hope you think and act as discussed now. Such righteous intelligence and attitudes promote long life and fame, create wealth and fulfil one's dreams and aspirations. The king who rules with such intelligence never causes his kingdom to fall into disaster. That king wins over the entire Earth and progresses day-by-day.'

To summarize, Dharm, i.e. integrity, justice and duty, were always at the core of all administrative and strategic decisions. Modernization of irrigation facilities, building infrastructure and use of machines, was an integral part of governance. In the sophisticated administrative structure of Bharat, even the remotest villages were as important as cities. Every aspect of society was respected, honoured and provided with policy-driven facilities to help them contribute to the nation. Together, they fulfilled the idea of *one* successful, prosperous civilization. The people of Bharat attached as much importance to spiritual fulfilment as they did to matters of security, finance, modernization and art. The roots of Bharat's Vedic culture allowed the 'Tree of Progress' to constantly grow and branch out into newer innovations and avenues of accomplishment.

Given the range and depth of Narad Muni's council, the praise showered on him at the beginning of Chapter 5 of the 'Sabha Parv' in the Ved Vyas Mahabharat is hardly surprising:[3]

Dev Rishi Narad understands the essence of the Vedas, Upanishads and other *shastra*s. He can elucidate the underlying unity of seemingly contradictory verses. He is joyfully welcomed and worshipped in all dimensions including heaven, Earth or the nether worlds by all beings. He is an unparalleled linguist who is a master of the construction of sentences, paragraphs, clauses and poetic metres in all their branches. He knows the physical, mental and other practical effects of the five groups of sounds. He is one of the greatest luminaries in the science of logic, justice, politics and warfare...

He has complete knowledge of all that has transpired even in the previous *kalpa* (For *kalpa*, see Chapter 4: 'How could the All-Knowing Lord Shiva not Recognize His Own Son?' and Chapter 9: 'Why is the Bungling Indra King of Gods?'). He has the divine attribute of knowing the past, present and future. He is the transcendental maestro in varied arts like the culinary arts, music, literature and drama...

He is also an unsurpassed scholar in various sciences like economics, sociology, metallurgy, psychology and body language. He is a *muni* who truly knows and understands God and seeks to inspire even the *rakshasa*s on the path of renunciation and realization. He is forever eager to help those seeking enlightenment. He is an unparalleled authority on the nuances of Dharm, and his word is accepted as proof by all. He has a complete understanding of the permanent and contextual duties of all the *varna*s. He can see all the 14 *lok*s directly and can go anywhere at will. He travels at the speed of his mind, using the aerial route which is accessible only to the most accomplished *yogi*s and *tapasvi*s. He is equanimous, ever courteous, never rude and ever pleasant in both speech and demeanour...

Ironically, Narad Muni's 'gossip' has only helped in the short or long run to establish Dharm in the world.

11

Was Karn a Victim of the Caste System?

Duryodhan, why should you feel
grateful or smaller to the Pandavs,
Now you are their king.
It was their duty to protect you.

The story of Karn brings to mind the image of a soul tormented by discrimination because he belonged to a so-called lower caste (See also, Chapter 20: 'What Was the Caste System in Ancient Bharat?'). Consider the following episodes from the Ved Vyas Mahabharat:

Karn received his early education from Dronacharya. Even at that time, Karn was friends with Duryodhan and treated Arjun as a rival.[1] In fact, Karn was the most educated warrior in the Mahabharat, as he studied not only under Dronacharya and Kripacharya with the Kauravs, Pandavs and other princes, but also independently under Rishi Parashuram.[2]

When Karn arrived in the amphitheatre—where the Pandavs and Kauravs had just finished displaying their military prowess to the people of Hastinapur—to prove that he, not Arjun, was the best archer in the world, contrary to some renditions of the Mahabharat, Maharishi Ved Vyas clearly mentions that Karn was allowed to display his skills without prejudice, and he performed the same *astra*s that Arjun had displayed earlier.[3]

Karn won the admiration of everyone in the crowd with his display. Yet, he wanted to challenge Arjun to a duel. Only then was he asked who he was. According to the prevalent custom, only a prince could challenge a prince.[4] And Karn was allowed to fight Arjun because Duryodhan anointed him, King of Anga, the province where he was born before being brought to Hastinapur for his education.[5] At that time, no one present in the assembly, including the royal family, the Brahmins, Dronacharya, Kripacharya, the Pandavs, the other Kshatriyas, and the general population, objected to Karn, a Shudra, being made the king of a province.

When Bhim sledged Karna for being a *sutaputra*, just before Karn was about to fight Arjun, Duryodhan stood by him, quoting from the *shastra*s. Nobody present in the assembly, including Bheeshm, Dronacharya, Kripacharya, the rest of the Pandavs, or the crowd there opposed Duryodhan. On the contrary, they were all full of praise for Duryodhan and Karn.[6]

However, by the time the duel between Karn and Arjun was to begin, the sun had already set, so it was impossible to have the duel after that.[7]

People regard Draupadi's rejection of Karn because he was a *sutaputra*—the son of a charioteer—as an example of caste discrimination but they forget that the same Karn had been duly invited and honoured at her *swayamvar* along with the other Kshtariyas present there[8] (See also, Chapter 14: 'Was it Misogynistic for Draupadi to Have Five Husbands?').

When Arjun won the challenge at Draupadi's *swayamvar*, all the Pandavs, including Arjun, were disguised as Brahmins.[9] The other Kshatriya kings and princes present on the occasion perceived a Brahmin succeeding where they had failed as a great insult. So, together, they attacked Arjun and Bhim. Hence, this event clearly indicates that all the kings along with Karn as the Kshatriyas (the so-called second highest caste) fought against the Brahmins (the highest caste). This clarifies that the *varna*s were not a hierarchy! As warriors, the Kshatriyas could not accept intellectuals triumphing over them in the use of weapons and warfare.[10]

Throughout the Mahabharat, Karn is referred to as 'Angaraj', 'Danveer' Karn, a great warrior and a deadly foe. The Pandavs respected his prowess and Yudhishthir spent sleepless nights thinking of the terrible threat that Karn's military expertise posed to Arjun.[11] Karn's being a *sutaputra* never overshadowed his military prowess.

Even during the *rajasuya yagya* that Yudhishthir performed, Shishupal abhorred the idea of Lord Krishna being honoured in the presence of the mightiest of Kshatriyas in the assembly. He suggested Karn's name along with those of stalwarts like Bheeshm, Dronacharya and Parashuram, as worthier than Krishna of the honour, despite Krishna being Shishupal's cousin.[12]

Despite all the honour that was bestowed on Karn throughout the Mahabharat, his burning desire to defeat Arjun was never satiated. He sided with Duryodhan in all the crimes the latter committed, including conspiring to burn the Pandavs—and their mother Kunti—alive in the Lakshagriha,[13] the devious game of dice, and the Kurukshetra War.[14] It was Karn who ordered Dushasan to disrobe Draupadi in the court of Hastinapur.[15]

For Karn, his status as king of Anga—donated to him by Duryodhan—was more important than upholding justice and righteousness. Karn pledged his loyalty to a selfish, greedy, ruthless and unfair man like Duryodhan, constantly fuelled the latter's hatred for the Pandavs and supported him with all his military prowess, just because he wanted to outdo Arjun.

12

How Could Hanuman Swallow the Sun?

yug sahsra yojan par bhanu...

[The Sun is situated at a distance of
thousands of yojanas beyond the age *(yug)*.]

—'Hanuman Chalisa', Verse 18

Hanuman swallowing the sun appears fantastical and puts to question the credibility of Sanatan history. However, Bharatiya scriptures have already answered the question headlining this chapter (See also, Chapter 18: 'How can Sanatan Dharm have Gods like Ganesh, Hanuman and Narasimha?').

Eight Siddhis

The scriptures mention eight types of *siddhi*s:

1. *Anima:* Ability to reduce one's size to the atomic level
2. *Mahima:* Ability to increase one's size infinitesimally
3. *Garima:* Ability to become heavier
4. *Laghima:* Ability to become lighter, to the point of being weightless
5. *Prapti*: Ability to instantly obtain anything one desires from anywhere
6. *Prakamya:* Ability to fulfil one's desires, increase one's lifespan and survive in impossible circumstances, like under water, without food or drink, etc.

7. *Isitva:* Lordship over creation
8. *Vasitva:* Control over everything, including the five elements

Patanjali's *Yoga Sutra*s indicate how these *siddhi*s can be developed within an individual:[1]

Janma: Birth/genetics
Ausadhi: Use of herbs
Mantra: Chanting of sacred mantras
Tapah: Austerities
Samadhijah: Meditation for extended periods of time

The Bhagavat Puran mentions the following primary and secondary *siddhi*s that can be attained by an aspirant through yoga and meditation.

Primary *siddhis*:

1. *Trikalajnatvam:* Knowing the past, present and future
2. *Advandvam:* Tolerating heat, cold and other dualities
3. *Para Citta Adi Abhijnata*: Knowing the minds of others
4. *Agni, Arka, Ambu, Visa, Adinam Pratistambhah:* Controlling the influence of fire, sun, water, poison, etc.
5. *Aparajaya:* Remaining invincible, unvanquished

Secondary *siddhis*:

1. *Anurmimattvam:* Remaining undisturbed by hunger, thirst and other bodily appetites
2. *Durashravan:* Hearing things far away
3. *Duradarshanam:* Seeing things far away
4. *Manojavah:* Projecting astrally, teleporting at the speed of thought
5. *Kamarupan:* Assuming any form desired
6. *Parakaya Pravesanam:* Entering the bodies of others

7. *Svacchanda Mrityuh:* Dying when one desires
8. *Devanam Saha Krida Anudarshanam:* Witnessing and participating in the pastimes of the gods
9. *Yath Sankalpa Samadhi:* Perfect accomplishment of one's desires

Parmahamsa Yogananda's *Autobiography of a Yogi* (1946) and Swami Rama's *Living with the Himalayan Masters* (1978) document such *siddhi*s and supernatural powers that are used and displayed even today by *sadhu*s and seekers of various religious and cultural orders throughout Bharat and other parts of the world.

Why Do Hanuman's Feats Appear to Be Fantastical?

The above question would find an unequivocal answer in Chapter 6 of the *Vaimanika Shastra* (Aeronautical Science).[2] In this chapter, Maharishi Bharadwaj mentions three categories of *viman*s, classified according to the *yug*s in which they are built and operated (See also, Chapter 22: 'Does science have its origins in Sanantan Dharm?' and Chapter 38: 'Basic Concepts of Sanatan Dharm').

Satya Yug: People are completely rooted in righteousness and hence so firmly anchored in their cosmic power that the eight above-mentioned *siddhi*s come naturally to them. Therefore, they do not need *viman*s. They can travel at the speed of wind anywhere in the world.

Treta Yug: People start becoming slightly corrupt. Hence, they begin to become isolated from their cosmic power. Therefore, many need *viman*s. But they can build and operate their *viman*s by using *mantra*s. Such *viman*s are called *mantrika viman*s.

Dwapar Yug: As people become even more Adharmic, they become so cut off from their cosmic power that they can build and operate *viman*s only by using Tantras—a combination of *mantra*s and metaphysical devices. Such *viman*s are called *tantrika viman*s.

Kali Yug/Kalyug (present day and age): With Dharm on the verge of extinction, people are so cut off from their cosmic power that none of the aforementioned means work, and people have to rely solely on mechanical devices and technology to build and operate their *viman*s. Such *viman*s are called *kritaka*—artificial—*viman*s.

Conclusion

What is considered fantastical today was a natural 'way of being' for almost everyone in the Satya Yug and many in the Treta Yug. Also, Hanuman was genetically predisposed to inherit superhuman powers as he was the son of Vayu, God of Wind.

As the Valmiki Ramayan states, Brahma ordered the gods to help Vishnu in his Ram avatar to eliminate Ravan:

> Let monkey-shaped progeny equalling Vishnu's valour be procreated and they shall be wizards of miracles and audacious ones; in travel, they shall have the speed of the wind; bestowed with intellect, they shall be the knowers of ideation, and with their divine physique, they shall be ineliminable; they shall be endowed with all the assaultive aspects of all missiles, and they shall be untiring in their efforts, like you (the gods) who thrive on ambrosia, unmindful of thirst and hunger. (1:17.3, 4, 6)
>
> The direct son of the God of Wind is the marvellous and adventurous Hanuman with an indestructible body,

and one identical in the speed of Lady Vinata's son, namely Garuda, the Divine Eagle vehicle of Vishnu, and among all monkey chiefs, he is the intelligent and the indefatigable one too. (1:17.16, 17)

13

Was it Fair for Ahilya to Be Cursed?

On your welcoming Ram...you will be divested of your greed... Then you will assume your own body...and be in my proximity, rejoicingly.

Another incident from the Ramayan that has ignited much debate involves Rishi Gautam cursing his wife, Ahilya. The following should resolve the debate once and for all.

The Episode

Ahilya was exceptionally beautiful and Lord Indra was infatuated with her. So intense was His desire for Ahilya that setting aside all propriety, one morning after Rishi Gautam left his hermitage for his ablutions, Indra took on the form of the *rishi* and entered Ahilya and Rishi Gautam's chamber in the hermitage. After having copulated with Ahilya, as Indra was leaving the hermitage, Rishi Gautam returned. At the sight of Indra, through his yogic powers, Rishi Gautam intuited all that had transpired and cursed both Indra and Ahilya.

Did Ahilya Know That It Was Lord Indra in Disguise?

The debate about whether Rishi Gautam was right in cursing Ahilya is directly related to whether or not Ahilya had seen through Lord Indra's disguise. If she had not recognized that it was Indra who had assumed the form of her husband, she had only acquiesced to the wishes of her husband. Hence, what transpired between her and Indra in disguise was not her fault, and the curse was unfair.

However, the Valmiki Ramayan mentions unequivocally—Ahilya knew that the man before her was not her husband; He was Lord Indra.[1] Indra had taken on the form of Rishi Gautam and spoken to Ahilya of His desire. But Ahilya had seen through the disguise and recognized Him immediately. Not only did she tell Him that she knew who He was, she also said that she was gratified that the King of Gods desired her and that she was happy to fulfil His wish.[2] In fact, before Indra left, she even warned him to watch out for Rishi Gautam and protect both Himself and her from the *rishi*'s ire.[3]

Ahilya had clearly given in to temptation. So, the fault was both Indra's and Ahilya's. Therefore, there was nothing unfair about Rishi Gautam cursing Ahilya. In fact, he first cursed Indra and then Ahilya.[4]

Relationship between Power and Restraint

One might argue, however, that a *rishi* could have been more forgiving. The counter to that is, a *rishi patni*—one powerful enough to see through Indra's disguise—should have exercised more restraint.

The more powerful, i.e. the more connected a being is with the universe or the elements, the more far-reaching is the impact of their thoughts and actions. To use an analogy, a live ember falling on sand has no effect, but the same ember falling on a stack of hay can start a fire, and the same ember falling on a heap of gunpowder can set off an explosion. While this ember of temptation may be forgivable for an ordinary individual, it is unforgivable for a mighty god and an almost equally powerful being.

Having said that, Rishi Gautam actually did forgive Ahilya. Attached to the curse was also her path to redemption—she would be absolved of her infidelity on receiving Lord Ram and offering Him her hospitality. Rishi Gautam also promised that thereafter, he and Ahilya would be happily reconciled.[5]

Had things transpired the other way around, Ahilya too would have been justified in cursing her husband, a powerful *rishi*, for his infidelity. There are instances in ancient Bharat where men too have been cursed. Emperor Yayati was cursed by his father-in-law, Rishi Shukracharya, with premature and excruciating old age because Yayati had cheated on his wife Devyani.[6] Lord Shani's wife, Damini, cursed Him with destructive vision when He neglected her while performing a *yagya*.[7] The rules of Dharm were equal for both men and women in ancient Bharat.

The *rishi*s of yore were known to do *tapasya* for thousands of years in forests and caves. It is believed that many still reside in the deep recesses of the Himalayas. What Ahilya was made to do, albeit as a curse, was not punishment but rather a *rishi*'s *tapasya*. She was *not* turned into a stone; the curse clearly stated that she would become invisible to the world, like a grain of dust, subsisting on nothing but air.[8] The 'stone' analogy came from the context of *tapasya*, i.e. subduing one's passions and senses—being a stone in the face of temptation—the most important step to spiritual progress. The Purans and the epics recount episodes in which powerful *rishi*s like Vishwamitra lost the spiritual splendour they had accumulated through *tapasya* when they allowed themselves to be seduced by *apsara*s sent by Indra. They had to begin their austerities all over again.

Had Ahilya evinced the desire to leave Rishi Gautam for another man, the incident might have played out differently, but this was just pure, carnal passion—something that a woman as powerful and spiritual as Ahilya should have been able to hold back from had she wanted to. Even Rishi Gautam had to perform intense *tapasya* after this incident as the bout of anger which made him curse Indra and Ahilya diminished his spiritual power.[9]

However, while narrating the incident, the Valmiki Ramayan does not judge Ahilya. It clearly mentions that Brahmarishi Vishwamitra ended his narration of Ahilya's story by actually praising her great *tapasya*, and by revering the spiritual power that it gave her.

It is also erroneous to say that Lord Ram had to touch the stone with His feet for Ahilya to be released from the curse. The Valmiki Ramayan mentions that the moment Ram and Lakshman entered the hermitage where Ahilya resided, she came into their view and it was the brothers who touched Ahilya's feet out of respect for her.[10]

The *tapasya* freed Ahilya of her past mistakes. Not only had she redeemed herself but she had emerged self-contained, powerful and blissful. Even the gods assembled in heaven, and showered flowers on her, celebrating her victory over her mind—the most difficult aspect of *sadhana*.[11] After Ahilya had rendered due hospitality to the visitors, a joyous Rishi Gautam himself appeared there to take his wife along with him to the Himalayas.[12]

The story of Ahilya serves as another reminder that Sanatan Dharm documents events with perfect candour, irrespective of whether the individual involved is a man, woman, god, *rishi* or an ordinary mortal. Unbiased, Sanatan documents the errors as well as the celebration of redemption.

14

Was it Misogynistic for Draupadi to Have Five Husbands?

...distribute it amongst yourselves...

The popular belief that Draupadi was *forced* to marry five men *only* to honour Kunti's thoughtless command is based on a false assumption. And yet, if that were true, it would be unfortunate and cruel. However, in the Ved Vyas Mahabharat, this episode has multiple dimensions, and Draupadi was not forced into any situation.

Draupadi's Birth

King Drupad had performed a *yagya* to beget a son capable of killing the invincible Dronacharya.[1] From the ceremonial flames emerged a young man named Dhrishtadyumna, who was ready to go into battle. An *akashvani* declared him to be a warrior par excellence and the answer to Drupad's prayers.

Then emerged a beautiful, dark-complexioned, fiery woman. The *akashvani* declared that she was Krishna, the most beautiful woman on Earth,[2] born only to help the *devata*s annihilate thousands of Kshatriyas and petrify the Adharmik Kauravs.[3] Drupad and the entire kingdom of Panchal welcomed the birth of this daughter who came to be known as Draupadi (daughter of Drupad). When the time was right, Drupad announced the *swayamvar* of Draupadi.[4]

Visit by Maharishi Ved Vyas

Around that time, the Pandavs were roaming the forests, residing in different villages disguised as Brahmins after narrowly escaping a murder conspiracy in Lakshagriha, hatched by Duryodhan. Since they were disguised as Brahmins, they had to beg for food and alms every day.

75 days before Draupadi's *swayamvar*, Maharishi Ved Vyas appeared before the Pandavs.[5] Except Vidur, no one knew that the Pandavs were alive. But Ved Vyas was *trikaal darshi*—he could look into the past, present and future of anyone. He told the Pandavs about Draupadi's previous birth and that she was destined to marry all five brothers.

Maharishi Ved Vyas explained that in her previous birth, she had done *tapasya* to get the perfect man as her husband. Pleased with her austerities, when Lord Shiva had appeared before her, she asked him to grant her the boon of the perfect man as her husband, but repeated her desire five times in her excitement.[6] Lord Shiva smiled at this and said that she would have five husbands in her next birth. The five husbands were the Pandavs.

The Swayamvar

During the *swayamvar*, in front of the entire assembly of kings, *devata*s, *gandharv*s and *rishi*s, Draupadi rejected Karn, the only man other than Arjun who could have won the contest, and Arjun won.[7]

Proposal for Marriage

When Arjun and Bhim returned with Draupadi to their abode, and told Kunti—whose back was turned towards them—'We have brought alms,' without looking, Kunti ordered, 'Whatever it is, distribute it among yourselves.' This was awkward for everyone. When Kunti realized what she had done, she was horrified, and immediately took Draupadi to Yudhishthir to consult him.[8]

Yudhishthir was clear that since Arjun had won the contest, he should be the one to marry Draupadi.[9] But Arjun did not want to marry just yet as he was younger than Yudhishthir, who was still unmarried (Bhim had married Hidimba because she herself had proposed to him). At the time, Yudhishthir glanced at Draupadi and the rest of the Pandavs. He remembered what Rishi Vyas had said about all five of them being destined to marry Draupadi, and he could see that somewhere each brother was reflecting on his words. Yudhishthir did not want any ill feeling between the brothers.

Through all this, Draupadi remained silent. The woman who had openly rejected Karn in front of an assembly of kings a while back, the woman who later reduced the entire assembly of hundreds of kings in court of Hastinapur into a shameful silence through her pointed questions—that Draupadi did not register any protest at the prospect of marrying all five Pandavs.

Such polyandric marriages were not unheard of in ancient Bharat. Jatila had married seven *rishi*s.[10] Varakshi had done *tapasya* and consequently married 10 brothers.[11] All these men and women were well respected in ancient Bharat.

The next day, when Yudhishthir informed Drupad of their decision—Draupadi marrying all the five Pandavs—he and Drishtadyumna did not agree.[12] At that time, Maharishi Ved Vyas appeared there again and informed Drupad about Draupadi's previous life and also shared the origins of the Pandavs.[13]

Previous Lives of the Pandavs

At some point in the past, four of the Pandavs were the Indras of heaven while Arjun was the son of the current Indra, and

Draupadi was the personification of Swarg Lakshmi, i.e. Goddess of Prosperity and Abundance. The five Indras were:

1. Vishwabhoot incarnated as Yudhisthir
2. Bhutadham incarnated as Bhim
3. Shibi (Indra of the time of the Mahabharat) who became Arjun's father
4. Shanti incarnated as Nakul, and
5. Tejasvi incarnated as Sahdev

Lord Shiva had ordained that the four Indras and Arjun would incarnate in the mortal world as brothers, with Swarg Lakshmi as their consort, with the specific task of helping Lord Vishnu annihilate the unrighteous and re-establish Dharm in the world. At that time, the Indras had decided which *devata*s would father them, and that is how things happened:

- Yudhishthir was the son of Yam, God of Death and Righteousness
- Bhim was the son of Vayu, God of Wind
- Arjun was the son of the current Indra called Shibi
- Nakul and Sahdev were sons of the Ashwin twins, the physicians of the gods[14]

Not only did Ved Vyas narrate this episode to Drupad, but he also showed him a vision of the same event. Only then did Drupad agree to Draupadi marrying the five brothers. Hence, Draupadi married each of the five Pandavs on five consecutive days.[15]

Rules of Marriage

The brothers laid down some rules regarding Draupadi.[16] She would stay in the palace of one brother for a continuous period of one year. Whenever she was alone with one of the brothers, anywhere in the palace or outside, the other brothers were not to see them together. If any brother did that, he would have to go into exile for 12 years, and adhere to celibacy during the period of exile.

Arjun had to go on such an exile. Once, Draupadi was alone with Yudhishthir in the armoury of the palace. At that time, a Brahmin arrived at the palace gates seeking help from the Pandavs. His cows had been stolen and he was in great distress. Arjun took it upon himself to help as he did not want to turn away any subject seeking help from them. However, Arjun's weapons were in the armoury of the palace. He knew the consequences of going in there, but for him, helping his subject was more important than avoiding the exile. He went in and took his bow and arrows without so much as looking at Draupadi or Yudhishthir, but he had violated the rule by entering the armoury, and hence, had to leave Indraprastha for 12 years after retrieving the Brahmin's cows and arresting the thieves.[17]

Conclusion

While kings and *rishi*s were known to have multiple wives, the idea of a woman having more than one husband in the historical past raises serious questions about whether she was forced into such marriage, or whether her honour, dignity and well-being were compromised in such marriages.

From the Ved Vyas Mahabharat, it seems clear that neither was Draupadi forced into the marriage nor was her well-being compromised, because all the five Pandavs and Draupadi herself adhered to the rules laid down for managing this marriage.

The Pandavs, with their Divine origins and accomplishments, and Draupadi with her Divine origin and the role she played in the events of the Mahabharat towards the end of the Dwapar Yug when Vishnu took on His eighth avatar (Krishna) all seem to belong to a period of 'Sanatan *itihas*' during which extraordinary things happened to create extraordinary results.

SECTION II
FROM SANATAN CULTURE

15

Why Does Sanatan Dharm Have So Many Gods and Goddesses? How to Know Which One to Worship?

O Parth! See my forms by the hundreds and thousands...
in every speck of Creation.

Such questions have been raised by many Hindus, particularly the youth. The truth is that the number of gods in Hinduism is not to create confusion but to offer the seeker a choice.

Concept of God in Sanatan Dharm

According to Sanatan Dharm, God is the formless Consciousness that creates, pervades and manages the entire cosmos and the millions of universes that exist within it. It is this Consciousness that takes on various forms for the management of Creation. The first few forms are:

1. Adi Shakti, Energy of Creation
2. Brahma, the Creator
3. Saraswati, Goddess of Knowledge
4. Vishnu, the Sustainer, Administrator
5. Lakshmi, Goddess of Wealth and Resources
6. Shiva, the Destroyer of all that is redundant to make place for a new Creation
7. Parvati, the Destructive Force in the Cosmos

Then Brahman takes on additional forms of the five elements, all the *lok*s or dimensions of existence, the physical laws of each dimension and the beings that inhabit them, including *devata*s, men, women, flora and fauna, etc.

So according to Hinduism, everything is God, including you and I (hence, Bharat has not just 33 crores but more than 134 crores *devis* and *devata*s, since all of us are gods). Life is therefore just a journey to help people recognize and experience their innate divinity, whether it takes them one lifetime, a hundred lifetimes or millions of lifetimes to complete this journey. This completion is the 'Moksh'.

Even though Hindus worship specific forms of God, subconsciously one believes in the formlessness and all-pervasiveness of God. Why would Hindus pray to a 'lifeless' stone or metal idol if they did not believe that the idol is a representation of an entity which is beyond the stone or metal, an entity they can communicate with? Why would Hindus mentally pray to Ram or Shiva even without visiting the temple or having an idol at hand if they did not believe that Ram or Shiva were part of the Cosmic Consciousness present everywhere?

Why Does Sanatan Dharm Have So Many Forms of God?

Hindu gods can be classified predominantly into four categories.

1. *Forms mentioned in the Purans and Vedas:* These are believed to be the primordial forms of God which existed even before Creation. They are Goddess Adi Shakti, Lord Brahma, Goddess Saraswati, Lord Vishnu, Goddess Lakshmi and Lord Shiva.
2. *Avatars:* Often, God would descend on Earth in specific forms to fulfil a particular mission—predominantly to protect Dharm:

Hiranyakashipu was given a boon—he could be killed neither by man nor beast; neither in day nor night; neither inside nor outside the house; neither by a weapon nor without it. Hence, Lord Vishnu took the form of Narasimha—part-lion, part-man—so He was neither man nor beast. He killed Hiranyakashipu at the twilight hour (neither day nor night) at the threshold of the palace (neither inside nor outside) with His nails (neither with a weapon nor without it).

Goddess Parvati had once incarnated as a fisherwoman called Mumba. When the fisherfolk realized who She was, they asked Her to remain their protector forever. Thus, She came to be known as Mumba Devi, the goddess after whom the city of Mumbai is named. Even today, there is a temple dedicated to Mumba Devi in the heart of the city.

Sanatan Dharm is the only civilization of the world with a millennia-spanning history. During this time, hundreds of such avatars were born. Hence, we have so many gods and goddesses.

3. *Emergence of certain gods in specific regions:* At times, saints and seers have been granted visions of *kuldevata*s or *kuldevi*s whose idols have appeared in certain regions as *swayambhu*—on their own without being sculpted by humans. These forms of God are worshipped in small and specific regions, normally no larger than a village or a district.

4. *Devatas:* These refer to the heads of the elements, of natural phenomena and certain sciences. For instance Surya is the Sun God, Vayu is the God of Wind, Varun is the God of Oceans and Rivers, Indra is the God of Thunder, Lightning, Storms and Rain, Dhanwantari is the God of Medicine, the Ashwin Kumars are the

twin physicians of Swarg, Bhu Devi is the Goddess of Earth, etc. (See also, Chapter 9: 'Why is the Bungling Indra, King of Gods?')

'33 Crore Gods'

There aren't 33 crore but rather 33 gods (12 Adityas, 11 Rudras, 8 Vasus and 2 Ashwins).[1] The word *'koti'*—which translates to 'crore' in Sanskrit—also means 'level of excellence'. Since everything is God, including humans, the level of excellence implies 'spiritual advancement or closeness to the Supreme Consciousness and hence, greater powers over natural phenomena.'[2]

Eight Vasus (deities of material elements)—Dyaus (sky), Prithvi (Earth), Vayu (wind), Agni (fire), Nakshatra (stars), Varun (water), Surya (sun), Chandra (moon).

Twelve Adityas (personified deities)—Vishnu, Aryaman, Indra (Sakra), Tvashtr, Varun, Bhag, Savitr, Vivasvat, Amsha, Mitra, Pushan, Daksh.

Eleven Rudras consist of the five *gyan indriya*s (organs of perception)—eyes (vision), nose (breath), ear (hearing), tongue (taste), skin (touch); five *karma indriya*s (organs of action)—mouth (*mukh*), hands (*hath*), legs (*prastra*), anus (*maladvar*), genital (*mutradvar*) and the self (*atma*).

The Ashwins are twin deities associated with medicine, health and the sciences.

Since all elements in nature are forms of the Supreme Consciousness (Brahman), it follows that these elements and phenomena are conscious, dynamic, and hence, personified by various *devi*s and *devata*s.

Which Gods to Worship?

The answer to this question is: the form(s) of God one likes the most.

Nowhere does Hinduism say that one god is better than the other, or that only one god can give us the specific thing we want. The 'Ram Raksha Stotra' presents Lord Ram as the Knower and Giver of all blessings a human could want; the 'Namakam' and 'Chamakam' of the Shri Rudram Mantra extols Lord Shiva in the same way; the 'Vishnu Sahasranam', presents Lord Vishnu; the 'Lalita Sahasranam', Goddess Lalita; and the 'Hanuman Chalisa' presents Lord Hanuman as the ultimate Protector and Giver of all kinds of material and spiritual blessings. Other texts dedicated to other gods serve the same purpose.

Since all gods are different forms of the same Supreme Consciousness, none is more or less powerful than the other. Hinduism gives us complete freedom to perceive God as we like. Some may think of nature as God; others may find Lord Ram's life to be an ideal and want to worship him; yet others may imagine God as a mother and worship Goddess Durga; for an artist, God might be Saraswati, Goddess of all Art, Skill and Knowledge; a dancer may feel inspired by Lord Shiva as Nataraj; for many, God may be a combination of strength and wisdom, and hence, they might worship Lord Hanuman.

Hinduism imposes no restrictions on which form of God to follow, including those of other faiths. Since everything is God, all names belong to God, all forms belong to God. Hence, Allah, Tao, Jehova, Ahura Mazda are as valid names for God as Brahma, Shiva, Saraswati, Durga, Adi Shakti, Ram or Krishna.

There is only one rule with regard to God in Sanatan Dharm—God resides in every speck of Creation. Hence, if one believes in God, one will not knowingly hurt or harm any part of Creation—flora, fauna, man, woman or even inanimate objects—and treat them all with love, compassion and respect.

Why Should One Choose a Form of God That One Likes?

What we like speaks to who we are. One person wishes to be a writer, the other dreams of being an architect, a third person wants to be a filmmaker, yet another one wants to run a business... We are happiest in the professions that truly resonate with who we are.

The same principle applies to the form of God we choose to pay reverence to. If we are comfortable with the form of God we choose, we enjoy a lifelong bond that gives us faith, strength and guidance to choose our path in life.

In the same family, one member may want to worship Lord Shiva, another might love the cuteness of Lord Ganesh, a third might draw strength from Ma Durga, a fourth may be inspired by the beauty and light of the sun, while yet others might want to follow Buddhism and chant '*Nam Myoho Renge Kyon*'. This is perfectly acceptable.

In fact, in Sanatan Dharm, it is not even necessary to choose a form of God. One can be an atheist and still be a Sanatani. The Sanatan way of life recognizes individual freedom and makes only two demands of its followers:

1. *To lead a life of Dharm:* Be fair, honest, compassionate and courageous, and create happiness for yourself and others.
2. *To know that one's destiny is in one's own hands:* People write their destinies based on the karma (actions) they choose to perform. Every action has an equal and opposite reaction. Hence, one has every right to cheat but one must know that someday, one will be

cheated too. People have the right to be kind and they must know that because of their kindness, someday good things will happen to them too.

In Sanatan, God is *not* a punisher of sins (See also, Chapter 27: 'Is God Punishing and Serious or Happy and Fun-loving?')... God is the creator of the 'Laws of Existence' that make people reap what they sow.

It follows from the core idea that since every being is the Cosmic Consciousness in a different form, each being is God. Therefore, God cannot impose His/Her will on anyone. God can only guide everyone through His/Her example, and the various forms and systems of knowledge in Sanatan— the Vedas, Upanishads, Purans, Ramayan and Mahabharat. Thereafter, people have to use their own intellect and free will to choose their path. This is the essence of one's relationship with God (See also, Chapter 31: 'Why Does Sanatan Dharm Not Give Ready-made Answers?').

How All the Gods in Sanatan Dharm Are Similar

Regardless of the form of God one chooses, all of them are the same. They all uphold Dharm. Whether they are ferocious or calm, within their temples they welcome every devotee with a smile. They are powerful enough to grant people whatever they wish. They all wish for people to be good human beings who live by the precepts of Dharm even without completely believing in them. None of these forms are superior or inferior to each other, or in any conflict with each other.

Conclusion

So, we can choose to worship God in the form we like to create an everlasting bond with an omniscient, omnipotent, omnipresent and eternal mother, father, friend, brother or sister! And regardless of whether or not we want to identify with a particular form of God, the fundamental principle of Sanatan is: *Our conscience is our god!*

16

Why Do Sanatan Gods Behave like Humans?

I will hide behind this pillar and when
Krishna comes with his gang to steal butter,
I shall catch him red-handed.

In many incidents in the epics and the Purans, Sanatan gods seem to succumb to very human emotions—Lord Ram worries and literally cries for Mother Sita after She is abducted by Ravan; Lord Krishna steals butter from the *gopi*s' homes; Lord Shiva is so consumed by grief on the death of His wife Sati that Lord Narayan has to destroy Her corpse to bring Shiva back; and Sati Herself dies a sad death.

But aren't gods supposed to be beyond life and death, beyond grief, worry, anger, joy, pain, fun, frolic and the rest of the scale of human emotions?

God in Sanatan Dharm

In Sanatan Dharm, God is formless. Brahman, (not to be confused with Brahmin, one of the *varna*s, and Brahma, Creator of the Cosmos) Parmeshvar, Parmatma, is the supreme, formless Consciousness in whom all universes are contained.

It is this Brahman that takes on the forms of various gods, goddesses, *devata*s, the various elements, animals, trees, birds, humans, and every animate and inanimate object in the universe. The discovery of the 'god particle' in quantum physics and the string theory corroborates this belief. God is formless, all-powerful, all-knowing, present everywhere, eternal and ever-blissful.[1]

Why Does Such an All-Powerful, Eternal God Behave Like Humans?

Imagine a formless entity. You have no way of knowing whether it is male or female. Since it has no body, you cannot interact with it either through speech or action. You may be able to speak to it through sheer belief in its existence but how do you decipher what it thinks? How can you know what it wants you to do and what it considers as right or wrong? How do you know that this all-powerful God understands your pain and does not discount it as mere human weakness? How do you know that God is ever-loving, ever-compassionate and your protector?

Incidents from the Ramayan, Mahabharat and Purans enable us to address the above questions. Surely, God is beyond pain and human struggle but when we see God going through 'human' strife and dilemmas and choosing to uphold Dharm despite all suffering, we understands what God wants from us; the kind of life God wants people to lead. When people see God leading a human life, they know that He/She understands their problems, and thus, develop affinity and love for God.

Lord Ram's longing for His wife shows how intensely a husband and wife must love each other. Despite all the challenges in His life, the choices He made taught mankind what an ideal son, elder brother, friend, king, warrior—and even an *ideal enemy*—must be like.

Lord Shiva's anguish for Sati shows us His love for Her. He could have forced Her to not go to King Daksh's *yagya*, but between an ideal couple there cannot be any element of force or servitude.

Lord Shiva could have brought Sati back to life, but He respected Her powers as Adi Shakti. She had chosen to go back to Her original form, because as long as She lived as the daughter of the arrogant Daksh, She had to obey and respect him as Her father even though he had heaped unforgiveable insults on Her husband. Painful though it was, Lord Shiva respected His wife and Her choices.

The episodes in the Purans and epics impart important lessons about people's day-to-day lives, explain what right living entails, and that upholding Dharm—being loving and compassionate, yet fighting evil—is above every human emotion or struggle (See also, Chapter 4: 'How Could the All-knowing Lord Shiva Not Recognize His Own Son?').

And what of the powers that these very gods exhibit in the same epics? Can they be ignored?

Lord Ram, who lived as a human being, also gave Kakabhushundi, the crow, a glimpse of the entire cosmos in His mouth as a baby, proving that He was indeed Lord Narayan. Lord Shiva—who lamented His wife's demise—also caused the dissolution of the entire cosmos within Himself during the 'Pralaya Kaal'. Adi Shakti who could not bear insults to Her husband is also the energy that animated the entire cosmos. Lord Krishna—who stole butter—also created clones of the *gop*s out of Himself in the blink of an eye when Lord Brahma abducted the original boys just to tease Him. Not even the families could make out that Krishna had created those boys. When Brahma returned the *gop*s after an entire year, the ones Krishna had created simply merged back into Him. And Lord Krishna—who built the city of Dwarka which was secured by the sea in order to protect His subjects from constant wars with Jarasandha—also showed His Virat Roop to Arjun and gave mankind the Bhagvad Gita, a comprehensive doctrine on how to lead a happy and ideal life.

God takes help from ordinary mortals in spite of being all-knowing and all-powerful, to give them the opportunity to do the right thing.

- Lord Ram gave the *rakshasa*s and the *vanar*s the opportunity to pick the right side but only the *vanar*s and Vibhishan took it.
- Lord Krishna gave all the kings of Bharatvarsha the chance to pick the side of Dharm in spite of their political motives. But not all of them sided with the Pandavs. However, Yuyutsu, one of Duryodhan's brothers, seized the opportunity and fought on the side of the Pandavs against his brothers. Sadly, Bheeshm, Dronacharya, Kripacharya and many others wasted this opportunity to pick the side of Dharm.

Difference between Purans and Upanishads

While many episodes of the Purans depict gods exhibiting human, mundane qualities, the Upanishads communicate profound truths of existence and the deepest understanding of reality.

This difference lies not so much in the content of the Purans and the Upanishads but rather in the people they are supposed to cater to. The Purans are meant for ordinary people dealing with the mundane rigmarole of life while the Upanishads are for evolved souls who have risen above the dualities of daily living and are able to contemplate the higher questions of life.

Conclusion

Sanatan gods pretend (as suggested by the word *'leela'*) to behave like humans in order to teach us how to lead a righteous life that creates *only* love, joy and peace for us and the world. When we see God undergoing struggles in His/Her various avatars we develop faith and affection for God and know that God understands our human struggles, empathizes with us and will always help us through them. Thus, we form a strong bond with God, one that not only gives us strength and reinforces our faith but also shows us the way to lead a meaningful and fulfilling life!

17

What Is the Shivling?

tat pranamaami sadaa shiva lingam

[I salute that eternal Shiva Lingam.]

—'Lingashtakam'

There is much conjecture on what is a Shivling. To begin with, some clarifications are required to understand the concept.

Shape of the Shivling

The Shivling is ellipsoid, egg-shaped or a seed-shaped oval. Such a shape is difficult to hold erect unless it is inserted within a stand or pedestal to give it stability. That is why what we see as an ellipse on the Shivling is only a part of the entire Shivling. The rest of it is embedded in the pedestal and hence not visible.

In Sanatan Dharm, the formless Brahman or Divine Consciousness—also called the 'Shiva Tattwa'—takes the form of Lord Brahma to create the universe; the form of Lord Vishnu to sustain it; and the form of Lord Shiva to dissolve the universe and cause the creation of a new one. Brahma, Vishnu and Shiva are all different aspects of the Brahman that existed before the universe came into existence and will continue to exist after it is dissolved.

Just as *Aum* is regarded as the voice of the Brahman,[1] the Shivling is regarded as its simplest visualization. Isn't the egg the simplest form of life? It has no organs, yet represents a living being in all its complexity, with eyes, ears, heart, muscles, veins, nerves, etc. This is true of a seed too. (Have you ever noticed how most seeds are similar in shape—ellipsoid?) Even our expanding physical universe is shaped like an ellipse.

One significant feature of this shape is that it has no definite beginning or end. It is therefore the best scientific representation of that which is expanding and eternal.

Symbolism of the Shivling

It is important to understand what a Shivling mean, and why it is constructed in the classical form seen in most temples—the pedestal, the ellipse and a cobra around it?

The Shivling has three parts: the base of the pedestal represents Lord Brahma, the top of the pedestal represents Lord Vishnu and finally the ellipsoid represents Lord Shiva. For ease of understanding, let us take the example of a seed. It contains the entire tree and its resultant flowers and fruits, but the seed itself has none of those constituent parts. This is the Shivling. It is pure static consciousness, i.e. Brahman or God before Creation. Then the seed begins to sprout roots, develop the shoot, stem and branches, marking the beginning of Creation. This is the 'Brahma Peetham'—the Brahma part of the Shivling or the phase of 'creation'. As the tree grows, it is provided with resources to help it grow, i.e. nutrient-rich soil, enough water and sunlight to nourish it. This is the 'Vishnu Peetham'—the Vishnu part of the Shivling or the phase of 'sustenance'. Finally, the tree has grown and lived well. It has borne fruit. Some fruits are eaten by birds, animals or humans, while others fall off the tree and eventually rot. But in all cases, what finally remains is the seed that contains the entire tree, yet is nothing more than a simple ellipsoid. The cycle is thus complete from seed to seed—it all begins and ends in Shiva.

The Shivling reminds worshippers that such is the nature of life and the world—we come from God, live in a world created and provided for by God, and ultimately, go back to God. We are all God's energy in different forms and our ultimate constant form is that of the formless God.

The cobra on the Shivling is representative of our 'Kundalini' which, according to yogic iconography, resembles a coiled serpent at the base of the spine. As the devotee becomes more spiritually advanced, the energy rises till it reaches the crown *chakra*. The culmination of this energy is what we experience as being Enlightenment, Moksh or Nirvana.

Each leaf of the *bilva patra* that is offered on the Shivling has three leaflets that are said to represent the Trinity—Lord Brahma, Lord Vishnu and Lord Shiva.

This is the crux of what the Shivling signifies—a simple yet profound representation of the eternal cycle of Creation, the endless cycle of life.

The energy that the Shivling represents is the combined energy of the entire cosmos. If one can keep water flowing over nuclear reactors, which hold an infinitesimally small part of cosmic energy, why can one not keep water flowing over this representation of God's infinite energy, even if symbolically?

What Is the Yoni?

The *yoni*, i.e. the pedestal also signifies 'Shakti' or energy. Without the flow of energy, neither creation nor sustenance nor dissolution is possible.

Just as 'consciousness' is represented by Brahma, Vishnu and Shiva, 'energy' is represented by Saraswati, Lakshmi and Parvati.[2] They are not separate but rather essential aspects of the same Supreme Being. Hence, the *yoni* being regarded as the representation of the 'feminine' is not a contradiction but a further elucidation of the same continuum wherein the formless and static Brahman merges with the dynamic Shakti and is stirred into action—creation of the cosmos, development and sustenance of the cosmos, and the ultimate dissolution of the cosmos back into Shiva.

In the Kollur Mookambika Temple in Karnataka, there is the Swayambhu Jyotirling in which the vertical right half of the represents Brahma, Vishnu and Shiva while the vertical left half represents Maha Saraswati, Maha Lakshmi and Maha Kali.[3] This signifies that the *lingam* is not about sexuality but rather a physical representation of Brahman, the formless Consciousness.

Why Is the Shivling Considered a Phallus and the Yoni the Female Genitalia?

That the Shivling represents physical organs is but a very simplistic view of the cosmos.[4] Any activity that a creature in this world undertakes requires both consciousness and energy. This combination of consciousness and energy is nothing but the union of Shiva and Shakti. It is the essential principle of all action in the universe, whether the task is as mundane as consuming food, as intellectual as writing a thesis or as spiritual as learning music or engaging in *tapasya*.

How can such a wide range of physical, mental, emotional and spiritual activities on the individual plane, the change of seasons, the motion of tides and other natural phenomena on the global plane, and the birth and death of stars, rotation and revolution of planets and other celestial bodies, etc. on the cosmic plane be restricted to just the act of sex? All of it is simply Consciousness which keeps the universe in order through the flow of Energy, i.e. the union of Shiva and Shakti.

The Ardhanarishwar form of Shiva and Shakti also signifies the same principle.

The Shivling is symbolic of a sublime cosmic principle that everything in our elipsoid universe is contained within the ellipse of the Shivling, i.e. within God or the Supreme Being as both Consciousness and Energy.[5] Even modern science acknowledges that before the Big Bang, all matter was condensed to a point called the 'Cosmic Egg', which is called the 'Hiranya Garbha' in the Vedas (See also, Chapter 22: 'Does Science Have its Origins in Sanatan Dharm?'). This Supreme Being is both the cause of it all as well as beyond everything. Thus, everything in this universe is a manifestation of God, i.e. a symbol or a *lingam* of God.

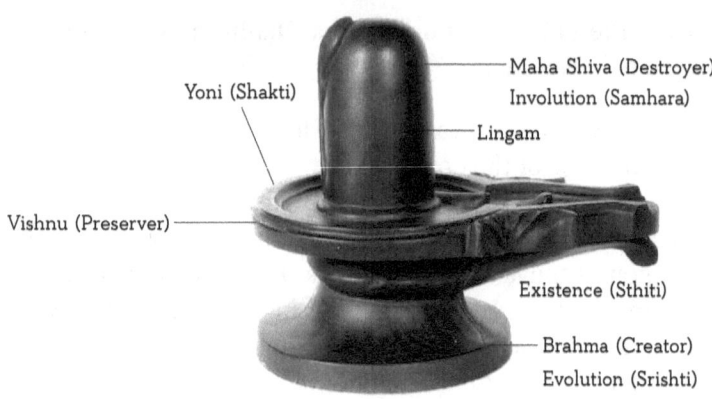

18

How Can Sanatan Dharm Have Gods like Ganesh, Hanuman and Narasimha?

sankata-mochana naama tihaari

[Monkey God, your name takes away all my troubles.]

—'Sankat Mochan Hanuman Ashtak'

Lately, many questions are being raised about the 'forms' of gods in Sanatan Dharm. This chapter attempts to address all those queries.

In the previous chapters, we have already discussed Ganesh (See also, Chapter 4: 'How Could the All-Knowing Shiva Not Recognize His Own Son?'), Narasimha (See also, Chapter 15: 'Why Does Sanatan Dharm Have So Many Gods? How Do We Know Which One to Choose?') and Hanuman (See also, Chapter 12: 'How Could Hanuman Swallow the Sun?').

Divine Creator

The Supreme Consciousness, notwithstanding the name it is addressed by, is the only Truth that exists. Everything else—all matter and anti-matter—are simply manifestations of that universal principle.

The same Supreme Consciousness manifests itself as gods and angels, man and woman, bird and beast, flora and fauna, earth and ether, fire and water, wind and mind. Everything and everyone is God. People are all divine beings experience humanity for some time till they go back to realizing that they themselves are God! Hindus call the state in which this Truth is finally experienced 'Moksh' and regard its attainment as the ultimate purpose of all life.

By undermining how Sanatan gods look, sceptics and critics suggest that God—who created countless universes and the countless forms of beings in them—is restricted in the number and kinds of forms to take; that God needs to justify the form of the manifestation to the servitors, who get to decide whether the choice is logical or plausible! Absurd and self-contradictory, isn't it?

19

What Was the Status of Women in Ancient Bharat?

*yatra naryas tu pujyante
ramante tatra devaata*

[Even gods rejoice in societies
where women are worshiped.]

—*Manu Smriti* 3.56

No *sanskriti* (culture) in the world—other than Sanatan Dharm—professes God as a woman. Sanatan regards Adi Shakti as Creator, Sustainer and Destroyer of the cosmos. Also, goddesses are associated with different aspects of existence— Saraswati is Goddess of Knowledge, Arts and Learning, Lakshmi, is Goddess of Wealth, and Durga is Goddess of Power, War and Strength.

Let us explore the status of women in ancient Bharat, systematically, over the following few sections.

Education

The Ramayan, Mahabharat and Purans are replete with episodes in which women debate with or remind men about the tenets mentioned in the *shastras*.[1] Thereby, one can infer that in ancient Bharat, women were as knowledgeable about the *shastras* as men were.

The practice of *swayamvar* allowed a princess to choose her husband from an assembly predominantly of kings and princes.

Her choice was based on the knowledge of each prospective groom's credentials which was possible only through her awareness of the political and social affairs of the country, across different kingdoms.

Texts such as the *Harita Dharmasutra*, *Asvalayana Grihya Sutra* and *Yama Smriti* suggest that girls who decided to study at a *gurukul* underwent the *upanayan*, a rite of passage, at the age of eight, and thereafter, were called 'Brahmavadini'.[2]

Music, dance, painting and warfare were as accessible to women as they were to men. For instance, Arjun had taught dance to Uttara, the daughter of King Virat, and to other women of the palace.[3] Chitralekha was taught painting by Dev Rishi Narad.[4] Kaikeyi was a warrior princess who saved Dasharath's life by taking him out of the battlefield and protecting him from the onslaught of demons while he was unconscious.[5] Tara, the wife of Vali, was a hymnist who was also renowned for her political acument.[6] Sita discussed war strategies with Hanuman when he visited Her in Lanka.[7]

Women were also known to recite the Vedas.

Tapasya

There are several instances of women performing *tapasya* for spiritual accomplishment. Satyavati and her daughters-in-law, Ambika and Ambalika, went to the forest for *tapasya*.[8] Vedavati—Mother Sita in Her previous birth—left home to perform *tapasya*.[9] Anusuya, the wife of Rishi Atri, performed *tapasya* for 10,000 years. Through the powers attained, she altered the flow of time when approached by the *dev*s for help. She turned the period of 10 nights into one night. She also revived an area ravaged by a decade of drought by causing River Jahnavi to flow there.[10] Amba performed *tapasya* to extract revenge on Bheeshm, and was reborn as Shikhandi. In this endeavour, she was supported by the greatest *rishi*s of the time who saw the injustice done to her and helped her wholeheartedly, even though Bheeshm was renowned for his military prowess.[11]

Yogic Powers

Women in ancient Bharat were accomplished in yogic powers. Vedavati defended herself from Ravan.[12] She also immolated herself in her own yogic energy (without the use of an actual fire) while vowing to be the cause of Ravan's death herself.[13] Vedavati was reborn as Sita. Of course, while Vedavati was an *anshavatar* of Goddess Lakshmi with only part of the latter's powers, Mother Sita had almost all of Goddess Lakshmi's powers.

Draupadi had the power to destroy the entire Kaurav clan with just the pronouncement of a curse, but she did not do so because she did not want to waste her yogic energy on people like Duryodhan who deserved to be vanquished and humiliated on the battlefield[14] (See also, Chapter 8: 'Duryodhan or Yudhishthir—Who Was the Real Villain?').

When Sita was still unmarried, a hermitess with ascetic powers prophesied to Her and Her mother that Sita would have to spend Her life in forests.[15]

Ahilya, the wife of Rishi Gautam had seen through Indra's disguise through her yogic powers.[16] (See also, Chapter 13: 'Was It Fair for Ahilya to Be Cursed?')

On many occasions, Goddess Durga and Goddess Kali forced even Lord Shiva into submission. When blessed by Goddess Parvati, Ganesh was invincible by even Brahma, Vishnu and Shiva[17] (See also, Chapter 4: 'How Could the All-Knowing Lord Shiva Not Recognize His Own Son?').

Women Scholars

Among the revered women scholars of ancient Bharat were Gargi, Lopamudra, Anusuya, Draupadi, Sita, Maitreyi,

Mandodari, Ahilya, Ubhaya Bharati, Damyanti, Queen Chudala (mentioned in the *Yoga Vashishta*) and Princess Hemalekha. Even in medieval times, saints and scholars like Meerabai, Muktabai, Sakubai, Janabai,[18] the Avvaiyar scholars in the South, Sarada Devi, Brahmani Bhairavi, Andal, Akka Mahadevi, among others, made tremendous contributions to Bharatiya music, literature, the Bhakti movement, Sanatan philosophy and education for men and women.

They were all skilled debaters. Among the most popular debates in Sanatan culture is the one between Rishi Yajnavalkya and Maitreyi on love and the *atma*, and the one between him and Gargi—in King Janak's court—on the nature of reality, the universe and Brahman. Both these profound exchanges are documented in the Brihadaranyaka Upanishad.

Gargi remained celibate throughout her life and she was recognized as one of the nine gems in King Janak's court. She composed many hymns of the Rig Veda.

Ubhaya Bharati was chosen as the judge of a debate between the most renowned scholars of medieval Bharat— Shankaracharya and Mandana Mishra.

Queens

When Lord Ram was leaving for the forest on the 14-year exile, their preceptor Vashishtha—one of the most powerful *rishi*s of Bharat—declared that in Ram's absence, Sita would rule Ayodhya. Instead, She decided to accompany Ram to the forest.[19]

After her husband, King Shantanu and her sons died, and Bheeshm refused to ascend the throne of Hastinapur, Queen Satyavati—Shantanu's wife—ruled the kingdom as the matriarch with the help of Bheeshm.[20]

Gender Roles

The Mahabharat mentions that Kunti looked after Rishi Durvasa like a son, a student, and a younger sister—a testament to the equality of genders in ancient Bharat.[21]

Draupadi described working women as *sairandhari*—women who earn their living and can protect themselves through their own virtuous and sensible conduct.[22]

Yudhishthir said that Draupadi was just the kind of partner one wanted so as to attain all four Purusharthas—Dharm, Arth, Kaam and Moksh. As a wife and queen, she was involved in all affairs related to the family and the kingdom, including righteous choices, economic policies, fulfilling aspirations of the subjects and spiritual living.[23]

Marriage and Sexuality

Right to Love and Choose a Life Partner

There are many instances in the epics and the Purans of women falling in love, openly acknowledging it and asserting their choice of husband, either in regular life or even by doing *tapasya* to get the husbands of their choice. Hence, a woman's right to choose a life partner was well acknowledged and respected in Sanatan culture.

When Ulupi professed her love and desire for Arjun, no one judged her for that.[24] Hidimba proposed to Bhim and even asked Kunti for his hand in marriage. Neither Kunti nor the Pandavs judged her and respectfully got Bhim married to her.[25] In an assembly of the most powerful kings of Bharat, Draupadi rejected Karn and none of the kings could oppose her; Draupadi's own kin stood by her decision.[26]

Draupadi called herself neither a devotee, nor a lover, nor a sister of Lord Krishna. She openly declared herself

Krishna's friend and Krishna reciprocated likewise. Nobody misunderstood or judged their beautiful bond.[27]

Usha, Krishna's grand daughter-in-law, went to the extent of having Aniruddh—Krishna's grandson—abducted to assert her love. While this appears a bit too extreme and even wrong, it clearly shows how open society must have been for a woman to dare to do this.[28]

When Rukmini realized that Lord Krishna had not been invited to her *swayamvar* and her brother was forcing her to choose Shishupal against her wishes, she sent a message to Krishna asking him to come and take her away. In fact, while she praised Krishna for the qualities that she knew he possessed, she also confidently spoke about her strengths and stated that she was 'equal' to Krishna in every way and that only he was 'worthy' of becoming her husband.[29] (See also, Chapter 1: 'Why Did Lord Ram Abandon Mother Sita?')

King Ashwapati gave his daughter Savitri the freedom to choose the man she wanted to marry. So, she travelled all over the country looking for a suitable match.[30]

Maiden Names after Marriage

In modern times it has become a celebrated feminist trend that women assert their identity by continuing to assume their maiden surnames even after marriage. But there are already so many instances in the epics where the women kept their maiden names as a mark of their individual identity. For example:

Draupadi's names and their meanings:

- *Draupadi:* Daughter of King Drupad
- *Panchali:* Princess of the kingdom of Panchal
- *Krishna:* The dark-complexioned one (she was regarded as the most beautiful woman of the world in her time)

- *Yagyaseni:* The woman who emerged from the sacrificial fire in the fullness of youth

Sita's names and their meanings:

- *Janaki:* Daughter of King Janak
- *Maithili:* Princess of the kingdom whose capital city is Mithila
- *Vaidehi:* Princess of the kingdom of Videha
- *Sita:* One who emerged from the furrow on Earth

Kunti's name and its meanings:

- *Kunti:* Daughter of Kunti Bhoj

There are more examples of women who were known by their original and maiden names throughout their life.

Importance of the Mother's Name for a Child

Mothers enjoyed an equally important status as fathers. Children of ancient Bharat were known as much by their mother's name as by their father's. Lord Ram was called Kausalyanandan (son of Kausalya), and the Pandavs were known as Kaunteya (belonging to Kunti) and Kuntinandan (sons of Kunti).

Sexual Gratification

In ancient Bharat, denying a wife seeking sexual fulfilment was regarded as a sin. A woman's satisfaction was as important as that of a man.[31] If—devoid of options—a woman sought help from a man to beget a child during the few days after menstruation (regarded as the best time to conceive), he had to comply with her wish (with the permission of his wife and family). Not doing so was akin to murder.

Arranged Marriage and a Husband's Duties

Though the scriptures gave the father the right to pick a groom for the daughter if she had not chosen someone suitable for herself, he was also obligated to find a groom who was worthy of his daughter and keep her happy.[32] Treating his wife with utmost respect—and providing amply for her and their children—was ordained as the highest duty of a husband.[33]

The Pandavs even pressed Draupadi's limbs when she collapsed due to exhaustion during an arduous walk in the Himalayas at the time of their exile.[34] Regardless of their greatness, goodness and prowess, failing to protect Draupadi tarnished the name of the Pandavs forever. Several kings expressed their disgust at Yudhishthir when he wagered her during the game of dice.[35]

When Damayanti married Nal in front of the *devata*s, everyone in the assembly congratulated them and praised Nal for the words he said to Damayanti: 'You have chosen an ordinary mortal like me over all the exalted *devata*s present here. Because of your extraordinary love, you will always find this husband of yours eager to fulfil your every command. I promise you that for as long as I am alive, I will love you.' Hearing these words, the four *devata*s who Damayanti had rejected were so happy that they granted eight boons (two each) to Nal.[36]

Forced Marriage and/or Rape

Forceful abduction of a protesting woman, taking advantage of a woman while she is sleeping, impassioned, or otherwise not in her senses, was regarded as a heinous crime.[37]

Raping and molesting a woman are regarded as the worst crimes in Bharatiya scriptures and invite nothing less than complete destruction and annihilation of the perpetrator.

The *rishi*s, *devata*s[38] and Marich had said this to Ravan in the Ramayan,[39] Krishna to Draupadi in the Mahabharat, and the same can be found mentioned in many other scriptures.[40]

Apsaras and Their Rights

Many *apsara*s (celestial women) emerged from the ocean during the 'Samudra Manthan'. While some chose different *devata*s and *gandharv*s as their husbands, others decided to remain unmarried and unattached. Nobody judged them for their decision. Even Indra, the King of Heaven, could not force them to seduce a particular individual. The consent of the *apsara* was essential.[41]

When Ravan raped the *apsara*s Rambha and Punjikasthala, though Lord Brahma could not kill him immediately due to Ravan's boon that no god or beast could kill him, he did pronounce a curse on Ravan that the next time he forced himself on a woman, his heads would explode into a thousand pieces. That is why Ravan could not violate Sita even though he had abducted her[42] (See also, Chapter 3: 'Ram or Ravan—Who Was the Better Man?').

Rights of Women in General

A reading of the types of sons as defined in the *Manu Smriti* provides valuable insights into the rights of women in society and the open-mindedness of Sanatan culture. The same has also been mentioned in the Mahabharat.[43]

Paunarbhava: When a woman chooses to remarry because she has either been deserted by her husband or widowed, her son is the *paunarbhava* of her new husband.

Kshetraja: When a husband is unable to beget a child because he is infertile, the wife may beget a child through another man with the consent of the husband. If the husband is deceased, the widow may beget a child with the consent of another important family member. Such a practice is called *niyoga*.

Putrika Putra: When a couple has no son, they can assert their right on their daughter's son as their own. Then he is regarded as the son of the woman's parents,

(Also, contrary to medieval distortions of Bharatiya culture, having a son though desirable was *not* necessary for things like performing the funeral rites or carrying the family lineage forward.)

Gudhaja: The child of a married woman—when the father of the child is unknown—will have all the rights of being family and is known as the *gudhaja* son of the woman's husband.

Sahodhaja: The son born to a woman who was pregnant before marriage is the *sahodhaja* son of the woman's husband.

Kanina: The son born to a woman out of wedlock is the *kanina* son of the man who eventually marries her.

Adoption and Acceptance of Daughters

King Romapada of the kingdom of Anga had adopted King Dasharath's daughter Shanta, as the former was without child. It was Shanta's husband Rishyasringa who performed the *putrakameshti yagya* for Dasharath.[44]

Kunti was the adopted daughter of King Kunti Bhoj. Her original name was Pritha and she had been adopted from Krishna's paternal grandfather King Shurasena.[45]

Drupad performed a *yagya* to beget a son who could defeat Dronacharya but from the *yagyavedi*, daughter Draupadi emerged alongside son Dhrishtadyumna. Drupad celebrated her emergence from the fire and she was wholeheartedly accepted as the princess of Panchal.[46]

King Ashwapati had performed a *yagya* to beget sons. Instead, Devi Gayatri blessed him with a daughter called Savitri, whom the king brought up with utmost love and affection.[47]

Even today, during Navratri festivities, on *ashtami*, the eighth day of the festival, the father washes the feet of the daughter.

Property Rights of Women

The *Apastamba Dharmasutra* recognizes the property rights of women. It gives women the legal right to inherit wealth from their parents. [48]

Sati in Ancient Bharat

No Sanatan scripture prescribes—or even endorses—Sati for widowed women.[49] Most Sanatan scriptures ignore Sati and the rest condemn the practice. In the Rig Veda, the funereal hymn (10:18.7)—regarded as the one which mandates Sati—actually says the following for a widowed woman:[50]

> The wife must sit next to the corpse of her husband, moisten her eyes with ghee and then get up and resume her rightful place in the world.

At such a time, any respectable, worthy man was allowed to offer himself in marriage to the widow.

The practice of Sati in ancient Bharat was negligible. The only Sati mentioned in the Mahabharat is that of Madri, wife of Pandu and mother of Nakul and Sahdev, who insisted on immolating herself on Pandu's funeral pyre.[51] She did this only because she held herself responsible for Pandu's death— Pandu had been cursed that the moment he copulated with a woman, he would die. Madri felt guilty about not stopping him from doing so. Brahmins who conducted the funeral rites for Pandu dissuaded Kunti from performing Sati and they did their utmost to dissuade Madri too from performing Sati.[52]

Even in modern Indian history, Sati was sparsely practised. Author and historian Meenakshi Jain states in her book *Sati* that between 1817 and 1827, Sati accounted for only 0.000027 per cent of deaths, i.e. 4,323 deaths for a population of 160,000,000.[53] There are even reports of family members attempting to coerce women out of their decision to commit Sati. Raja Ram Mohan Roy, who was instrumental in getting Sati banned during the colonial period, had also expressed private apprehension about the direct legislative intervention by the British authorities and would have preferred a more indirect strengthening of structural obstructions against the practice.

Post-Independence (as of 2016), there have only been 40 instances of Sati in Bharat.[54]

Gender Equality while Dispensing Justice

While worshipping women and respecting their social rights was inherent to Sanatan society, crimes committed by women were also treated at par with those committed by men.

Lord Ram killed the *rakshas* Tataka (also called Tadaka) who was torturing peace-abiding *rishi*s in the forests;[55] Lord Vishnu killed Shankaracharya's mother who wanted to destroy Earth;[56] Ayyappa destroyed the demoness Mahishi who was wreaking havoc on Earth;[57] and Indra eliminated the ogress Manthara.[58]

Emotions and Genders

In ancient Bharat, expressing of emotions was neither regarded as a sign of weakness nor un-manly. It was considered a natural process of life and relationships. If Draupadi bewailed her insult, Yudhishthir too collapsed in agony at having caused such unforgiveable torment to his wife and brothers. While an anguished Mother Sita shed tears for Lord Ram, the latter also wept in His longing for Sita, while Lakshman tearfully bemoaned his brother's plight.

However, we must remember that Sanatan heroes, no matter how deeply invested in a relationship, never overturned the practice of Dharm even in the face of great—oftentimes personal—adversity. So, while Sita pined for Ram, She did not accept Hanuman's suggestion to carry Her back to Him, because it was Ram's mission to annihilate all unrighteous demons in the world. Thus, He *had* to wage a war against Ravan and his army and vanquish them. Similarly, despite seething for revenge, Arjun still questioned the 'rightness' of the war and needed the Bhagvad Gita to convince him that the Kurukshetra War was in the interest of Dharm.

Conclusion

In ancient Bharat, women were respected as individuals and both the husband and wife accepted each other and lived together bonded by mutual respect and dignity, not just for themselves but for each other's families and the overall cause of Dharm as well.

20

What Was the Caste-system in Ancient Bharat?

brahmana-kshatriya-visham shudranam cha
parantapakarmani pravibhaktani
svabhava-prabhavair gunaih

[The duties of the Brahmins, Kshatriyas, Vaishyas and Shudras are distributed according to their qualities, in accordance with their own individual natures.]

—Bhagvad Gita, Chapter 18, Verse 41

The word 'caste' comes from the Portuguese word *'casta'* and is not of Bharatiya origin. It was systematically and deliberately introduced in Bharata by the British to execute their policy of 'divide and rule'. Any prevalence of untouchability and caste discrimination in medieval times was a grave distortion to the original *varna vyavastha* of ancient Bharat.

The Varna Vyavastha

The term *'varna vyavastha'*, used in Sanatan scriptures means a system of organizing society in a way that the various professions required to keep it thriving are matched with the basic nature, talents and inclinations of individual members of that society. The reason for this classification, that began in the Vedic era, and continued down to the medieval times, was to ensure that only those with genuine passion and talent for a particular occupation took it up and society grew and prospered as a whole.

When we take up occupations which we love, we perform them with passion and joy in the pursuit of excellence, increasing the chances of individual success and national progress. No profession falls beyond the ambit of the *varna vyavastha*.

Those inclined towards intellectual pursuits—teachers, philosophers, spiritualists, researchers, scientists, mathematicians and medical researchers—were collectively called Brahmins. Their profile automatically included performing Vedic rituals. Among these rituals, there were specialists who conducted various types of *yagya*s; not all *rishi*s could perform all *yagya*s. For instance, even though Vashishta, the *guru* of King Dasharath's clan was a 'Brahmarishi', the *putra kameshti yagya* that Dasharath organized to beget sons was performed by Rishi Rishyasringa who lived in another kingdom.

Individuals with a natural talent for leadership, administration, military strategies, statesmanship and politics were collectively called Kshatriyas.

Those with a flair for business, trade, economics and wealth creation were collectively called Vaishyas.

Shudras constituted the service industry and encompassed a plethora of occupations—engineers, doctors, architects, sculptors, musicians, artists, dancers, craftsmen, weavers, builders, masons, clerks and labourers. They constructed the temples of Bharat as engineers and architects. They designed and sculpted the exquisite statues and carvings on them. Therefore, it is unlikely that they would have been prevented from entering temples or regarded as untouchables in ancient Bharat.[1]

What Sanatan Scriptures Say about Varnas

The Supreme Being (God) exists enveloping the entire manifest universe, cognizing through every mind, seeing through every eye and working through every limb. Essentially, the entire universe is the Supreme Person[2] ('Purusha Sukta', Verses 1 and 2).

Brahmins represented the head or the 'power of thought and discrimination' of this being; Kshatriyas represented the two arms or the 'power of protection and preservation'; Vaishyas represented the two thighs or the power of acquisition and disbursement; and the Shudras represented the feet or the 'power of support and movement'.

"Then the moon was born out of the Supreme Person's mind, the sun out of His eyes, Indra from His mouth and Vayu from His breath."[3]

This verse itself says that all *varna*s were different aspects of *one* 'Supreme Person'. Can one truly regard the head to be more important than the arms, thighs or feet? Aren't all aspects of one's body equally essential, and interdependent?

The duties of the Brahmins, Kshatriyas, Vaishyas and Shudras are distributed according to their qualities, in accordance with their *gun*s (and not by birth).[4] Tranquillity, restraint, austerity, purity, patience, integrity, knowledge, wisdom and belief in a hereafter—these are the intrinsic qualities of work for Brahmins.[5] Valour, strength, fortitude, skill in weaponry, the resolve never to retreat from battle, large-heartedness in charity and leadership abilities are the natural qualities of work for Kshatriyas.[6] Resourcefulness and charity are the qualities Vaishyas are expected to possess,[7] and the best way for Shudras' progress is to serve society according to their calling.[8]

By fulfilling their duties, born of their natural

predisposition, human beings can attain perfection.[9] By performing one's natural occupation, one worships the Creator from whom all living entities have come into being, and who pervades the whole universe. This way, a person easily attains perfection.[10]

The Padma Puran says that God is not concerned with the time or place where one performs devotion. God only sees the love in people's hearts. All souls are the children of God, who is willing to accept everyone with open arms, provided they come with genuine love.[11]

Texts such as *Sushruta Sutrasthana* mention that students from all four *varna*s were to be included in the formal education process and also state that the *upanayan* rite of passage was open to everyone.[12]

The knowledge of the Vedas was open to all, but the conduct of Vedic rituals was left to the Brahmins. It is like saying that everyone is allowed the knowledge of how the human brain functions but only a qualified neurosurgeon is eligible to conduct a surgery.[13]

Varna-Fluidity and Equality in the Ramayan, Mahabharat and Other Texts

Sumantra, prime minister in the court of King Dasharath and Lord Ram, was born a Shudra as a *sutaputra*. He advised on stately and administrative duties—and helped execute them—but was also Dasharath's charioteer.[14] Hence, even though he accepted a *varna* different from which he was born into, he took pride in his origins.

The Valmiki Ramayan contains an elaborate description of the four castes in Ayodhya. In the four-caste system, from the first to the last, everyone was a worshipper of deities and guests, was also faithful, illustrious, valiant and brave. There was no citizen in Ayodhya who had not mastered the six branches of knowledge[15] (See also, Chapter 26: 'What Were Prosperity and Society like in Ancient Bharat?').

The tribal king Guha was a childhood friend of Lord Ram; tremendous respect and admiration existed between them. Their mutual affection was also honoured by Lakshman, Sita and Bharat.[16]

Brahma Rishi Vishwamitra was born a Kshatriya. He was called King Kaushik before he renounced his kingdom and took to *tapasya* after which he became a Brahma Rishi.[17] He revealed the sacred 'Gayatri Mantra' to the world which is still revered as the most powerful of all *mantra*s in Sanatan Dharm.

Rishi Valmiki—though born a Brahmin—was a dacoit called Lohaganja (Ratnakar by some accounts) who was inspired by the Sanat Rishis to renounce his wayward life and do *tapasya*. Eventually, he became one of the most exalted *rishi*s of Bharat. He was tasked by none other than Lord Brahma Himself to document the Ramayan and is renowned as the 'Adi Kavi'—the first poet of ancient Bharat.[18]

Shabari was born in a tribal family but led her life as a *yogini* in the hermitage of Sage Matanga. She was charged with the exalted task of welcoming Lord Vishnu in His Avatar as Ram into the sacred hermitage, after which she attained salvation in front of Lord Ram.[19]

Before the *ashvamedh yagya* and the *putrakameshti yagya* performed by Dashrath, the following were the instructions issued by Brahma Rishi Vashishta for the welcoming of guests for the ritual: People of all the *varna*s had to be honourd well honoured and given their due respect, and no disrespect could be shown even when overcome by passion or anger at anyone.[20] The most exceptionally respectable were the men and architects preoccupied with the works of the ritual, and they had to be well-treated with funds and food.[21]

Ravan was born to Rishi Pulastya and the demoness Kaikasi. He was a born Brahmin and lived his life like a Kshatriya.[22]

In the Mahabharat, Narad Muni asked Yudhishthir whether he looked after all four *varna*s in his kingdom with the same justice, fairness and generosity as his forefathers did.[23] Shudras attending Yudhishthir's *rajasuya yagya* were repeatedly referred to as 'Shudra Mahatmas'—Exalted Shudras.[24]

While Sanjay was Dhritarashtra's charioteer, there were many instances of him pointing out his and Duryodhan's unfair treatment of the Pandavs.[25] Dhritarashtra's second wife, was of the Vaishya *varna*, and her son was Yuyutsu—the only Kaurav to have switched over to the side of the Pandavs.[26] Queen Satyavati, the matriarch of Hastinapur was the daughter of the fisherman chief, a Shudra.[27] Though born in a Kshatriya clan, Lord Krishna was brought up by Vaishyas and Shudras—milkmen and farmers in Gokul. His foster father Nanda was a close friend of King Vasudev, Krishna's biological father. Maharishi Ved Vyas was the son of Rishi Parashar and the fisherwoman Satyavati.[28] In the Chandogya Upanishad, Jabala's son Satyakam is inducted into Vedic studies even though Jabala does not know who Satyakam's biological father is.[29] All of this shows the close, unbiased bonds that existed among the different *varna*s and how they were not determined by birth but by occupational preference and life roles.

In the epics and the Purans, there are many instances of intermarriage among the various *varna*s. Emperor Yayati married Rishi Shukracharya's daughter Devyani; Shantanu married the celestial Devi Ganga and also the fisherwoman, Satyavati; Arjun married the *nag* princess Ulupi, etc. In Draupadi's *swayamvar*, even Brahmins were allowed to participate after all the Kshatriyas had failed (See also, Chapter 11: 'Was Karna a Victim of the Caste System?').

Many individual races in the Sanatan scriptures do not

belong to any *varna*, e.g. the demon Maya Danav, who constructed the Maya Mahal for the Pandavs at Indraprastha, the *vanar*s of the Ramayan, celestials like the *gandharv*s, *nag*s, *devata*s, *vasu*s, *rudra*s, *aditya*s, *prajapati*s. All are known to have been friends with each other and adept in the Vedas, the art of warfare, engineering, art, architecture and economic pursuits.

Conclusion

*Varna*s were about individual qualities, and the *varna* that one chose was in accordance to one's predominant personality, and the choice of occupation congruent with that personality to promote individual and societal excellence and progress (See also, Chapter 21: 'Why Do Brahmins Seem to Be Given More Importance in Hinduism?').

21

Why Do Brahmins Seem to Be Given More Importance in Sanatan Dharm?

brahmano'sya mukhamasid bahu rajanyah krtah

[The Brahmins represented the Supreme Person's Head or His Power of Thought and Discrimination.]

—'Purusha Sukta', Verse 13

The Ramayan, Mahabharat and Purans are full of instances in which giving charity to Brahmins and revering them are considered among the highest duties of kings and emperors. This begs a question, if *varna*s were only categories of professions and not hierarchies, why do Brahmins seem to be given more importance (See also, Chapter 20: 'What Was the Caste System in Ancient Bharat?')?

The answer lies within the question itself. Except the Brahmins, the other three *varna*s had sustained sources of income. Kshatriya kings had their treasury and their soldiers and administrative officers received regular salaries. Vaishyas had goods to sell and profits to make. Shudras as doctors, engineers, architects, musicians, dancers and performers had a contractual income, and as labourers, workers, masons and craftsmen, earned salaries.

Brahmins were the only ones who had no ready-to-sell assets to generate an income. Broadly, the categories of functions performed by Brahmins were research, teaching, managing temples and conducting regular rituals. Through these functions, they made tremendous contribution to the social, scientific and spiritual fabric of society.

Social: Brahmins fulfilled several social responsibilities. The rituals that they conducted on both celebratory and sorrowful occasions brought people together as a community, fostering a sense of oneness and camaraderie.

Temples were not just places of worship but offered a space where people came together for debates and discussions, music, dance and drama performances, charity, community dining, banking and celebration of festivals. Notable ancient temples had a *mandapam*—a hall for such gatherings. Many temples even ran *gurukul*s and Veda *pathshala*s.

Education was free for all in ancient Bharat. This meant that as *acharya*s, Brahmins or teachers had to rely on state grants for a living.

Scientific: Brahmins conducted research and experimentation in various branches of knowledge like medicine, astronomy, physics, mathematics, cosmology, economics, sociology, psychology and philosophy, among others. These pursuits required relentless work and continuous funding for indefinite periods of time.

Also, the *rishi*s and Brahmins of ancient Bharat were adept at removing pollutants and killing germs in the environment through the scientific use of herbs, fire and specialized sound frequencies called *mantra*s (See also, Chapter 23: 'What Are Yagyas?').

While quantum physicists are beginning to understand the effect of vibrations within and around us, *rishi*s and Brahmins were applying this science every day millennia ago. It is needless to emphasize the impact these rituals had on the overall health and well-being of society.

Spiritual: Faith in God or the magnanimity of the universe lends a higher meaning to life and gives a sense of purpose and 'beyondness' to an individual. People who believe that there is something more profound than the mundane existence of everyday life become more resilient, positive and creative, for they are not borne down by the regular vicissitudes of life. These attitudes in society were fostered by Brahmins through the elucidation of spiritual, philosophical and metaphysical teachings in the scriptures.

The functions performed by Brahmins were essential for creating a healthy, vibrant and progressive society. Yet, they led challenging lives, staying mostly in hermitages in forests, wearing garments made of tree bark or ordinary cloth, and adorning themselves only with religious symbols like the *tulsi mala* and *rudraksha*. They lived on forest fruit and tubers, and led extremely disciplined and devout lives.

Like the other *varna*s, Brahmins too had families. Additionally, they also had to maintain students and disciples for their elaborate research, experiments and rituals. Yet, as mentioned earlier, they had no assets to sell to maintain a regular flow of income.

Why then has the only *varna* which had no option but to depend on charity and grants for its subsistence been so demonized in Bharat over the last few centuries? Demonizing Brahmins was essential for the British to divide Bharat because Brahmins, by virtue of the functions they performed for society, were at the core of Bharat's scientific, cultural and social excellence.

Islamic invaders burnt Bharat's libraries—in Nalanda, Vikramashila and Odantapura, among others—and destroyed tomes of Sanskrit texts, demolished its temples and forced its people to convert to Islam.

The British capitalized on this decimation of Bharatiya culture by demonizing Brahmins, making victims out of Shudras and creating a distorted narrative that defined the *varna* system as a hierarchy and not professional categories. Tragically, robbed of the Sanskrit texts—an important part of their historic-cultural legacy—Bharatiyas played right into the hands of the British.

22

Does Science Have its Origins in Sanatan Dharm?

*dvevidye veditavye para chaiva aparaa cha
atha paraa yayaa tadaksharam adhigamyate*

[There are two types of knowledge to
be acquired by man—one pertaining to
the material world and the other transcendental
which leads to the Imperishable Reality.]

—Mundaka Upanishad 1:3.5

Science is a universal system of knowledge, and no single culture or civilization can lay proprietary claim to it. However, it is logical to assume that the earliest scientific treatizes must have originated in the oldest civilizations of the world, provided there is evidence of scientific study and its application in such civilizations.

Why Does Sanatan Dharm Not Have a Date of Origin?

The reason why it is difficult to pinpoint the exact year of the origin of Sanatan Dharm in modern terms is because, Sanatan existed millennia before the invention of the Gregorian calendar. The calculation of time according to Sanatan moves in cycles of *yug*s spanning millions of years. At the end of each cycle, the Vedas are said to dissolve into the consciousness of Brahma, the Creator, and are revealed once more when the next cycle of Creation begins. That is why the Vedas are believed to be lakhs of years old.

Even in recorded Sanatan history, the timelines are enormous. For example, the Ramayan clearly states that Lord Ram ruled for 11,000 years while the Ramayan itself must have happened at least 10,000 years ago. Ram's father Dasharath had ruled for 60,000 years. Yet, 38 previous generations of Ram's Iskhvaku dynasty have been mentioned, with the histories of many meticulously detailed in several scriptures, including the Mahabharat, the Ramayan, the Bhagavat Puran, Skanda Puran and Padma Puran, among others. The Vedas are regarded as the very basis of the scientific, social and spiritual aspects of life. Therefore, one may conclude that Sanatan culture is as old as the Vedas, which implies that it is hundreds of thousands of years old, and still surviving. In fact, the very term 'sanatan' means 'eternal.' It is difficult to imagine that such a culture has survived all this time without profound practical, scientific and mathematical knowledge and their successful application.

Time-scale in Sanatan

Indicated below is a part of the time-scales according to the *shastra*s:[1]

- $26^2/_3$ *truti*s = 1 *nimesh* = 8/45 second
- 18 *nimesha*s = 1 *kastha* = $3^1/_5$ seconds = 8 *vipala*s
- 30 *kastha*s = 1 *kaal* = $1^3/_5$ minutes = 4 *pala*s
- 30 *kaal*s = 1 *muhurta* = 48 minutes = 2 *ghatika*s
- 30 *muhurta*s = 1 day and night = 24 hours = 60 *ghatika*s
- 30 days and nights and odd hours = 1 *pitrya* day and night = 1 month and odd hours
- 12 months = 1 year = 365 days, 5 hours, 30 minutes, 31 seconds = 1 *daiva* day and night

- 365 *daiva* days and nights = 1 *daiva* year
- 4,800 *daiva* years = 1 Satya Yug = 1,728,000 human years
- 3,600 *daiva* years = 1 Treta Yug = 1,296,000 human years
- 2,400 *daiva* years = 1 Dwapar Yug = 864,000 human years
- 1,200 *daiva* years = 1 Kali Yug = 432,000 human years
- 12,000 *daiva* years = 1 Chatur Yug (four *yug*s)
- 12,000 Chatur Yugs = 1 *daiva yug*
- 2,000 *daiva yug*s = 1 day and night of Brahman
- 365 Brahmic days and nights = 1 year of Brahman
- 71 *daiva yug*s = 1 *manvantar*
- 12,000 Brahmic years = 1 Chatur Yug of Brahman
- 200 *yug*s of Brahman = 1 day and night of Parabrahman
- ...and so on

Aspects Inferred from the Time-scale

The scale of calculation is enormous—from nano-seconds to millennia.

The Upanishads, from where this calculation has been taken, are a part of the Vedas whose date of creation remains unknown. If one were to go by the aforementioned calculation of time, even in the current *yug* cycle, excluding the number of years in the present Kali Yug, the Vedas are at least 10,800 *daiva* years (3,888,000 years) old!

It is believed that the Vedas were never written by a human. They are called *shruti*s, which means 'heard'; they were *revealed* to different *rishi*s at various points of time from the consciousness of Lord Brahma—a phenomenon which is said to occur every time creation takes place anew.

One sees mathematical principles of fractions and decimals in this system.

That 365+ days (12 months) make a year, 30 days make a month, and 24 hours make a day was known to Bharatiyas millennia ago. And since this information is acknowledged in modern times to be accurate, one can logically infer that the other time-scales must be accurate too.

*Devata*s do not exist on the earthly plane; they belong to another dimension of existence. This system gives us the duration of their day and night too. So, it spans multiple dimensions. It was only in the early part of the nineteenth century that Western scientists began to grapple with the idea of multiple dimensions of existence.[2]

In Hindu temples, one hears chants in praise of God: '*ananta koti brahmanda nayaka*' which means 'The Lord of Infinite Number of Universes'. Possibly, Bharat was aware about the existence of multiverses.

How Advanced Was Sanatan Culture in Other Sciences?

The table below provides a fair idea:

Number	Subject	Shastras
1.	Physics including Gravity, Construct of the Cosmos, etc.	*Vaisheshika Darshanam* was written by Maharishi Kanad Kashyap circa 600 BCE, at least 1,700 years before Isaac Newton, 800 years before Galileo and 1,600 years before Al-Biruni.

Number	Subject	Shastras
2.	Human Anatomy and Medicine	Shiva Puran Garbha Puran Ayurveda The Vedas and Purans are of unknown antiquity but the Purans must have been compiled at least 5,000 years ago, since Maharishi Ved Vyas—who compiled them—was born at the time of the Mahabharat.
3.	Economics, Business Administration and Political Science	*Arthashastra* is an Upaveda of Atharva Veda (Unknown Antiquity).
4.	Music, Dance, Literary and Visual Arts, Stagecraft	*Natya Shastra* (also called *Natya Veda*) was taught by Lord Shiva to Bharat Muni (Unknown Antiquity). Gandharv Veda is an Upaveda of Sama Veda (Unknown Antiquity). Linga Puran is at least 5,000 years old.
5.	Astronomy	*Jyotish* is the science of light. All astronomical studies are based on light as its speed is the highest. Astrology is only one of the many applications of *jyotish* (Unknown Antiquity).

Number	Subject	Shastras
6.	Logic	*Nyaya Darshan,* also called *Tarka Shastra*, was compiled by Akshapada Gautam circa 600–200 BCE but references to *Tarka Shastra* are found in the Mahabharat as well.
7.	Warfare and Defence	Dhanur Veda is an Upaveda of Yajur Veda (Unknown Antiquity).
8.	Architecture and Engineering	- Shilpa Shastra - Agama Shastra - Sthapatya Veda - Vastu Shastra - Skanda Puran - Agni Puran (Unknown Antiquity)
9.	Sculpture	Shilpa Shastra (Unknown Antiquity)
10.	Debating	*Nyaya Darshan,* also called *Tarka Shastra*, compiled by Akshapad Gautama circa 600–200 BCE.
11.	Grammar	*Vyakaran* was an essential aspect of Vedic Studies. It was also detailed by Panini in his *Ashtadhyayi*, based on the *Shiva Sutras* taught to him by Lord Shiva (Unknown Antiquity).
12.	Aeronautics	*Vaimanika Shastra* was written by Maharishi Bharadwaj (Unknown Antiquity).

Number	Subject	Shastras
13.	Literary Rhythm	*Chhanda*s were an essential part of the Vedas. In 200 BCE, Maharishi Pingalacharya documented and elaborated on the *chhanda*s in the *Chhandas Shastra*.
14.	Phonetics	*Shiksha* was an essential aspect of Vedic Studies.
15.	Etymology	*Nirukta* was an essential aspect of Vedic Studies.
16.	Matter and its Properties that make up the Natural World	*Sankhya Darshan* was written by Kapil Muni circa 300 BCE.
17.	Agriculture, Horticulture, Botany	*Vrikshayurveda* was a component of the Agni Puran compiled by Surapala in 1,000 CE.
18.	Gemology	Garud Puran
19.	Toxicology—Antidotes to Poisons	Garud Puran

What follows provides a glimpse of what is contained in the respective scriptures. The actual texts contain much greater detail, and many of them also cover a plethora of other sciences.

Jyotish: Study of Light

Jyotish is not astrology. *Jyoti* means light; hence, *jyotish* is the study of light in the cosmos, which then also implies the study of astronomy. Astrology is just one application of astronomy.

The *kundali* and the *panchang* in *jyotish* work with planetary positions in the natal chart of an individual or a place. The calculations are made in degrees of relative positions of the various planets and constellations.

Thus, it establishes that the *rishi*s knew of the existence of the sun, as well as the revolving and rotating planets in the solar system. They knew about the constellations of stars and understood that planets have orbits. In order to calculate their relative positions at a particular point of time, they needed to know the distances and speeds at which each planet travels.

Ashtadhyayi: Grammar

Panini's *Ashtadhyayi*, an exposition of Sanskrit grammar written in the sixth century BCE, i.e. almost 2,600 years ago, is the world's earliest, most comprehensive document on grammar and linguistics known to mankind. This has been acknowledged by renowned linguists in universities in Europe and the US.[3]

> This representation method and especially the actual list constructed by Panini, which is called the *Siva Sutra*s, earns universal admiration. The legend says that God Siva revealed the *Siva Sutra*s to Panini in order to let him start developing his grammar of Sanskrit.[4]
>
> —Wiebke Petersen

> Among grammars, Panini's description of Sanskrit takes up an outstanding position. On the one hand, not only is it one of the oldest recorded grammars but also one of the most complete grammars of any language [...][5] Modern linguistics acknowledges it as the most complete generative grammar of any language yet written, and continues to adopt technical ideas from it.[6]
>
> —Paul Kiparsky

Chhandas Shastra: Literary Rhythm

Chhandas Shastra, compiled by Maharishi Pingalacharya in 200 BCE, elucidates another aspect of Vedic learning, i.e. a collection of advanced mathematical algorithms in which words of any length can be fitted into an endless number of lines to render poetic metres that are delightful to read, enigmatic to chant and easy to remember.[7]

These algorithmic metres were responsible for the unbroken oral tradition of passing the Vedas from generation to generation before Maharishi Ved Vyas compiled and classified them into the four documented forms we know today.

An algorithm in the *Chhandas Shastra*, Chapter 8, *sutras* 21, 22 and 23, mentions two types of syllables—short and long—their patterns identifiable all across Sanskrit *shlokas*. This algorithm has the mathematical formula of 2^n where n is the number of letters in the word.[8] This formula gives us the binary number system of 1 and 0 which is the root of all computing in the modern world.

Pascal's triangle created by Blaise Pascal of France circa 1700 CE is the *meru prastar* created by Maharishi Pingalacharya in the *Chhandas Shastra*, Chapter 8, *sutras* 26 and 27, at least 2,500 years ago.[9]

Going by conservative estimates, *Chhandas Shastra* was written about 2,500 years ago in 200 BCE. *Chhandas* being the rhythmic metres of the Vedas, have to be much older than 2,500 years. But even at 2,500 years, they qualify as the oldest such mathematically articulated system of poetry, with many applications in advanced mathematics as well.

The *meru prastar* is a ready-reckoner for binomial theorems of mathematics like $(a + b)^2$, $(a + b)^3$, $(a + b)^4$, and so on. The mathematician Fibonacci, famous for the Fibonacci sequences in his book *Liber Abaci* written in 1202 CE, clearly stated that he had taken this particular sequence of numbers from the *meru prastar* of ancient Indian mathematics. In fact, he proudly mentioned strict adherence to the Indian method. He stated that he wrote the book only to introduce the Hindu numerical system and the Sanatan-Arabic way of mathematics to Europe, and claimed no credit for himself.[10] The *meru prastar*—which contains the Fibonacci sequence—is what gives us the golden ratio, the fundamental building block of nature, art and life itself!

Maharishi Pingalacharya's *meru prastar* was created in 200 BCE, translated by Omar Khayyam of Persia circa 1000 CE, Yang Hui of China circa 1300 CE, Niccolo Tartaglia of Italy circa 1500 CE, and circa 1600 CE by Blaise Pascal of France.[11]

The *meru prastar* is also foundational to the tenets of algebra, infinite series, binary number system, combinatorics and many more mathematical principles, with applications in the fields of machine learning, genetics, statistical physics and electronic computing.[12]

Garbha Upanishad and Shiva Puran: Foetal Development

The Garbha Upanishad and Shiva Puran document the entire process of conception, including the sperm's movement, the egg's fertilization, and the foetus's development.[13] These scriptures also detail the stages of foetal development week-wise, month-wise and trimester-wise, in line with what contemporary science says about foetal development, pregnancy and childbirth.

These scriptures behold a developing foetus as a receptacle of 'consciousness', that part of Brahman that is embedded in this particular *soul* or *being* or the '*atma*' that will become the human to be born. Therefore, even before the child's body is developed, consciousness has chosen this particular 'womb' to manifest this particular life. Hence, the baby is alive even before the brain is developed.

It is for this reason that ancients spoke of the importance of the mother's *sanskar*s and insisted that the mother read, hear and speak of sacred, positive, happy and constructive things, and that the mother be kept joyful, as these vibrations would be captured by the consciousness of the developing baby, affecting his/her personality, values and attitudes in life.

The scientific truth of consciousness in a developing foetus has also been discussed and proven by the new-age biologist Dr Bruce Lipton in his book, *The Biology of Belief* (2005).[14]

Vaisheshika Darshan: Atomic Structure of Matter

This treatise discusses the atomic structure of matter and the behaviour of atoms. An article in *East-West*, April, 1934, presents a summary of the *Vaisheshika Darshan*'s scientific knowledge:

> Though the modern 'atomic theory' is generally considered a new advance of science, it was brilliantly expounded long ago by Kanada, 'the atom eater'. The Sanskrit *anus* can be properly translated as 'atom' in the latter's literal Greek sense of 'uncut' or indivisible. Other scientific expositions of the *Vaisesika* treatises of the B.C. era include (1) the movement of needles toward magnets, (2) the circulation of water in plants, (3) *akash* or ether, inert and structureless, as a basis for transmitting subtle forces, (4) the solar fire as the cause of all other forms of heat, (5) heat as the cause of molecular change, (6) the law of gravitation as caused by the quality that inheres in earth-atoms to give them their attractive power or downward pull, (7) the kinetic nature of all energy; causation as always rooted in an expenditure of energy or a redistribution of motion, (8) universal dissolution through the disintegration of atoms, (9) the radiation of heat and light rays, infinitely small particles, darting forth in all directions with inconceivable

speed (the modern 'cosmic rays' theory), (10) the relativity of time and space.[15]

Vaisheshika regarded atoms as possessing an incessant vibratory motion—exactly what the String Theory of quantum physics says. *Vaisheshika* philosophers also reduced time to its furthest mathematical concept by describing the smallest unit of time *(kaal)* as the period taken by an atom to traverse its own unit of space.

Ayurveda: Medicine and Life Sciences

'Ayur' means 'life' and *'veda'* means 'knowledge'. Thus, Ayurveda is not just the knowledge of disease, it is also the knowledge of life and its physical, mental, emotional and spiritual dimensions.[16] The basic branches of Ayurvedic treatment are:

1. *Salya Chikitsa:* Surgery, including—
   a. Removal of foreign bodies, e.g. kidney stones
   b. Repairing of organs and limbs, e.g. plastic surgery
   c. Removal of damaged organs, e.g. cataract
   d. Puncturing of organs, e.g. letting out pus
   e. Types of incisions
   f. Design of surgical instruments
2. *Salyaka Chikitsa:* ENT, oral and dental ailments; way back, Ayurveda understood the interconnectedness of ENT (ear, nose and throat) in the way modern medicine does
3. *Kaya Chikitsa:* Treatment of regular fevers and minor seasonal ailments
4. *Vish Chikitsa:* Toxicology
5. *Bal Chikitsa:* Paediatrics
6. *Graha Chikitsa:* Treatment of mental and emotional trauma and psychiatric disorders
7. *Rasayan Chikitsa:* Preparation of medicines, therapies and procedures for their administration to patients

8. *Vajikaran Chikitsa:* Treatment of sexual disorders

Each of these eight branches have five dimensions:

1. *Sutrasa:* General instructions and training for doctors
2. *Nidan:* Diagnosis
3. *Sareer:* Anatomy and physical processes
4. *Chikitsa:* Finding herbs, testing their medicinal properties, formulae for preparing medicines with herbs, storing them and administering them in ways specific to different types of ailments and therapies
5. *Kalpa:* Listing possible side-effects, toxins, poisons and preparation of antidotes

Vedic biology classifies organisms into the following categories:

1. *Udbij:* Sprouting from a seed
2. *Andaj:* Born in an egg
3. *Jeevaj:* Born in womb
4. *Swedaj:* Born in heat, sweat or dirt[17]

Genetics too was well advanced and the Chandogya Upanishad fully explained the phenomena of conception—the fertilization of the ovule in the female (*reta*) by the semen of the male (*raja*), thus forming the fertilized egg in the womb, the subsequent development of the egg into the foetus, and later, into a fully developed organism.[18]

Vedic physiology subdivides '*pran*' or the vital air in the human system into five parts:

1. *Pran:* Air, working in the lungs and particularly responsible for respiration
2. *Apan:* Air working in the colon and bladder, particularly responsible for excretion and urination
3. *Saman:* Air working in the abdomen, particularly responsible for digestion of food and drink

4. *Udan:* Air operating in the larynx, particularly responsible for the voice
5. *Vyan:* Air operating in the limbs, particularly responsible for their physical activity and blood circulation

Vedic biology extended from the feelings of living beings, such as pain, pleasure, elation, depression, joy of life and fear of death, to plant life as well. Thus, there are *rishi*s like Manu speaking of trees and plants as having full consciousness within them and, therefore, being capable of experiencing both pleasure and pain.

Dhanur Veda: The Art and Science of Warfare

Dhanur Veda elucidates on various types of weapons, body postures of the warrior while shooting/attacking different types of targets—stationary, moving towards the warrior, moving away from the warrior in different directions, various shapes of arrowheads and spears, and the relationship between the weight and flexibility of a particular weapon in inflicting the intended damage.[19]

It also gives the following elements and count of the battle formation called *akshauhini sena*. One *pankti*, the first unit of ancient military formation, consists of:

- One chariot
- One elephant
- Three cavalry
- Seven foot soldiers

Multiples of this first unit become an *akshauhini* troop, which consists of 21,870 chariots, 21,870 elephants, 65,610 cavalry, and 109,350 foot soldiers.

It also contains the description of a complex system of *shastra*s—physical weapons and *astra*s—which are methods channelizing various energies of nature to inflict damage on the opponents.

[...] Soviet Scholar, Dr A.A. Gorbovsky [...] observes by the stanzas that describe the disaster caused by such astras, [now loosely termed as a well-crafted bow with skyrocketing arrows,] as below:

> *A blazing shaft which possessed all the effulgence of smokeless fire was let off... all directions were enveloped by darkness... the very elements seemed to be perturbed... the sun seemed to turn... the universe, scorched with heat, seemed to be in fever... the survivors lost their hair and nails... for years the sun and sky remained shrouded with clouds...*

The narration goes on. This is the account of the Brahmastra, as in the Mahabharata... Thus, the Dhanur Veda may be taken as the canon of missile sciences, which *fortunately* has not been handed over to successive generations, lest Earth would have been annihilated by now. In the Ramayana too [...] there are elaborate accounts of such astras...[20]

Isn't it ironic that while the world stares at biological and ecological warfare, people still consider the utilization of natural forces as *astra*s to be mere fantasy?

If anything, referencing modern science should make people more open-minded and accommodating of the scientific advances mentioned in Bharat's ancient scriptures, as modern science is only taking us back to what had already been documented!

Nyaya Shastra: The Science of Logic

According to the *Nyaya Shastra*, there are 14 forms of gaining knowledge.[21] One of those forms is called *praman*, i.e. evidence of truth.

*Praman*s are of six types:

1. *Pratyaksha* (Experience): When one tastes sea water, one knows it is salty and that river water is not.
2. *Anuman* (Logical Guess): Looking at the exquisitely carved and sculpted temples of ancient Bharat, one can logically infer that the makers were brilliant sculptors, artists, architects and engineers.
3. *Upaman* (Similarities or Confirmed Examples): Since it is common knowledge that most living creatures need water to survive, a water-hole in the forest is the most likely place where a tiger may be spotted, especially in summer.
4. *Arthapatti* (Extrapolation of Facts): On seeing clusters of dark clouds and smelling the fragrance of moist earth, one knows it is likely to rain.
5. *Anuplabdi* (Thinking of Opposites): On seeing, hearing, touching, tasting and smelling the visible world, one tries to grasp how to perceive an 'invisible world' that one cannot see, hear, touch, taste or smell (Quantum physics would be completely at home in this *praman*—evidence of truth).
6. *Sabda* (Discussion and Documentation): This is the most commonly used method of acquiring knowledge—studying what is already known and perhaps gaining new insights into each field.

Consider the following *sutra* from the *Nyaya Darshan*:

> When someone wants to inform another of a particular event out of inference, the inference that the person makes has five aspects: *Pratigya, Hetu, Udaharan, Upanay,* and *Nigam*.[22]

The following example should help understand this *sutra*. Let us say, there is fire on a mountain. The flames are obscured by a rock, but the smoke is visible. Now if a person infers that there is fire on the mountain because of the smoke, that inference has the following five aspects:

1. *Pratigya* (Commitment to a Hypothesis):
   'There is fire on that mountain.'
2. *Hetu* (Purpose/Reason):
   'There is smoke visible on it'
3. *Udaharan* (Example):
   'Like when smoke is seen in the kitchen, one also sees a fire there.'
4. *Upanay* (Relationship between Reason and Inference):
   'Because one can see smoke on that mountain, there is fire there.'
5. *Nigam* (Conclusion):
   'There is fire on that mountain.'

Two types of logic can exist as a result of such an inferred conclusion:

1. *Anukul Tarka* (Appropriate Logic):
   'Had there been no fire on the mountain, there wouldn't have been any smoke seen on it.'
2. *Pratikul Tarka* (Inappropriate Logic):
   If on seeing steam coming from a lake, a person concludes, 'Because there is steam coming from the lake, it must be on fire.'

The above *sutra* in the *Nyaya Shastra*, is mentioned here only to illustrate the intellectual depth and sophistication of Bharatiya thought.

Vaimanika Shastra: Aeronautics

This Sanskrit text, though now unavailable, was translated into English by J.R. Joyeser.[23] *Vaimanika Shastra* was originally authored by Maharishi Bharadwaj who also features in the Ramayan and in many other Puranic incidents that took place much before the Ramayan. In the introduction to the text, Maharishi Bharadwaj says that he has drawn from the science in the Vedas and the work of many other *rishi*s before him, like Narad, Narayan, Shownak, Garg, Vaachaspathi, Chakrayani, Dhundinath and Valmiki in the field of aeronautics and engineering. This text is further enhanced with a commentary 'Bodhananda Vritti' by Maharishi Bodhananda, a disciple of Maharishi Bharadwaj.

*Viman*s also find a mention in the Ramayan, Mahabharat and Purans. Though the *Pushpak Viman* that Ravana used to abduct Mother Sita is the famous aircraft, there are several references to *viman*s in other texts.

During Draupadi's *swayamvar*, the *devata*s arrived in the city of Panchal in their 'aerial vehicles' or *vimans*.[24] At the time of Mother Sita's *agnipravesh*, the *devata*s assembled in the skies in their *vimans* (See also, Chapter 5: Why Did Sita Undergo the Demeaning Agnipariksha?)[25] to entreat Lord Ram to stop Mother Sita from entering the fire. King Shalva had attacked Lord Krishna's city, Dwarka, in a *viman*. In fact, this *viman*, called 'Saubh', appears to be a spaceship, as Krishna tells Yudhishthir that it was stationed in the sky for several days and Shalva would attack and fight the army of Dwarka from there. Shalva and his army were staying on the spaceship which was 'as big as a city.'[26]

The *Vaimanika Shastra* has eight chapters that are divided into 100 sections, 500 principles for building and riding aircrafts, and 3,000 verses. There are detailed chapters on the training of pilots, the clothes they should wear, the food they should eat, the dangers associated with flying and the effects of natural forces on the physical and mental abilities of pilots. The text also details combat strategies like spying on enemy planes, and defensive and offensive manoeuvres in aerial warfare.

The *shastra* divides the atmosphere into five regions, which are the seven upper *lok*s as mentioned in the Atharva Veda, and states that there are altogether 519,000 airways usable by the *viman*s in these regions. It also details the forces that affect the plane, including gravitational pull of the Earth, sun, moon and other celestial bodies, wind speed, atmospheric pressure, etc.

The *shastra* provides information on the melting of metals and the preparation of 16 types of metal alloys that are heat absorbent, pressure resistant, lightweight, unbreakable and fire-resistant, as suitable for making *viman*s. These metals include lead, mercury and borax.

12 kinds of motions are defined for *viman*s. These include proceeding, shuddering, mounting, descending, circling, speeding, circumambulating, receding, side-wise motion, anti-clockwise motion, remaining motionless and performing miscellaneous motions.

The manufacture of *viman*s is explained with cross-section diagrams, and the system includes electricity, copper wires, switchboards, pistons, tubes, cylinders, etc.

Maharishi Bharadwaj's *Yantrasarvasva* presents fascinating information about machines. It defines 32 types of machines for generating electricity through various means, including friction, heating, waterfall, combination and solar rays, among others. Among these, the *samayojaka* (production by combination) is considered the most suitable for *viman*s. The process of its manufacture is explained by Agastya Muni in the *Shakti Tantra*, also known as Energy Device.

A prototype of a *viman* mentioned in the *Vaimanika Shastra* was tested at the University of California, Irvine by aerospace engineer Travis Taylor and was found to be flight-worthy.[27] In 1895, Shivkar Bapuji Talpade is said to have constructed the world's first *marutsakha viman*, based on the drawings and manual for the *shuka viman* in the *Vaimanika Shastra*.[28] He flew it up to a height of 1,500 feet on Bombay's Chowpatty eight years before the Wright Brothers flew their first plane.[29]

Vrikshayurveda: Botany, Agriculture, Horticulture

This scripture has 12 chapters.[30]

Chapter 1

'Bhumi Nirupan' (Soil Selection, Fertility and Classification)
This chapter discusses:

- Types of soil and their individual properties
- Fertility of soil and techniques to make infertile soil fertile
- Requirements in terms of water, micro-organisms, etc. for the health of the soil
- Suitability of a particular type of soil for a particular plant or tree, and management of soil health and plant/tree health

Chapter 2

'Bijo Bijoptivithi' (Classification and Preservation of Seeds)
This chapter discusses:

- Process of germination
- Classification and gradation of seeds
- Selection of the right quality of seed
- Preservation of different types of seeds

One method for seed preservation suggested here is by exposing the seeds to medicated smoke that acts as an anti-microbial agent.

Chapter 3

'Padapavivaksha' (Plant Morphology and Physiology)
This chapter discusses:

- Biology and anatomy of plants
- Plants and trees feeling hunger and pain

Chapter 4

'Ropan Vidan' (Life in Plants)
This chapter discusses:

- Senses in trees and plants
- Processes of stimulation of the senses in trees and plants

This chapter also suggests that plants have their own nervous system—their roots—inside the soil. It states that the difference between humans and plants is that plants have their heads below ground and humans above it.

Only in the current millennium are modern botanists studying roots to understand how neurons in the human brain grow and function. They are realizing that indeed, there might be parallels between their workings, just as it is now known that trees communicate with each other.[31]

Chapter 5

'Niscan Vidhi' (Techniques of Irrigation)
This chapter discusses:

- Techniques and methods of irrigation, depending on the type of soil, plant or crop, the climate of the place, the availability of water, etc.
- Detailed calculation of the amount of water needed by a particular tree or plant at various stages of its development

- Different methods of fertilization of undeveloped and underdeveloped trees and crops
- Diseases of trees, plants and crops

Chapter 6

'Poshan Vidhi' (Techniques of Fertilization)
This chapter discusses:

- Types of fertilizers
- Techniques to prepare fertilizers for various types of trees and crops in the initial stages of their development
- Methods to administer the fertilizer into the soil/plant

Chapter 7

'Drumaraksha' (Protection of Plants)
The chapter discusses:

- Techniques to save trees and crops from extreme weather conditions like storms
- Medicinal plants to treat trees with broken branches to save the rest of the tree

Chapter 8

'Taru Chikitsa' (Diagnosis and Treatment of Plant Diseases)
This chapter discusses:

- Various methods of treating plants or trees suffering from pest infestations and other diseases

Chapter 9

'Upavan Kriya' (Planning Home Gardens)
This chapter discusses:

- Designs for gardens including artificial hillocks, fountains, creepers, flowers, etc.

- Building of a *latagraha,* a type of greenhouse, for the cultivation of selected medicinal and aromatic plants with a huge yield of perfumed blossoms and flowers

Chapter 10

'Nivasasanna Taru Shubhashubha Lakshan' (Trees to Be Cultivated Near Homes and Those to Be Stayed Away From)
This chapter discusses:

- Types of trees to plant close to home and those that should be planted away from home
- Directions in which various trees must be planted

Chapter 11

'Chitri Karan' (Grafting, Cutting, Genetic Engineering)
This chapter discusses:

- Ways to infuse properties like colour, yield, fragrance in plants
- Techniques for fusing two or more varieties of trees or plants to get a new variety
- Ways to make a plant bloom throughout the year, make a non-fragrant flower fragrant
- Ways to make a plant mature faster
- Change the shape and form of trees

Chapter 12

'Taru Mahima' (Dependence of Humanity on Trees)
This chapter discusses:

- Importance of trees for human life and the cycle of nature
- Necessity to protect trees
- Diktats on the *punya* of planting trees with edible fruits

The following quote from this chapter and the Matsya Puran depicts how important trees were considered in ancient Bharat, and how environmentally conscious people were back then.

> 10 Wells = 1 Tank
> 10 Tanks = 1 Lake
> 10 Lakes = 1 Child
> 10 Children = 1 Tree

Apart from *Vrikshayurveda*, systematic and detailed scientific documentation on good agricultural and field collection practices, encompassing important issues like soil selection, plant propagation methods, irrigation and watering methods, plant nourishment, plant diseases and management, etc., can be traced back to other Bharatiya scriptures like the Rig Veda, Atharva Veda, Agni Puran, Vishnu Puran, *Satapatha Brahman*—most of these scriptures are millennia old—and other scriptures like the *Brihat Samhita, Amarakos, Upavan Vinod, Krishi Prasar* which are at least 2,000 years old.[32]

The methodology on crucial issues determining the quality and efficacy of soil suitable for cultivation and collection of drugs, proper identification of herbs, period of collection of those herbs, seasons for collection, parts used, preservation methods, etc. have been detailed in Ayurveda, *Charak Samhita, Sushruta Samhita, Bhavprakash, Sarangadhar Samhita,* etc. Each of these scriptures are at least 1,200 to 1,500 years old.

Parallels Between the Vedas and Modern Cosmology

Before Creation/Before the Big Bang

The following is a translation of verse 1 of the 'Cosmogenic Hymn' from the Rig Veda.[33]

> Non-Being then existed not, nor Being:
> There was no air, nor heaven beyond it.
> What motion was there? Where? By whom directed?
> Was water there and fathomless abysses?

> *nasadasinno sadasittadanim nasidrajo no vyoma paro yat kimavarivah kuha kasya sarmannambhah kimasidghanam gabhiram*

This hymn talks about the mystery that existed before Creation.

Nobel Laureate, Dr Steve Wienberg—who presented the classic Big Bang theory in what is now known as the 'standard model'—said:

> There is an embarrassing vagueness about the very beginning of the Universe [...] However, it is at least logically possible that there was a beginning and that time itself had no meaning before that moment (of the Big Bang) an absolute zero of time—a moment in the past beyond which it is, in principle impossible to trace any chain of cause and effect.'[34]

Needless to say, the Rig Veda and Dr Wienberg are saying the same thing. And this congruence goes further. According to Vedanta, the universe is eternal. It has neither a definite beginning *(anadi)* nor a definite end *(ananta)*. The Supreme Being or Cosmic Consciousness that is Brahman projects the universe in endless cycles of Creation, Sustenance and Dissolution. Each such cycle is called a *kalpa* (see, the timescales mentioned earlier in this chapter). According to the Vedic proposition:

> *dhata yatha purvam akalpayata*[35]
>
> [At the beginning of the *kalpa*, the first cause ideated, as it did all along before and projected the universe.]

kalpa-kshaye punasthaani kalpaadau visrajraamyaham[36]

[At the end of each *kalpa*, Creation merges into the Cosmic Consciousness again, and then Brahman brings it forth once more to start the next cycle.]

Modern science has long conceded the aforementioned view of the Vedas. Dr Weinberg himself suggests that:

One possibility is that the present expansion of the Universe may have begun at the end of a previous age of contraction [...] Looking further back, we can imagine an endless cycle of expansions and contractions stretching into the infinite past with no beginning whatever.[37]

To be convinced that the universe is created in cycles, one simply needs to observe nature—our breath is in cycles of inspiration and expiration, the eternal cycle of day and night, the waxing and waning of the moon, all seasons come in cycles, precipitation is a cycle from the moisture of the ocean condensed into clouds, coming down as rains into rivers that find their way back to the ocean. If perceivable nature moves in definite cycles, surely the universe might too!

Vedanta extrapolates this cycle to the *jivatma*; the individual soul—if the individual soul or consciousness has emanated from the Cosmic Consciousness, surely the cycle is complete only when it merges back into the Cosmic Consciousness. This is what is called Moksh, Mukti, Nirvana or Liberation. Therefore, Sanatan is *not* mere philosophy but science itself, based on the thorough understanding of natural phenomena!

It is equally significant that in the Upanishads, the longevity of one *kalpa* or one day of Brahma, Creator of the Universe, is about 4,329 million years. Curiously, that is close to the age of the solar system which modern science estimates to be about 4,500 million years.[38]

The Point of Creation—The Big Bang

According to the following verse of the 'Cosmogonic Hymn' of the Rig Veda:

na mrtyur asidamrtam na tarhi na ratrya ahna asit praketah anida-vatam svadhaya tad ekam tasmad dhanyan na parah kim canas

[The One breathed calm and windless by self-impulse;
There was not any other thing beyond it.
The empty space that by the void was hidden,
That One was by the force of heat engendered.][39]

This verse implies that this Cosmic Consciousness or Brahman or the Supreme Being breathed not air, but its own inherent essence. To draw an analogy, this is just like the sun which is visible by its own light. Likewise, Brahman is alive because of its own life essence. This is the state of awareness—'I am'—with its infinite potential for creation.

This verse says exactly what the Big Bang theory standard model does. According to this theory, the entire mass and energy forming the galaxies as we see them today, was compressed at the beginning of Creation into a small volume, which science calls the Cosmic Egg and Vedanta calls the Hiranya Garbha. The Cosmic Egg exploded in such a cataclysmic outburst that in the words of Dr Weinberg:[40]

It was not like the familiar explosion on earth starting from a definite centre [...] but an explosion which occurred simultaneously everywhere, filling all space from the beginning, with every particle of matter rushing apart from every other particle.

At that time, the heat generated was about 100,000,000,000 degrees centigrade. It is interesting to note that the aforementioned Vedic hymn states: 'That One was by the force of heat engendered.'[41]

Vedanta is clear that the Supreme Being had to have *existed* and is *sentient* or *living* because Existence cannot come out of Non-Existence nor Being from Non-Being. No non-sentient, non-intelligent force can bring forth a universe of such complexity, beauty, order and balance.

It further says that since the Cosmic Consciousness is the 'stuff' of Creation, all Creation has a Consciousness that is aware of and can perceive itself and the world.

That inanimate objects could be sentient seems like fantasy. Yet it has been proven by none other than the world-renowned physicist, botanist and inventor Jagdish Chandra Bose, who proved to the modern scientific world that plants were sentient and alive. He also invented the crescograph, an instrument that magnifies an object ten million times its original size as opposed to the microscope that magnifies objects a few thousand times only.

J.C. Bose was knighted for the invention of the crescograph and other inventions in 1917. In his speech at the opening of the Bose Institute of Research,[42] he said:

> I dedicate this institute not merely as a laboratory but as a temple. In the investigations, I was unconsciously led into the border region of physics and physiology. To my amazement, I found boundary lines vanishing, and points of contact emerging, between the realms of the living and the non-living. Inorganic matter was perceived as anything but inert; it was a thrill under the action of multitudinous forces.
>
> [...]
>
> A universal reaction seemed to bring metal, plant and animal under a common law. They all exhibited essentially

the same phenomena of fatigue and depression, with possibilities of recovery and exaltation, as well as the permanent irresponsiveness associated with death. Filled with awe at this stupendous generalization, it was with great hope that I announced my results before the Royal Society—results demonstrated by experiments. But the physiologists present advised me to confine myself to physical investigations, in which my success had been assured, rather than encroach on their preserves. I had unwittingly strayed into the domain of an unfamiliar caste system and so offended its etiquette.

According to Vedic thought, the universe is not an inanimate physical entity. Rather, it is a projection of the creative potential of the Brahman. This Brahman is the source of all energy and it manifests its own self as all of matter or anti-matter at all times, in all places. Modern science supports this view too.

The physicist Dr Roger Jones says:[43]

Modern space-time is very reminiscent of the causal body in the Hindu spiritual hierarchy. This is a place of Consciousness or being above the ordinary physical plane. The causal body includes all of what we, today, should call space and time, past, present and future [...] and forms a continuum of all human beings, creatures and things.

The aforementioned idea of a sentient, conscious cause of the universe is well demonstrated in the 'double-slit' experiment of quantum physics that has baffled scientists, since it proves that all things being constant, the mere presence of an observer changes the result of the experiment!

According to the Vedas, the creation of the 'Pancha

Mahabhut', five elements, followed a certain order (indicated below). One cannot help but marvel at the simple, logical sophistication in explaining the increasing complexity of Creation:

1. *Akash* or Ether/Space came first, through which sound first travelled. Sound can only be heard.
2. *Vayu* or Wind came next. Wind could be heard and felt.
3. *Tejas/Agni* or Fire was the third element. Fire could be heard, felt and seen.
4. *Jal/Aapa* or Water was the fourth element. Water could be heard, felt, seen and tasted.
5. *Prithvi* or Earth was the fifth element. Earth could be heard, felt, seen, tasted and smelt.

A string of verses in the Krishna Yajur Veda called 'Mantrapushpam' deals with the inter-relations between the above elements. Consider just the following two lines:

- Fire is the source of Water.
- Water is the source of Fire.

While these lines appear to be contradictory, unscientific and fantastical, if one were to observe natural phenomena, it would be difficult to deny that the 'fire' or heat in the sun is the source of the cycle of precipitation and rainfall. Also, rain or 'water'-bearing clouds cause lightning which has enormous heat or 'fire'

From these hymns that were used during Vedic rituals, one can logically infer that they were *not* about superstitions but scientific application of the principles of nature and the universe (See also, Chapter 23: 'What Are Yagyas?')!

Aum and the Big Bang

The cosmic sound that followed the Big Bang has been identified by Vedanta as 'A-U-M' or *aum*. *Aum* is regarded as that indestructible, transcendental, vibrating sound that carries the creative power of Brahma. Hence, *aum* is called 'Shabd Brahma' or 'Nad Brahma'—'Sound of Brahman'. This primordial sound is said to be ceaselessly reverberating in the universe as the hum at the end of the chanting of *aum*.[44]

Modern science too has identified this primordial sound, glorified in Vedanta. In 1965, using a high-powered antenna, American radio astronomers Arno Penzias and Robert Wilson detected in space a sizeable amount of micro-wave sound that they describe thus:

> The sound was independent of direction, unaffected by the time of the day or, as the year went on, by season. It did not seem to come from one galaxy but [...] coming equally from all directions [...] Thus, in a sense, its antenna is a box, the box is the whole Universe.[45]

Science also holds that the starting point of Creation after the Big Bang was the condensation of the pre-galactic matter when the turbulence of the mass exceeded the velocity of sound. Sound is thus postulated by science as the origin of the universe just like *aum* is the Nad Brahma (Sound as Creator) or the origin of Creation in Vedanta.

Much after the Big Bang: While the Universe Was Still Forming

Vedanta is clear that the same Supreme Consciousness or Brahman projected itself into the manifest universe. This means that everything in the universe is Brahman itself.

Brahman has two aspects: Shiva and Shakti. Shiva is

pure Cosmic Consciousness, which exists only as a static creative potential, and Shakti is pure Cosmic Energy that is dynamic and causes vibrations, movements and change, to bring forth the entire cosmos and everything within it. Shakti is the source of all energy in all its forms immanent in Creation; Shakti is indestructible, eternal and all-pervading. Nothing can add or take away from it.[46] This is exactly what the first law of thermodynamics says, 'Energy can neither be created nor destroyed. It can only be transformed from one form to another.'

Therefore, it is clear that everything in the cosmos is a manifestation of Shiva and Shakti—the dual aspects of Brahman: Shiva is Space, Shakti is Time; Shiva is Consciousness, and Shakti is Energy. They are two aspects of the One. This is beautifully depicted in the image of the Ardhanarishwar, the cosmic form of the Brahman, and even in the Shivling (See also, Chapter 17: 'What Is the Shivling?').

When Prof. Brian Josephson, Nobel Laureate in Physics, was asked how the universe was created, he replied, 'I cannot add more to what is said in Indian philosophy.'[47]

After the Big Bang: Creation of Matter

The next verse of the 'Cosmogonic Hymn' of the Rig Veda says:

> *tiraschino vitato raamiream adhah swid asid upari swid asitretodha asan mahiman asantsvadha avastat prayatih parasta*
>
> [From this engenderment, beams of light shot forth
> Up and down, Gross matter was formed and Nature too
> Expanded in directions all, as the Sentient One
> Spread itself everywhere—high and low, here and beyond.][48]

This verse not only accurately explains the aftermath of the Big Bang in gross, physical terms; it also identifies the One Brahman as the *cause* of the universe and the manifestation of itself *as* the universe.

Hence, it is clear that Vedic cosmology is in line with the findings of modern physics. Yet, the Vedas are millennia old while these developments in modern physics are barely a century or two old.

Quantum Physics and Vedanta

Noted physicist Dr Fritjof Capra says:

> The most spectacular aspect of sub-atomic physics is the creation and destruction of material particles. Modern physics shows that movement and rhythm are essential properties of matter, that all matter, whether here on earth or in outer space, is involved in a continual dance. This dynamic view of the Universe is similar to that of modern physics and, consequently, finds its most beautiful expression in India in the image of Shiva Nataraja.[49]

Capra further substantiates this viewpoint by quoting the Sinhalese theorist and metaphysician, Ananda Muthu Coomaraswamy, who played a pioneering role in taking Indian art to the West:

> Shiva dancing, sends through inert matter pulsing waves of awakening sound, and lo! matter too dances, appearing as a glory round about Him. In the fullness of time, still dancing, He destroys all forms and names by fire and gives new rest. This is poetry, nonetheless, it is science.[50]

Vedic theory thus gives a logical account of the great event with which Creation began, consistently following its basic thesis of a conscious, supremely intelligent reality as the cause of the cosmos. This spiritual approach, therefore, is not theological but, as consistently emphasized earlier, in line with modern scientific thought.[51]

There are amazing parallels between Vedanta and the theory of relativity too. However, in the interest of the present narrative, the reader is invited to explore information available on the subject on various platforms.

Contributions of Bharatiya Experts to Mathematics, Astronomy, Science and Medicine

Mathematics and Astronomy

Baudhayan calculated the value of Pi.[52] He is also credited with inventing the Pythagoras theorem documented in Baudhayan's book, *Sulba Sutra*, estimated to have been written circa 800 BCE, about 300 years before Pythagoras.[53]

Aryabhata was the first mathematician to discover zero and, consequently, negative numbers. Additionally, he was the first scientist to calculate the exact distance between Earth and the moon. As an astronomer, he proposed that Earth rotates on its axis and revolves around the sun, asserting that the sun itself is stationary. He also suggested that celestial bodies in the solar system shine by reflecting the light of the sun. Furthermore, he provided a scientific explanation for the phenomena of eclipses. A student at Nalanda university, he later became its head. His work was documented in his book *Aryabhatiya*, written in 499 CE.[54]

Brahmagupta elucidated negative numbers and the operations of zero, explaining place values in multiplications. He is recognized as the creator of several principles in algebra, geometry, trigonometry and algorithmics. These contributions are documented in his two books, *Brahma Sputa Siddhanta* and *Khandakhadyaka*, which introduced Bharatiya mathematical systems to the Arabs circa 628 CE.[55]

Bhaskaracharya's work is documented in *Siddhanta Shiromani*, which he wrote at the age of 36 in 1150 CE. The book comprises several volumes, including 'Lilavati', named after his daughter, which covers the principles of calculating progressions, measurement, permutations, and features the *chakra* method for solving quadratic equations—later referred to as the inverse cycle by European mathematicians. This volume was translated into English by James Taylor in the nineteenth century. Another volume, 'Bijaganita', discusses important concepts such as zero, infinity, positive and negative numbers, and indeterminate equations, including what is now known as Pell's equation, which he solved using the *kuttaka* method. Notably, he resolved the problem $61x^2 + 1 = y^{261}x^2 + 1 = y^{261}x^2 + 1 = y^2$, a challenge that would elude Pierre de Fermat and his European contemporaries for centuries. Additionally, 'Goladhyaya' is dedicated to the mathematics of spheres, while 'Grahaganita' calculates the speeds of planetary motion, using principles of trigonometry. This significant work was translated into Persian by Safdar Ali Khan in 1797.[56]

Mahaviracharya compiled many important mathematical concepts in his work *Ganit Sara Sangraha* circa 850 CE, creating what is considered the first modern textbook of mathematics. The modern method of calculating the least common multiple (LCM) was first published in his book. Logs, exponents, set theory, quadratic equations and fractions were discussed in ancient Jain literature between 500 and 100 BCE. Remarkably, this occurred centuries before the Scottish mathematician John Napier, who is credited with the discovery of logarithms, published his work.[57]

Science

Kanad is known as the father of atomic theory that has been documented in the *Vaisheshika Darshan*.

Varahamihir was a geologist, hydrologist, ecologist and astrologer. He was among the first scientists to propose that the presence of six specific animals and 30 plants indicated the presence of underground water, with special emphasis on termites and other wood-eating organisms that he suggested could dig deep underground to find water for their colonies. Additionally, he was among the pioneers to document the science of earthquakes, proposing that factors such as underground water, cloud formation, planetary influences, and unusual animal behaviour could serve as indicators of seismic activity. His works are documented in *Pancha Siddhantika*, *Brihat Samhita* and *Brihaj Jataka*, all written between 500 and 600 CE.[58]

Nagarjun discovered a gold-like element that is still used in artificial jewellery. Additionally, he detailed procedures to extract metals such as gold, silver, copper and tin.[59] His work is documented in his book *Rasaratnakara* written in the tenth century.

Medicine

Sushruta studied dead bodies to research human anatomy and detailed over 1,000 diseases, including 26 types of fevers, eight types of jaundice and 20 types of urinary problems. In his work, he described over 700 types of plants and their medicinal uses, outlining the properties of different parts, such as roots, stems, leaves, flowers, bark, resin and juice, as well as methods of use like crushing, boiling and consuming them raw. He provided clear, step-by-step procedures for performing plastic and ophthalmic surgeries, removing a foetus, extracting bladder stones and repairing a damaged rectum—procedures that closely resemble contemporary surgical practices. Furthermore, he listed and illustrated 125 surgical instruments that are still used by modern surgeons. His work is documented in the *Sushruta Samhita*, written circa 1000 BCE. The Australian College of Surgeons has a rare English translation of this text. And the Royal Australian College of Surgeons in Melbourne, where he is considered the 'Father of Surgery', has erected a statue in his honour.[60]

Charak was the first to describe immunity, metabolism and digestion as important aspects of health, emphasizing the significance of preventive healthcare. Additionally, he documented the fundamentals of genetics. His work is recorded in the *Charak Samhita*, written between 100 and 200 BCE, which also includes references to earlier ancient works in Ayurveda, such as those composed by Agnivesh, circa 800 BCE.[61]

If Bharat had all this knowledge, how did it just disappear?

Bharat suffered over 1,000 years of invasions and foreign rule, first by a series of Muslim rulers who destroyed its temples, scriptures and libraries, and then by waves of Europeans, particularly the British, who severed its ancient knowledge from its citizens by supplanting Sanskrit with English and the Western system of education, while denigrating everything Bharatiya. Today, most Bharatiyas would be hard put to read the Bhagvad Gita unless it is a translation of the original in Sanskrit.

From the perspective of Sanatan Dharm, Kali Yug, the present age is one in which Dharm is on the verge of extinction. Imagine how disastrous it would be if the evil forces of today had access to the material secrets of the universe and knew how to apply the ancient knowledge of communicating with the elements, using forces of nature for material advantage! Hence, obscuring powerful knowledge from those not wise or Dharmic enough to use it for the benefit of all seems like the most compassionate form of Divine Providence.

This obscured knowledge is once again emerging as the world moves towards the forthcoming Golden Age in which humanity will be worthy enough to receive it.

What Makes Sanatan Culture Scientific?

Non-dogmatic Outlook

Hindus have no dogmatic concept of the 'Word of God' apart from the syllable *aum*. In Hinduism, every individual is God and one's own conscience is the 'Word' of that 'God'. So, as long as we follow our conscience and do what is right within the context of our unique circumstances—and strive to become the best of who we can be—we are on our way to experiencing the reality that we *are* God.

Culture of Debating and Questioning

Hindus have always welcomed debates. The fine art of debating was developed in ancient Bharat as *shastrartha,* meaning the interpretation of scriptures. These debates were regularly organized by kings in their courts or temples. Scholars from all ideologies were allowed to freely participate in these debates with almost no rigid protocol. The only objective of these debates was to foster new ideas and fresh ways of perceiving life, nature and science.

Most Sanatan scriptures are in the form of questions and answers. Questioning was regarded as a virtue and a doorway to knowledge. Even the most profound, spiritual exposition for a human is said to begin with a question: 'Who am I?'

Obviously, people belonging to this culture are logical, curious and scientific.

Educational Institutions

As mentioned earlier, Bharatiyas built some of the world's oldest universities, like Takshashila, Kashmir Smast, Sharada Peeth, Nalanda, Odantapura, and Vikramashila. Numerous *gurukul*s educated both men and women. These educational institutes offered a vast array of subjects like science, philosophy, economics, art, physics, astronomy, mathematics, literature, metaphysics, psychology and martial arts. Nalanda itself taught over 108 subjects, including economics, astronomy, medicine, political science, physics and chemistry.

Students from all over the world were not only welcomed to these seats of learning but were also educated free of cost in a harmonious environment that fostered intellectual and spiritual pursuits. In fact, for the entrance examinations in Sanskrit, students from all over Asia would join preparatory classes and learn Sanskrit to gain admission into these universities.[62]

Conclusion

Science and Sanatan Dharm are synonymous; the scientific advances of ancient Sanatanis are older and more progressive than most recorded cultures or civilizations till date. The Maharishis and *rishi*s—Vashishta, Valmiki, Agastya, Bharadwaj, Gautam, Vishwamitra, Kapil, etc.—mentioned in our epics and Purans also authored some of the *shastra*s mentioned in this chapter. Even if we do not understand all this knowledge yet, it is clear that a culture that produced such stupendous scientific achievements could not have built its entire cultural edifice on myths and fairytales.

Western Scholars and Scientists on Bharat's Scientific Advances

- 'All science is transcendental or else passes away. Botany is now acquiring the right theory, avatars of Brahma will presently be the textbooks of natural history.'—Robert Charlton Emerson[63]
- Sir Monier Williams—in the 'Introduction' to his Sanskrit-English dictionary (1899)—wrote, 'The Hindus have made considerable advances in Astronomy, Arithmetic, Botany, and Medicine, not to mention superiority in grammar, long before some of these sciences were cultivated by the most ancient nations of Europe. Hence, it has happened that I have been painfully reminded during the progress of this dictionary that a Sanskrit lexicographer ought to aim at a kind of quasi-omniscience.'[64]
- 'All history points to India as the mother of science and art. This country was anciently so renowned for knowledge and wisdom that the philosophers of Greece did not disdain to travel thither for their improvement... The tranquility of their minds, even in the most trying circumstances, is expressed by a constant smile that sits gracefully on their placid countenances. The Hindus are naturally the most inoffensive of all mortals... In politeness and gracefulness of deportment and speech an Indian is much superior to a polished Frenchman.'—William Mackintosh[65]
- 'Sanskrit is the source of all other languages. She is the parent of every dialect from the Persian Gulf to the China Seas and even Latin and Greek. She is the language of the most venerable and unfathomable antiquity, signifying the dawn of civilization.'—Nathaniek Brassey Halhed[66]
- 'I am amazed at the mathematical exactness of the stone instruments at Raja Jai Singh's observatory at Banaras. The

Asiaticks had climbed the heights of science before the Greeks had learnt their alphabet.'—Sir Robert Barker[67]
- 'Even the highest and farthest reaches of modern Western mathematics have not yet brought the Western world even to the threshold of ancient Indian Vedic Mathematics.'—Prof. D.C. Morgan[68]
- 'We believe, consequently, that no department of study, particularly in the humanities, in any major university can be fully equipped without a properly trained specialist in the Indic phases of its discipline. We believe, too, that every college which aims to prepare its graduates for intelligent work in the world which is to be theirs to live in, must have on its staff a scholar competent in the civilization of India.'—Prof. W. Norman Brown[69]

23

What Are Yagyas?

sarva-bhutesu yah pasyed
bhagavad bhavam atmanah
bhutani bhagavaty atmany
esa bhagavatottamah

[One who sees God everywhere and in all
beings is the highest spiritualist.]

—Srimad Bhagavatam 11:2.45.20

Since all Creation is the energy of Brahman or the Supreme Consciousness, all aspects of nature are personifications of that energy, and therefore, alive and sentient. These personifications are called *devatas*.

Energy can neither be created nor destroyed. It can only be altered/converted from one form to another by altering vibrations.

What Does a Vedic Yagya Entail?

The requirements for different types of *yagyas* are elaborate and extend beyond the scope of a basic exploration of these rituals. Broadly speaking, a *yagya* involves several essential components. First, there is the *yagya-kund*, or *vedi*, which must have precise dimensions specific to the type of *yagya* being performed. Additionally, only Vedic scholars with expertise in conducting specific *yagyas* can perform these;

not all Brahmins are qualified to perform every kind of *yagya*. The construction of the *yagya* hall is also tailored to the specific requirements of the *yagya*, including the kind of pillars, materials, dimensions and orientation. Furthermore, offerings must be made into the fire, accompanied by Vedic *mantra*s that are pertinent to the specific *yagya* being conducted. Finally, charity is an important aspect of the ritual and is observed both during and after the *yagya*.

What Does a Yagya Accomplish?

A *yagya* uses the nine elements of Creation to alter vibrations and hence, make energy in a particular location, at a particular time, beneficial, thereby accomplishing the specific goal of its performance. For instance, many *yagya*s were performed for favourable natural phenomena like sufficient rain, better crop yield, prevention of storms and other natural calamities. Most *yagya*s were done by kings for the general good of the subjects.

The nine elements that *yagya*s cater to are:

1. *Akash* (Space/Ether)
2. *Vayu* (Air)
3. *Tejas* or *Agni* (Fire)
4. *Aapas* (Water)
5. *Pruthvi* (Earth)
6. *Dikh* (Direction)
7. *Manas* (Human Mind)
8. *Kaal* (Time)
9. *Atma* (Soul)

The alteration in vibrations in the aforementioned elements for favourable results was done through the chanting of powerful sound frequencies called *mantra*s, by having the subjects concentrate on them with faith and sincerity of intention.

The idea about thoughts, intentions and sound frequencies affecting physical reality around us is increasingly being recognized in the modern world. This understanding is supported by various phenomena, such as cymatic patterns, i.e. patterns made by sound vibrations in surrounding molecules of water, flour and sand, etc. Just by looking at the patterns, one can make out whether the effects of the specific sound frequencies are positive or negative.

Another example is Kirlian photography that captures the aura around an individual and a space—the colours of the aura are affected by the physical, mental, emotional and spiritual state of the individual. Also, quantum physics and the double-slit experiment in which the result of the same experiment can be altered by the mere presence of an observer is another example of this phenomenon.

Scientific Studies on Yagyas and Mantras

Many studies have been conducted on the effects of the sound vibrations of Vedic *mantra*s and of Vedic rituals on individuals participating in the rituals and the environment around the rituals. Given below are two such studies: the first is on the *agni chayana yagya* and the other on the 'Gayatri Mantra'.

Study on the Agni Chayana Yagya

Venu Menon—on behalf of *Illustrated Weekly of India*, 27 May 1990—covered the performance of a Vedic *yagya* in Kundur, Kerala. It drew parallel to another, similar performance, which was carried out by Vedic scholar, Prof. Frits Staal, in 1975.

Staal sought assistance from several American funding agencies—including the Smithsonian Institute and the Rockefeller Foundation—and organized the *agni chayana* ritual in 1975. Despite innumerable hurdles, he managed to persuade the elderly *Nambudris* (scholarly priests of Vedic lore) to put together a team of ritualists old and young, train them thoroughly and rehearse for several months, before finally putting up a performance for filming and documentation.

Staal followed this up with the publication of his two-volume book, *Agni: The Vedic Ritual of the Fire Altar* and *The Mantra*, which attempted to analyse the Vedic hymns. According to him, a Vedic ritual is very different from a health cure, a psychoanalyst's session, an anthropological meeting or a religious service. A Vedic ritual follows its own principles. He stated that a Vedic ritual requires very detailed and specific knowledge and estimated that the extent of specialized knowledge needed to put the sacrificial altar together ritually was on par with the technical knowledge required to build an aeroplane. 'The bird shaped is in fact a kind of aeroplane...' he said, 'only it takes off in a different way...'

During the *yagya*, scientific evaluations were also made by experts from Canada, in association with the Prague Institute of Czechoslovakia, on the physical and metaphysical impacts on the performers of the ritual. Mrs Rose Mary Steel, from London, took hundreds of Kirlian photographs of not only the performers but also the visiting people—and their fingertips—to record the aura or the electromagnetic radiation around the human organism. Significant changes were detected both in individuals who attended the ritual and in the surrounding environment. These were measured by taking readings of the humans' pulse, colours of their auras, and the degree of electromagnetic radiation and air quality across within a kilometre radius of the ritual spot.

Usually at the end of any Vedic ritual the *yagya* hall, a thatched shed, is offered into the fire as *purnahuti* (complete oblation into fire), which was usually followed by rain. 'The association between the *yagya* and rain is indelible,' noted

Venu Menon, as both the 1975 and 1990 renditions of the yagya were concluded with a shower.

Study on the Gayatri Mantra

There are many Gayatri Mantras dedicated to different deities in the Vedas. The chief among them however, is the 'Mahamantra':[1]

aum bhurbhuvah suvah tatsaviturvarenyam
bhargo devasya dhimahi dhiyo yo nah prachodayat

Krishna Himself has said in the Bhagvad Gita that among *mantra*s, He *is* the Gayatri Mantra.[2]

Dr Rama Jaysundar, PhD, University of Cambridge, UK conducted the following experiment using Magnetic Resonance Imaging (MRI) Spectrography on 30 volunteers for a period of nine months.[3]

- The first three months were dedicated to the baseline study.
- The next three months was when the experiment was conducted.
- The last three months was for follow-up study.

MRI Spectrographs were taken of all volunteers, every week, over the nine months. The MRI aimed to observe the asymmetry in the distribution of neurochemicals in both hemispheres of the brain, and any changes that occurred in them through the period of the study. The 30 volunteers were divided into three groups of 10 volunteers each:

- *Group 1:* Chanted the Gayatri Mantra in Sanskrit during the Brahmamuhurta (between 2.30 a.m. and 3.00 a.m.) 108 times for 3 months
- *Group 2:* Chanted the English translation of the Gayatri

Mantra during the Brahmamuhurta 108 times for 3 months
- *Group 3:* Did not chant anything

Results

1. Those who chanted the Gayatri Mantra showed far greater alignment in the distribution of neurochemicals in both hemispheres of the brain.
2. Those chanting in Sanskrit showed an even greater symmetry in the distribution of neurochemicals in the brain than those who chanted the English translation of the Gayatri Mantra.
3. Moreover, the symmetry between the chemical distribution of both hemispheres was maintained in the group chanting the Gayatri Mantra in Sanskrit even *after* they had stopped chanting it on the completion of three months of the experimental phase of the study.

From the results it is clear that the frequencies of sound provided by the Gayatri Mantra chanted in Sanskrit lead to significant and beneficial physiological changes in brain chemistry even after one stops chanting it.

Alignment in the two hemispheres of the brain is said to provide the individual with the following benefits:

- The mind becomes more awakened.
- Intuition develops, allowing individuals to take important decisions easily.
- The brain forms more neural pathways, enhancing overall intelligence and wisdom.
- The mind becomes calm and peaceful.
- Memory is greatly improved.
- Creativity, insight and concentration are enhanced.

- The mind is free from anxiety, depression, anger and other forms of negativity.
- The feeling of power, expansion and oneness with the universe is enhanced.

Aside from this, the Gayatri Upanishad lists numerous benefits of chanting the Gayatri Mantra, which include:

- Activating and energizing the five sheaths of human existence.
- Harmonizing the distribution of the elements in every organ of the human body.
- Activating and energizing the *chakra*s.
- Activating and energizing the five physical processes of a human body.
- Awakening the *kundalini*.
- Making the individual all powerful, happy and blissful.[4]

(See also, Chapter 38: 'Basic Concepts of Sanatan Dharm')

Attitude Towards Yagyas in Ancient Bharat

In ancient Bharat, *yagya*s were done not as a replacement for hard work but rather as an aid to it by kings and Brahmins with expertise in conducting a particular *yagya*, and only if a kingdom had more than enough resources to conduct it. A *yagya* could never be done at the cost of the subjects' well-being. And of course, an activity done in order to 'please' the forces of nature could not by itself hurt nature.

In fact, in the Mahabharat, Maharishi Ved Vyas once requested Yudhishthir—while the Pandavs were in exile in the forest called Dwaitavan—to shift to another forest as the *yagya*s being performed by the 10,000 Brahmins staying with him, were beginning to deplete the herbs in the forest. The very next day, the Pandavs moved to another forest called Kamyavan.[5]

Yagyas Beyond Rituals

Sanatan regards the macrocosm as merely an expansion of the microcosm. Therefore, any action done in sincerity and for the good of all concerned by any individual is a *yagya*. In the Bhagvad Gita, Chapter 4, Verse 24, Lord Krishna says:

> *brahmarpanam brahma havir brahmagnau brahmana hutam brahmaiva tena gantavyam brahmakarma samadhina*[6]

> [For those who are completely absorbed in God-Consciousness, the oblation is Brahman, the ladle with which it is offered is Brahman, the act of offering is Brahman, and the sacrificial fire is also Brahman. Such persons, who view everything as God, easily attain Him.]

This means that the activity, its doer, its object, and the resources used for it are all God, i.e. everything is God. And such persons who bear this in mind before doing anything, ultimately realize that they are God.

The human body itself is regarded as a *yagyashala*: our thoughts, words and deeds are oblations that we offer in the fire of life and reap the benefits thereof. Every temple is a *yagyashala* and the human body is the temple of *atma* or God. Therefore, no external ritual is compulsory for anyone, nor is a *yagya* the replacement of one's duty to choose only Dharm, i.e. righteousness above all else.

24

What Do Rituals in Sanatan Dharm Mean?

yad bhaavam tad bhavati

[As the feeling, so is one's reality.]

—Popular Sanskrit verse

Sanantan Dharm has many rituals, from daily *puja*s at home to elaborate, public *puja*s and *yagya*s, each with its own set of rules with regard to the purpose and the deity being worshipped. However,

1. What do these rituals mean? Are they necessary?
2. Why should one make offerings to the Lord when everything already belongs to him/her?
3. What kind of a god needs people to offer things to him/her in order to bless them?
4. Is puja simply a bribe? What kind of a god accepts bribes?

Given the vast variety of rituals in Sanatan Dharm, discussing each ritual would require extensive writing. Hence, here is a quick overview of the concept of rituals in Sanatan.

What Sanatan Dharm Says about Rituals

There is a concept in Sanatan Dharm called *manas puja* which says that if you do not have the time or resources to do a full-fledged physical *puja*, simply do it mentally. It is believed to be as potent as when it is done physically with all the paraphernalia. It makes no difference which kind of *puja* you perform as long as it is done with love and faith.

In the Bhagvad Gita, Chapter 9, Verse 26, Lord Krishna says:

*patram pushpam phalam toyam yo me bhaktya prayachhati
tadaham bhaktyupahritam ashnami prayatatmanah*

[If one offers to Me with devotion a leaf, a flower, a fruit, or even water, I delightfully partake of that item offered with love by My devotee in pure consciousness.][1]

The Vedas are full of rituals to be performed for various reasons on different occasions but the Upanishads, which are also a part of the Vedas, explicitly say that to know Brahman, no rituals are necessary. This is not a contradiction; it simply means that one can choose how to reach out to God, through rituals or meditation, contemplation or intellectual enquiry, by regarding one's work as worship, or by simply being in love with God (See also, Chapter 38: 'Basic Concepts of Sanatan').

Rituals cannot absolve you of the basic requirements of spiritual evolution that entails winning over your weaker impulses and being an honest, fair, good and happy human being, i.e. choosing to act in accordance with Dharm.

About 2,500 years ago, Shankaracharya, who gave Sanatan Dharm the doctrine of Advaita, led a movement to explain to Sanatanis that it was not the the rituals that were important but rather their *essence*, i.e. recognizing that you are one with Creation and the Creator. Shankaracharya is exalted as one of the greatest *guru*s of Hinduism.

Science and Logic Are Important Considerations in Rituals

The Shivling is an ellipse which is the exact mathematical shape of our expanding universe. Thus, it signifies infinite cosmic energy. If one can pour water over nuclear reactors, which deal with an infinitesimally small portion of cosmic energy, why can one not pour water or milk over this representation of infinite God Energy? When one looks at energy as an aspect of God rather than a manipulative tool in the hands of humans, one would use that energy responsibly (See also, Chapter 17: 'What Is the Shivling?').

The *jap mala* has 108 beads; 108 is a sacred number in Sanatan Dharm because it is obtained by multiplying 9 x 12. The number '9' is called the 'Para-Brahma Sankhya' because when it is multiplied by any number, the total of the digits of the answer is always '9'. For example:

$9 \times 6 = 54; 5 + 4 = 9$
$9 \times 17 = 153; 1 + 5 + 3 = 9$

Therefore, just as 9 remains 9, no matter how many times it is projected in various digits, the Brahman remains whole even if it projects itself in the myriad forms of matter and anti-matter in the cosmos.

Number 9 is arrived at by adding up the following realities of the universe:

- The '3' *Gun*s: *Satva, Rajas* and *Tamas* (All beings personify a combination of these three *gun*s)
- The '3' Aspects of Reality: Time, Space and Causation
- The '3' Aspects of Existence: Creation, Preservation and Dissolution.

Together, these define the basis of the phenomenal universe.

The 12 in 108 comes from the 12 signs of the zodiac. In Sanatan Dharm, the 12 signs or *nakshatra*s also signify the 12 Adityas, the respective parts of the sun that face Earth during different cosmic alignments. And the sun or 'light' is what allows us to perceive and function in the phenomenal world.

Hence, 9 × 12 means the perception and understanding of the ever-changing images of our phenomenal world on the screen of the eternal, unchanging Brahman.

While taking the name of God 108 times, people remind themselves consciously and sub-consciously that the physical world is just a temporary projection of the Brahman, and in reality, they *are* Brahman.

We are advised to meditate facing east because it aligns us with the flow of the magnetic energy on Earth and brings us in harmony with the cosmic energy.

The *yagya*s in Sanatan Dharm had *vedi*s which were built to precise mathematical calculations, based on the longitude and latitude of the location, combined with geometric diagrams of the energy frequencies of various *devata*s. Today, this is known as 'sacred geometry' in the West.

The peepal is considered sacred in Bharat for being one of the few trees that releases oxygen 24 x 7, while the tulsi plant releases ozone along with oxygen.

Ringing the temple bell creates beautiful vibrations that put the right and left brain in alignment, making the individual more receptive to the spiritual energy of the space.

Sanskrit as a language is a sophisticatedly designed series of sound frequencies. Today, the world talks about sound energy, music therapy, etc. Bharatiyas have been using these in the form of *mantra*s for millennia (The findings of a study on the 'Gayatri Mantra' are given in Chapter 23: 'What Are Yagyas?'; See also, 'Aum and the Big Bang' in Chapter 22: 'Does Science Have its Origins in Sanatan Dharm?').

Steps to a Simple Home Puja

In elaborate *puja*s, there are nine *supari*s which represent the nine planets; this is just one of the symbolic representations in a puja. Those who find this silly need to acknowledge that in the modern world, logos and emoticons are symbolic of something far bigger and grander than the logos or emoticons themselves!

Each item used in a *puja* has a reason for being chosen to represent a particular deity or celestial body. However, let us consider the following steps of a simple home *puja*.

1. *Ringing the bell:* As explained earlier, it removes random thoughts and allows one to concentrate.
2. *Invoking the deity:* This is like inviting God to spend time with you. Usually, a copper *kalash* half filled with water is kept for the *puja*; it is believed that various gods manifest within the *kalash*. Water is used because:
   - Water signifies Varun Dev.
   - 3/4th of planet Earth and 3/4th of the human body is water.
   - Water is known to absorb vibrations as revealed by the contemporary science of cymatics.
     Hence, after the puja, this water is sprinkled throughout the home and also partaken of by members of the family. It is known to have healing and positivity-increasing effects on individuals and the household.
3. *Offering ablutions:* Washing the feet of one's guests was an ancient custom in Bharat, done to offer them respect and to relieve them of exhaustion. Treating a guest with utmost respect has always been one of the highest form of duties in Sanatan Dharm. (See also 'Pancha Yagyas' in Chapter 38: 'Basic Concepts of Sanatan Dharm')

4. *Lighting a flame and incense; offering flowers and whole, uncooked rice mixed with turmeric:* When a revered guest comes home, one must ensure that the home is clean, well lit, well decorated, smelling nice and well stocked with eatables to make the guest feel welcome.
5. *Offering naivedya*: Refreshments are the most important aspect of hospitality.
6. *Offering clothes and adorning the idol:* It is still customary in many families in Bharat to offer a gift to a guest as a gesture of respect and affection.
7. *Offering things considered dear to the concerned deity (tulsi to Vishnu, hibiscus and dhruva to Ganesh, bilva patra to a Shivling, etc.):* When we love a particular friend or relative, don't we go out of our way to offer them things that are dear to him/her?
8. *Prayer:* This is like conversing with a friend who has come home.
9. *Aarti:* It is like saying goodbye with respect, adulation and realization. *Aarti* comes from two words *atma* (soul) and *rati* (engrossed in). Therefore, *aarti* means being engrossed in all aspects of the soul. The flame of the *aarti* always points upwards, signifying one's evolution towards a higher reality. An *aarti* signifies the light of knowledge—that one is an eternal, Divine being, having a temporary human experience. The flame also dispels the darkness of ignorance or the mistaken belief that one is only this body and that this world perceived through one's senses is the ultimate reality. In many *puja*s, the flame of the *aarti* is produced by burning camphor, as it leaves no residue on being burnt; it simply becomes one with the flame, just as humans must become one with God.

When God Is Already Present Everywhere, Why Conduct Rituals to Invite God?

When we know a best friend is always there for us, why do we still call them or meet them virtually every day?

A ritual is not about what God wants or what one offers Him/Her. A ritual is about wanting to spend time with a friend or a relative one reveres and about contemplating the reality of the true purpose of existence. When one makes these simple offerings with love, one develops a bond with God. The very idea that by offering a puja to a stone or metal idol, one is connecting with God, means that that one is connecting to the formless, omnipresent Consciousness of which that idol represents

A *puja* is like using a keyboard or touchscreen to access the invisible infinity of data on the internet.

Psychological Benefits of Puja

1. On a good or a bad day, just looking at a home-temple, decorated with flowers, illuminated with the light of a *diya*, and redolent with divine fragrance induces a feeling of well-being and peace.
2. This is a subconscious reminder that there is someone out there for us, someone all-powerful to give us a much-needed anchor in a rudderless world.
3. Just performing a simple ritual happily can give us much peace.

During a Puja/Ritual, What to Pray for and How?

While speaking to our best friend, are we careful with words? Do we hold back on how we are feeling, or what is happening in our lives? We don't. So, what is the use of holding back from an entity that knows every thought, every intention that crosses our minds and every detail of what is going on in our lives?

Faith in God introduces a sense of well-being and joy in life and rituals help us develop that faith by making us connect with God at a very human level. However, no ritual can compensate for the karmas we choose to perform in daily life! This is Sanatan—a life of righteousness or Dharm is the offering dearest to the Lord!

25

When God Is Everywhere, Why Should One Visit a Temple?

ishavasyam idam sarvam

[The entire universe is contained
in and pervaded by God.]

—Isho Upanishad, Verse 1

Of course, God is everywhere. So why should one visit a temple?

A Hindu temple is not just a building constructed on a piece of land. The *Agama Shastras* and the *Shilpa Shastras* provide detailed mechanical and engineering instructions for the construction of a temple. Meticulous calculations are made on the magnetic and rotational forces of the Earth, the type of soil, the astronomical energies of the space, and the overall vibrations of the location. Only a location with the energy most conducive to human well-being is selected as the temple building site. During construction, sacred *yantras*—geometric representations of the energy frequencies of the various *devatas*—are embossed on energy-emitting metal sheets and instated in that space. The rationale is that for a human being to experience peace, bliss and elevated personal strength, the rhythms of his/her mind and body must align with the rhythms of the cosmos.

Every aspect of a temple, including the material used to sculpt the idol, the stones used for the building, its size, the height of the *gopuram*—every detail of the space is designed to achieve perfect alignment between individual and cosmic energy. Hence, a temple is a scientifically designed, metaphysical, high-energy space of well-being that is accessible to all.

In ancient Bharat, a temple was not just a part of a town; it was its focal point as the most vibrant and positive structure in the settlement.

Besides being a place of worship, a Hindu temple is the abode of the enshrined deity. The installation of an idol in a temple is consummated with a Vedic ritual called *pran pratishtha*—inviting the deity to reside inside the idol, thereby transforming it into a living, Divine Entity.

That is why the daily rituals in a temple are akin to those in a vibrant household—waking up in the morning, ablutions, adorning the deity with attire and jewellery, preparing the *naivedya*, among others. Just as one enters a regular household by knocking the door or ringing the bell, one enters a temple by ringing the bell.

A temple is also an important part of Sanatan cultural identity. Through their devotion and service, the *pandit*s in the temple keep Sanatan cultural practices alive.

Whether in a good mood or not, when one visits a temple and beholds the idol of God adorned in silks, jewels and flowers, then hears the chants of *mantra*s punctuated by the ringing of temple bells, and sees the *pandit* performing *aarti* with the sacred flame, or distributing flowers and *prasad*, while devotees are deep in prayer or eagerly offering flowers and sweets to God, one is filled with deep faith in a higher power.

When people pour their hearts out to God, the smiling face of the Lord assures them that their problems are now in the hands of the one who shall help resolve them. They are filled with a sense of peace, security and well-being. This, in turn, reduces their stress so that they can resolve their problems.

And when one exchanges smiles with people coming in and out of a temple, one experiences what a powerful, unifying force this simple gesture is for Sanatanis as a community.

Conclusion

A temple is a space designed to receive and transmit the most positive earthly and spatial energy, augmented with healing sound frequencies and a pleasing altar for the smiling deity adorned in finery, enhanced by a burning flame and beautiful flowers...in short, a space of well-being. Visiting a temple is to connect with our glorious heritage and support its custodians. Every Hindu should visit a temple at least once a week, dressed in traditional attire. It may also be a good idea to ask the *pandit*s about the deity of the temple and their practices. In this way one can learn about this great culture and understand it better.

26

What Were Prosperity and Society like in Ancient Bharat?

nu no rasva sahasravat tokavat pustiimad vasu
dyumad agne suviryam varsistham anupaksitam

[Grant us indeed, Agni, wealth that may be
counted by thousands, and comprising
progeny, sustenance, brilliant riches,
and vigour, and be never-ending and
be countless and in-exhaustible.]

—Rig Veda 3:13.7

In Sanatan Dharm, one of the four primary goals of Purushartha, human existence, is wealth:

1. *Dharm:* Righteousness
2. *Artha:* Wealth
3. *Kaam:* Desires
4. *Moksh:* Liberation

Given below are excerpts from the Valmiki Ramayan that describe the wealth and society of Ayodhya, King Dasharath's capital, and Kishkindha, the city of Sugreeva. Similar descriptions exist in the Mahabharat and Purans as well.

Ayodhya and Its Residents

'A great kingdom named Kosala, a joyous and a vast one, well flourishing with monies and cereals, is snugly situated on the riverbanks of Sarayu.'[1]

'A world-renowned city is there in that kingdom, which is personally built by Manu, the foremost ruler of mankind.'[2]

'That glorious city with well-devised highways is twelve *yojana*s (96 miles) in length and three *yojana*s (24 miles) in breadth.'[3]

'That city shines forth with well-laid great royal highways that are always wetted with water, and with flowers strewn and scattered on them.'[4]

'That city is surrounded with gateways and archways; the front yards of buildings are well laid; it is lodged with all kinds of machinery, weaponry and craftsmen, and King Dasharatha dwells in such a city.'[5]

'Ayodhya accommodates groups of danseuses and theatrical personnel, and she is surrounded everywhere with gardens and groves of mango trees, and her wide fort-wall is like her cincture ornament.[6]

'Ayodhya is an impassable one for trespassers, or for other invaders, owing to her impassable and profound moats, and she is abounding with horses, camels, likewise with cows and donkeys.'[7]

'With the throngs of thousands of provincial kings who come hither to pay dues, she is verily lustrous with residents of various other countries, and with traders, too. In such a city Dasharatha dwells.'[8]

'Buildings are ornamentally studded with precious gems, and with such multi-storied skyscrapers she is adorned, and filled with them she is like Amaravati, the capital of Indra.'[9]

'Amazing is Ayodhya for its lay-out is like a game board called *Ashtapadi*, (possibly a chessboard) and with its flocks of beautiful women moving thereabout, where all kinds of precious gems are heaped up, and where its seven-storied buildings are picturesque.[10]

'The housing is very dense and there is no place or ground unutilized, and all are constructed on well-levelled lands, and rice-grain is plentiful while the drinking water tastes as sweet as sugarcane juice.'[11]

'That city is resounding with the drumbeats of great drums, and with musical rhythm instruments like *mridanga*, cymbals, and string instruments like *veena* etc., and on earth she is uniquely the best city.'[12]

'Ayodhya is like a hovering space station attained by sages by their ascesis, and its edifices are well planned and it is teeming with the best people.'[13]

'They, the skilful archers of that Ayodhya, will not kill with their arrows, one that does not have either a father or a son, one who is alone, one who is fleeing, or by listening to the sound of the target, as is done in sonic-archery, and their skills, acumen and handiness are thus benevolent.'[14]

'She, that Ayodhya is encompassed with Vedic scholars who always worship the ritual fire by enkindling the three kinds of ritual-fires continuously; no one in Ayodhya is not adept in the Vedas and their six ancillary subjects. The people of Ayodhya are virtuous like sages, generous, charitable and always abide by the truth.'[15]

'All the ladies and gentlemen in that city are virtuous in mind, self-controlled ones, they are all self-satisfied like great saints, and both in their conduct and character, they are blameless.'[16]

'In that city none is there without his earrings, headgear, or garlands; every person enjoys the finest things, takes their regular oil-baths and adorns their body with sandalwood paste, exotic creams and perfumes.'[17]

'None is famished, an uncharitable one in his nature; there is no one whose body is unadorned with ornaments like bracelets or chest plates, and there is none without a heart.'[18]

'There is no atheist, no liar, and none is less learnt in Vedas, and no one is found to be jealous, or disabled, or unscholarly person.'[19]

'Whoever it may be, either a gentleman or a lady, none is without wealth, even none without elegance or devoid of devotion to their king, in Ayodhya.'[20]

'In the four-*varna* system, everyone is a worshipper of deities and guests and everyone is also faithful, illustrious, valiant, and courageous.'[21]

'That city is always full with vigorous and mountain-like elephants bred mainly from three classes viz., Bhadra, Mandra and Mriga. And inter-bred among these three main classes are Bhadra-Mandra, Mandra-Mriga, Bhadra-Mriga and the like.'[22]

'The ministers for the great soul from Ikshvaku kings of King Dasharatha, are epitomised ones of their tactfulness, adroitness and are always obliged to undertake welfare activities of their king and the kingdom.'[23]

'Eight ministers are there for that valiant and glorious King Dasharatha, who are clean at heart and are involved in the works of the king and kingdom at all time.'[24]

'Two venerable saints of eminence are religious ministers for they are authorities in Vedic rituals, namely Vashishta and Vamdev, who are the acquiescent with religious matters, and apart from these two some more religious ministers are also there.'[25]

'All the ministers are well-versed in scriptures, they shun bad deeds, skilful ones in their duties with their senses regulated. Those great souls are affluent, knowers of all sciences, firmly courageous, and they are distinguished and quiet souls, and those ministers are true to their word. They are magnificent, patient and famed ones and they smile before they converse.'[26]

'They are efficient in administration and their friendships are well examined by the king, and those ministers impose punishment even on their sons, if the situation demands it.'[27]

'The ministers are renowned for their expertise, and even in foreign countries they are famous for their intellectual determination in all affairs.'[28]

'Accompanied with such of those effectual and good-natured ministers the exalted king Dasharatha ruled the Earth.'[29]

Ram's Procession to Dashrath's Palace

'Rama, adorned as in an auspicious festivity, took permission from Sita and started from his palace along with Sumantra.'[30]

'Then, that prince, the best of men, met his friends in the middle chamber. He saw all the people who came there to behold him, approached nearer to them, greeted them and mounted the excellent chariot, which was resplendent like fire and covered with tiger's skin.'[31]

'That chariot sounded like thunder. It was not congested. It was decorated with gold and jewels. Its splendour was like that of Meru Mountain, stealing the eyes. Excellent horses were tied to the chariot, which was moving quickly. That Rama shining with splendour like Indra, the Lord of Sky, mounted such a chariot and went forth quickly.'[32]

'Thereupon, hundreds and thousands of important people mounted on excellent horses and soldiers mounted on elephants, then followed Rama.'[33]

'Valiant persons, dressed in armour adorned with sandal and aloe perfumes, wearing swords and bows, declaring the arrival of Rama, went in front of Rama to receive him.'[34]

'While Rama, the annihilator of enemies, was going, well-adorned women standing in porticoes of palaces, sprinkled flowers on him from all sides.'[35]

'By the king's propitiousness, this Rama today is going to obtain this Earth and the wealthy kingdom. All our desires are going to be fulfilled because Rama will become the ruler.'[36]

'While bards and panegyrists were moving in front, praising with great respect, invoking blessing, eulogised by the most excellent instrumentalists, Rama, like Kubera the God of Wealth, went with resounding horses and elephants.'[37]

'Rama saw the great royal road which was spotlessly clean, having diamonds and various vendible commodities. It was full of male and female elephants, horses and chariots. There was abundance of people gathered at road junctions.'[38]

'Rama entered that excellent royal route, which was filled with sandal, superior aloe-wood, excellent perfumes, silk and linen cloth, heaps of them, unpierced pearls, excellent things made of crystal, splendid with various kinds of flowers and eatables, and which was not congested.'[39]

'Hearing the various blessing words spoken by his friends, he went acknowledging all those people suitably.'[40]

'Get coronated today, take the path followed by your grandfathers and great grandfathers and rule the kingdom.'[41]

'If Rama becomes king, we shall be more happy than when his father ruled and also when his grandfathers ruled.'[42]

Lakshman's Visit to Kishkindha

'Glorious Lakshmana has seen the splendid Kishkindha which is a colossal cave crafted with jewels, replete with flowered orchards and richly rife with gemlike-*objects d'art*.'[43]

'Kishkindha is compacted with mansions and multi-storied buildings that are embellished with various precious stones, and it is enlivened with blossomed trees that bear fruit of every relish and of every season, and Lakshmana has seen such a Kishkindha.'[44]

'That city is brightened with *Vanara*s who, with their prepossessing appearances, are attired in marvellous garlands and garments, and who can change their guise just by their wish, as they are the children of gods and *Gandharva*s, and Lakshmana has seen such a city.'[45]

'She is perfumed with the fragrances like sandal-scent, true aloe-scent, and the scents of lotuses, and her wide avenues are highly exhilarated with the bouquet of flower-liquors and grape wines, and Lakshmana has seen such a sweet-scented city Kishkindha.'[46]

'In that city, Lakshmana of Raghava dynasty has seen buildings that are not single-storied but multi-storied, semblable with Mt. Vindhya and Mt. Meru, and he even saw mountain-rapids with pure water.'[47]

'On the kings-way, Lakshmana has seen the exquisite mansion of Angad, likewise the lavish mansions of distinction about the other *Vanara* chiefs, namely Dvivid, Gavaya, Gavaaksha, Gaja, and Sharabha, Vidyunmali, Sampati, Suryaksha, Hanuma, and that of the noble-souled Nal, and even those of Virabaahu, Subaahu, Kumuda, Sushena, Lt. Taara, Jambavanta, Dadhivaktra, Nila, Supatala, and that of Sunetra.'[48]

Conclusion

The civilization of ancient Bharat was known for its opulent, lavish, tasteful and elegant life, with every *varna* enjoying prosperity and dignity. Yet, it was rooted in Dharm, and in the highest philosophy of the Vedas, with the deepest understanding of profound spiritual truths.

27

Is God Serious and Punishing or Happy and Fun-loving?

tat twam asi

[Thou Art That!]

The Cosmic Consciousness called Brahman is said to have three qualities—*Sat:* Truth (God is Truth and likes seekers to be truthful within themselves and with others); *Chit:* Awareness (God knows all and expects seekers to gain knowledge about Him/Her and the world); and *Ananda:* Bliss (God is ever blissful and wants seekers to be happy and spread happiness).

In Sanatan Dharm, God is not the punisher of sins; God is only the creator of laws that are enforced when required. Since everything and everyone is God, God does not interfere with anyone's free will. The episodes of the Purans and God's various avatars teach humankind the right path of living. It is entirely up to people whether they choose to follow the right path or not.

The various gods in Sanatan are proponents of the arts. Lord Shiva is the Nataraj; he dances with Goddess Parvati and plays the *damru* and the *veena*; Goddess Saraswati holds the *veena* and is the Goddess of all Arts; Lord Hanuman is a great poet, scholar and musician, and Lord Krishna plays the flute. *Natya Veda*, the world's oldest doctrine on stagecraft and drama was created by Lord Shiva.

Lord Krishna's ordinary day included picnicking in the forests, treating cows, birds and trees with affection and care, playing with his friends, and pulling pranks.

Given below is a description of the streets of Ayodhya after the coronation of Lord Ram was announced in the Valmiki Ramayan:[1]

> Hilarity filled the streets with people stampeding them and with the flurry of actors, dancers, singers and instrumentalists, as well as other onlookers, and there on the streets widely strewn are all kinds of gems appreciating the artists.

Music, dance, art, drama, fun, laughter, beauty, joy are an integral part of the Sanatan rituals. Science too upholds the fact that the universe indeed is a concert of joy and love (See also, Chapter 22: 'Does Science Have its Origins in the Sanatan Dharma?'). While describing interacting particles in the quantum field, Capra[2] says the following:

> Even the so-called stable structures that build up the material Universe do not remain stable but oscillate in rhythmic movements [...] the whole Universe is thus engaged in a continual cosmic dance of energy. Today, physicists term this dance as an "Energy Dance", "Cosmic Dance" or "Dance of Creation and Destruction."

This ties in beautifully with the concept of Shiva Nataraj—Dancing Shiva in the imagery below of this 'Cosmic Dance' discovered by modern science and described by Coomaraswamy:[3]

> 'This dance inspires Brahma (the Creator) to ensure rhythm in Shiva's dance by playing the *'taal'* or cymbals, while Vishnu (the Sustainer), accompanies Him with

beats on the *'mridanga'* or drum; Goddess Saraswati, the Source of All Knowledge and Wisdom, plays on the *'veena'*, while Goddess Lakshmi, the Goddess of all Resources supplies the tune by singing; Indra, the Lord of Pleasures, plays on the flute. All the rest of the gods are said to gather around and go on witnessing this Shiva dance of Creation-Preservation-Annihilation that goes on from the beginning of Time into Infinity.'

This symbolic image of the Dance of Shiva signifies the majesty and beauty, rhythm and melody, music and harmony, love and joy in Creation and the nature of the Creator or the Cosmic Consciousness that has manifested in all the above forms. Even beyond this, there is one easily witnessed, undeniable evidence of what God is like—nature!

Look at the sheer variety in nature. It is not just present in the numerous beings that are a part of it but also in the nature of these beings—there is cuteness and tenderness, colour and vibrance, love, harmony and balance! The stony mountain happily allows the flowy river to cut through it, the ocean and the sun share cloud, rain and rivers in what is essentially a long-distance friendship! The tastes, the smells, the sounds, the seasons, the scenery! Gentle winds, raging storms! Oh! She is beautiful in every color, in every form! All we need to do is be attuned to Nature. That in itself could become a spiritual experience of our connection to the Cosmic Consciousness or Brahman.

> How can you not be moved in tenderness
> By the delicate quivers of a flower, in a gust of wind!?
>
> How can you not be mesmerized, in awe
> At the myriads of stars, eons away, still
> Twinkling a 'Hi' from a speck in the infinite night!?

> How can the expanse of the ocean not feel like your soul!?
> How can you not know You are One with the Whole!?
>
> How can that bungling little bird not give you a smile!?
> At the tap of rain, how can your feet not want to dance
> Or run a breathtaking mile!?
>
> How can the gush of a river not thrill your Being!?
> How can the music of nature not make your heart sing?
> Don't you hear that whispering call,
> Telling you, it is You Within it All!?
>
> The mountain, firm as it stands, welcomes the delicate flakes of snow,
> The lion ferocious as it is, longs for that cool breeze to blow
> Every speck of nature is breathing 'n' alive!
> Pulsating with You in a Concert called Life!
>
> How can you not feel One with the Whole!?
> How can you not see, it is You Within it All!
> The Universe is throbbing and Alive!
> Pulsating through you, in a Concert of Love,
> A Concert called Life!!!

We are all a part of this grand symphony called Creation and when we look at God from that standpoint, we know that just like the nature that He/She Created, God is gorgeous, magnanimous, powerful, sweet and grand!

All God wants is for people to see that He/She is as much within them, as within every speck of nature. After creating this beautiful cosmos for all, God wants people to lead a perfectly balanced life by being respectful, loving, fair, strong, compassionate and happy.

28

Why Do Sanatanis Fast?

harir daata harir bhokta harir annam prajapatih
harir viprasharirastu, bhoonkte bhojayate harih

[The giver, partaker, the food itself, the body,
The one who eats and the one who feeds all are Hari.]

In Sanatan Dharm, no fast is compulsory. In most families, only one person fasts, if at all. There is no diktat on fasting for any specific period; it is an individual choice. While certain rituals and festivals require fasting, the rituals themselves are not mandatory.

Moreover, during most fasts, certain food items can be consumed. Some fasts allow one full meal in the day and small intermittent meals of milk, fruit, etc. over the rest of it. So, fasting is less about staying hungry and more about eating *sattvic* food.

Reasons for Fasting

People fast for one of the following four reasons:

To have a wish fulfilled: Is this about bribing God? Not at all. God has nothing to gain from people remaining hungry or denying themselves certain types of food. Fasting is about self-control and the intensity of the wish. In ancient times, people did *tapasya* for years on end in remote forests and mountains, away from their families, constantly meditating on the god/goddess they venerated, subsisting on minimal nourishment to have their deep, unearthly, celestial wishes fulfilled. However, such peope were far more attuned to nature and well-versed in yogic practices to be able to undertake such intense *tapasya* without harming themselves. *Tapasya* being difficult in Kali Yuga, a means of fulfilling everyday wishes is fasting on particular days. However, no Sanatani scripture mentions that fasting is a replacement for hard work.

To commemorate Puranic itihas: Among family and friends, people celebrate certain occasions with specific rituals, like a surprise for a sister's birthday, going back to the place of the first date on an anniversary. Everyone is a part of God's family, hence how can commemorating events related to God—as documented in the Purans or epics—be mere superstition? For instance, Monday in Sanskrit is 'Somvar'—the day of the moon. Since the speed of the moon is the lowest compared to the speed of the other planets in the solar system, the sequence of the days of the week began with assigning the moon as the deity of the first day of the week (Texts like the *Surya Siddhant*, *Aryabhatiya* and Bhagavat Puran— based on the principles of astronomy—elucidate scientific reasons for the names and deities related to the rest of the days of the week. But that discussion is beyond the scope of this book.) In the Purans, Somvar was also the day when Goddess Sati worshipped Lord Shiva for the first time, and on the same night, Lord Shiva healed the moon that had been cursed by Prajapati Daksh with a degenerative disease, and was dying. Since Shiva had fulfilled the wish of all those who were praying for the moon to be healed so that the world could be saved from the natural imbalance caused by its death, that night is called 'Mahashivratri', and Somvar is regarded as the day of the week when the Lord fulfils his devotees' wishes. So, devotees fast on the day preceding the night of Mahashivratri as a ritual, and also on Mondays to have a wish fulfilled, as an exercise in self-control, or to connect with their favourite god. With regard to all rituals and festivals, the eatables prescribed on specific days are perfectly aligned with the season, and the consequent need of the human body to consume or avoid certain foods.

To detox by fasting on certain days: For instance, fasting on 'Ekadashi', i.e. the eleventh day of the lunar cycle when the moon is 3/4th visible in its waxing phase and 3/4th invisible during its waning phase, has been prescribed as a day of cleansing and detoxing the body. Hence, no heavy, carb-rich or pungent food is consumed on that day. For good health, a detox twice a month makes sense, doesn't it? In the Bhagvad Gita, Chapter 15, Verse 14, Lord Krishna says:

> *aham vaishvanaro bhutva praninam deham ashritah*
> *pranapana-samayuktah pachamy annam chatur-vidham*
>
> [It is I who take the form of the fire of digestion in the stomachs of all living beings, and combine with the incoming and outgoing breaths, to digest and assimilate the four kinds of food.][1]

According to this *shlok* from the Bhagvad Gita, if God himself is the 'digestive fire' within a being, how can consuming healthy and delicious food be a sin and how can tormenting and weakening the body by denying it nourishment be a virtue?

The four kinds of food as per the Shastras are

1. *Bhojya:* Food that has to be bitten and chewed, like chapatis and vegetables.
2. *Peya:* Food that is liquid or semi-solid and has to be drunk or swallowed, like water, yoghurt and fruit pulp.

3. *Chausya:* Food that needs to be sucked, like sugarcane and candy.
4. *Lahaya:* Food that needs to be licked, like lemon, ice-cream and honey,

To gain spiritual control of the mind: Of all the senses (eyes, ears, nose, skin and tongue) control of the tongue is the most essential as it is responsible for two functions: speech and taste. Therefore, the misuse of the tongue can drive an individual towards falsehood, hurting and scandalizing others through uncontrolled, thoughtless speech, and towards addiction to unwholesome and unhealthy things, through uncontrolled, thoughtless consumption. Hence, the ancients sought to control the tongue by observing silence and fasting for specific periods. Our power of speech can be our biggest friend or our deadliest enemy depending on how we choose to use it. Of course, we all know that no amount of exercise can give the desired results without a healthy, wholesome and controlled diet!

Conclusion

Fasting is about self-control; it underscores one's commitment and intensity of desire to fulfil a wish or perform a ritual. It also commemorates Puranic *itihas* and connects people to their favourite gods. Fasting may also be done simply to detox the mind and body. For those who believe in God, the detox becomes an exercise to keep the body—which is the abode and the temple of God—in good health. It also helps people gain mastery over their impulses by resisting temptation.

29

Why Do Sanatani Gods Ride Animals?

mooshika vahana nandi vahana singh vahini

God is present in every speck of the cosmos. In the blink of an eye, God can appear anywhere. So why would God's various forms need animals to travel on?

Significance of Gods Riding Animals

Gods do not need animals as vehicles. Many Puranic episodes detail how various animals became vehicles of various gods. It is interesting to understand the Dharmic and logical import this phenomenon holds for worshippers of a particular form of God.

When one sees a god riding a tiger, a bull, a rodent, an eagle, etc. one believes that god has managed to tame the wild instincts of that animal. *That* is the *essence* of becoming God—controlling one's animal instincts. To put this idea in perspective, it is necessary to establish the difference between animals and humans.

An animal is driven by instinct; hence it has minimal control over its impulses, be it the impulse to kill, eat, copulate, etc. It must act on its impulses with no thought of right or wrong.

A human being on the other hand has intellect—the power to think, choose and decide. A human being need not be driven purely by the instincts of fear, hunger (for food, greed or anything else) or sex. A human being must consider the right and wrong of what he/she decides to think, speak and do. And it is when a human being completely controls his base instincts that he/she becomes God.

Complete Control Over One's Senses: Living in Self-denial, Poverty, or Lack?

Looking at the pictures and idols of Hindu gods and goddesses riding their animal vehicles, one sees that they exude power, wealth, wellness and happiness. A human being can be truly successful and free only if they refuse to be enslaved by their base instincts, which drag them from one selfish desire to another never allowing for a moment's respite, peace or joy.

While we must enjoy life and aspire to success, joy and prosperity, we must do so in ways that are balanced and beneficial to us and the world at large and not in ways that are harmful. Life is not about self-denial; it is about ensuring that ambition does not become greed, fear does not overtake the courage to do the right thing, the need for success does not supersede humanity, and a pursuit of pleasure does not degenerate into lust or addiction. We must understand that nothing worthwhile can be attained if one is a slave to the body, mind or senses.

Lessons for Humans

The phenomenon of animals and birds being closer to God than human beings clearly indicates that to respect God in *any* form is to respect nature and all her creatures. Had we understood this, we might have been more careful with the way we treated our environment.

If an animal, so driven by instinct, can be so close to God, surely, we humans with our ability to choose, decide and do the right thing, and with our power to influence the world, have the potential to not just be close to God but to realize that we *are* God!

30

If We Are God, Why Do We Not Feel Like God?

aham brahmasmi

[I am God!]

The answer to the question headlining this chapter has been beautifully expressed in the following analogy:

> A sculpture already exists within the block of stone. All the sculptor does to make the idol emerge from within it is to chisel away the unwanted parts of the stone that hide it.

The same works for us as humans. Yes, we are God. But over eons of lifetimes, we have picked up impulses which inhibit the expression and experience of our godliness. Also, modern mainstream education has taught us that we are advanced animals; it has never told us that we are all Divine. Hence, we have forgotten this truth.

The impulses that deny humans the experience of being Divine are selfishness, greed, attachment, ego, hate, fear, jealousy and insecurity. We cannot become God until we chisel these impulses out of our psyche.

Our own life experiences often bear out this simple truth. Traits like selfishness, fear, greed, arrogance jealousy take away our peace, and make us restless, because they contradict our inherent godliness. We must realize that we must treat others the same way we treat ourselves because all beings are One.

On the other hand, when we operate from a space of fairness, righteousness, love and compassion, we feel happy, joyous and fulfilled because these qualities are in sync with their basic godliness.

Hence, though 'Moksh' or feeling like God may seem like a profound, extraordinary experience, it begins with the small nothings of everyday life—choosing to be understanding instead of judgmental, accommodating instead of critical, respectful instead of condescending, doing the right thing instead of succumbing to that which is convenient.

Moment by moment, day by day, lifetime by lifetime, Dharm is the path to Moksh. The more people live in Dharm, the more they connect with their innate Cosmic Consciousness.

How Does a Person Know What Dharm Is?

Sat—God is the Eternal Truth: Since humans are God, they need to be honest and fair. They must respect all as equals because the truth is that humans are all One. Every difference, therefore, is simply another creative expression of God.

Chit—God is Ever Aware: As gods themselves, people must be aware of the workings of their own minds. What motivates humans? What drives them? Love or fear, selfishness or compassion, respect or judgement, righteousness or greed?

Ananda—God is Ever Blissful: People can be God if they are driven by love, by the desire to be happy and by creating happiness, as long as that happiness does not hurt or harm the general good.

Once I asked a teacher of the Bhagvad Gita, 'How do I know that I am doing well on the spiritual path? I wish God would give me some kind of a report card.' She smiled and said, 'Your report card is the answer to this one simple question: *Are you happy and at peace with yourself?*'

31

Why Doesn't Sanatan Dharm Give Ready-made Answers?

tamaso ma jyotir gamaya

[Lead me from the darkness of ignorance
to the light of wisdom.]

—Brihadaranyaka Upanishad 1:3.28

Wouldn't it be so convenient if we just had a ready reckoner, a checklist that we could tick every day and be assured of spiritual and material success? Imagine having detailed instructions for what to eat, what not to eat; what to wear, what not to wear; what to drink, what not to drink; how to pray, how many times to pray, what to pray; what to think, how to think; what is right, what is wrong... Life would be so much easier and simpler, wouldn't it? But at what cost?

Pitfalls of an Instruction Manual

Cost of Ready Instructions

If one looks at nature, every being is unique. This individuality is even more pronounced in humans. Therefore, deciding every aspect of a human being's existence is like telling a child to memorize that 10 + 10 = 20 without giving him the opportunity to reason out how or why that is so.

For children, life is sorted, but only as long as the number is 10 and the sign is +. But the moment the number and/or the sign changes, they will not know what to do. And if the child's psyche has been pumped with a false sense of superiority and ego—because they know that 10 + 10 = 20—they will regard any alternate question as wrong, not realizing that under the garb of being given solutions, they are being robbed of their freedom, denied the right to use their intelligence and divested of their right to grow! What can be more tragic?

If you think that this example is too simplistic then you already acknowledge that human beings are extremely complex—with unique combinations of experiences, emotions, dreams, inclinations, personalities, circumstances, relationships, duties, knowledge, talents, attitudes, perspectives, etc. Hence, there cannot be a one-size-fits-all approach to creating a meaningful life.

The Solution

The answer to the problem is to teach the child concepts rather than solutions and urge them to use their own intellect and wisdom. If the child understands the concept of numbers, proportions, increase and decrease, and learn to use their intelligence, they will be able to work with any set of numbers, with any sign in between them. This is the difference between believing and seeking.

Sanatan Dharm is the way of life for a seeker rather than for a believer; spirituality is seeking, not blindly believing. That is why Sanatan focuses on concepts like:

- *Dharm* (Righteousness)
- *Karma* (Action)
- *Moksh* (Liberation)
- *Shakti* (Energy)
- *Spandan* (Vibration)
- *Brahman, Paramatma* (Cosmic Consciousness)

- *Srishti* (Creation)
- *Maya* (Illusion)
- *Gyan* (Knowledge)
- *Bhakti, Prem* (Love)
- *Shanti* (Peace)
- *Ananda* (Bliss)
- *Atma* (Soul)

And so on.

These concepts are meant to be studied, contemplated upon, worked with and experienced by every individual in their own way, applied to their unique circumstances and personality.

For me, the difference between religion and spirituality is:

Religion is knowing; spirituality is being.

Religion requires unquestioning faith; spirituality requires questioning your faith.

Religion assigns a particular name to God; spirituality understands that all names belong to God.

Religion is the belief in a god without; spirituality is the search for the God within.

Religion constructs a heaven, a church, a temple, a mosque for God; spirituality sees every speck of Creation as the abode of God.

Religion forces the seeker to follow; spirituality urges the seeker to flow.

Religion is a set of rules; spirituality is a set of values.

Religion finds manifestation in rituals; spirituality finds purpose in love and compassion.

Religion is a candle, a *diya*, or fire; spirituality is just light.

Religion demands loyalty; spirituality demands humanity

Religion is about scriptures; spirituality is about conscience.

Religion judges people as sinners; spirituality accommodates people as learners.

Religion is about pleasing God; spirituality is about loving God's creations.

Religion creates differences; spirituality celebrates oneness.

Religion plucks flowers; spirituality plants gardens.

Human beings can survive without religion, but we will destroy ourselves without spirituality.

Spirituality can be confusing at times as there are no ready solutions and there are multiple possible answers to the same conundrum. However, rather than being about not having the answer, our confusion and fear is regarding the correctness of the answers we come up with. Hence, it is easier to let someone else decide for us.

But then, we are human beings and not robots. Each one of us is different, unique and free! Our destination may be the same—happiness, love, fulfilment—but our paths are different. We just have to deal with it!

32

Does Sanatan Dharm Focus on Afterlife?

tasmai tvam iha jajnise adrstas purusa
mrtyave tasmai tva ni hvayamasi

[This (is) the dearest world of the gods, unconquered.
Unto what death appointed, O man, thou wast
born here, we and it call after thee: do not die
before old age.]

—Atharva Veda 5:30.17

Sanatan Dharm focuses on karma. People's happiness, sadness, and the general circumstances in this earthly life depend on the karma that they have performed in their current and previous lives. According to Sanatan, karma includes thoughts, words, deeds and intentions, and the ultimate determinant of the quality of one's karmas is one's own conscience.

Sanatan Dharm and Earthly Life

If Sanatan Dharm considers everything as God, how can it consider one world better or more important than the other—whether it is heaven or Earth?

According to Sanatan, the ultimate purpose of human life is 'Moksh', not heaven. Moksh is the concept of realizing that one *is* God. When one attains this realization, one does not have to be born again. The path to Moksh is Dharm.

Dharm means living a comprehensively joyful life, while remaining fair, loving and compassionate. If people are supposed to live in joy in this world, it means this world is important, even more so than any supposed heaven or hell.

Lord Ram epitomized leading an ideal life in *this* world of humans. He was never known to speak or preach about basing one's karmas on the desire to go to heaven.

The Bhagvad Gita speaks of fulfilling one's responsibilities towards society in this world because it is one's duty, and not because one wants to secure a place in Heaven.

Right living in Sanatan is not a one-size-fits-all dogma. It depends on various circumstances. People have to consult their conscience and make choices that promote the greater good of everyone involved. Hence, one cannot equate a particular action as sin or merit by itself unless all circumstances within and around the person are taken into account (See also, Chapter 31: 'Why Doesn't Sanatan Dharm Give Ready-made Answers?')

Attaining Moksh means becoming *Satchidananda*—becoming God.

How can one experience ultimate bliss by creating misery for oneself or for others? Since Creation itself is God, hurting God's Creation is to hurt God! Therefore, the idea of hurting God's Creation to please God and be rewarded by him after death is absurd.

Conclusion

Sanatan Dharm is clear that a human being's duty is to *this* world, the afterlife of heaven or hell being only a byproduct of the way one chooses to live *this* life. That too is temporary since every being will have to return to the earthly plane to lead a life based on their karmas in their previous lives, till they realize that one is innately Divine. The focus, therefore, is on loving *this* world; the afterlife will take care of itself.

33

Why Would Hinduism Be Under Attack?

dasyutkrsta janapada
vedah pasanda dusitah
rajanas ca praja bhaksah
sisnodara para dvijah

[(In *Kali Yug*) Cities will be dominated by thieves,
the Vedas will be contaminated by speculative
interpretations of atheists,
political leaders will virtually consume the citizens,
and the so-called priests and intellectuals will be
devotees of their bellies and genitals.]

—Srimad Bhagavatam 12:3.32

Be it the systematic killings of Hindus in Kashmir, Bengal, and other regions of Bharat and the world, the belittling of Hinduism in a global conference on 'Dismantling Global Hindutva' and calling for its eradication, or hurling other insults at it through subtle anti-Hindu propaganda, it is undeniable that Hinduism—the third largest religion of the world—is indeed under attack, and has been so, for the past 800-odd years.

The accomplishments of Hindu *rishi*s, kings, queens and patriots have sometimes been undermined in history textbooks. Sanatan festivals such as Diwali and Holi are often presented as a threat to the environment—as though all pollution in the year happens only on Diwali night, and the water table is depleted only on Holi. Hindu festivals like Karva Chauth and Raksha Bandhan are portrayed as regressive for women, and there have been instances when the idols of Hindu gods and goddesses have been desecrated, their temples vandalized, and derogatory jokes and comments made on them in movies and general public discourse.

Why would anyone have a problem with a philosophy that believes in *'vasudhaiva kutumbakam'*—the world is one family?

Relationship between Religion and Power

Surely all religions have humanitarian and philanthropic objectives, and have been invaluable in furthering civilization. Today, however, religion has become the greatest source of power in the world by controlling how people think. It allows corrupt religious leaders to mould and influence millions of followers worldwide in order to fulfil the nefarious ambitions of their political and financial masters.

Religious leaders do this by defining the 'abstract' in ways that instil both fear and aspiration in the minds of their followers, such that they are willing to do anything that is asked of them to avoid God's punishment and receive God's grace. Fear and aspiration are created using the following means:

1. *God:* This omnipotent entity punishes followers for their sins and rewards them for their virtues.
2. *Scriptures:* For some religions, these contain the commandments of God, detailing the actions that may eventually lead a believer to heaven or hell.
3. *Priests:* They claim to understand God's commandments the best and can help the followers navigate life to ensure a place in heaven after death.
4. *Rules and Rituals:* These make religions interfere with

the private affairs of their followers by dictating their choices—how to pray, what to pray for, what to eat, what to wear and how to behave in daily life.

Together, these dos and don'ts control the lives of people who look to religion for guidance and support. To some degree, all religions do this— but none of the aforementioned means work in Hinduism to wield any kind of control on the followers.

Why Hinduism Doesn't Seek to Control

Concept of God: Like many religions, Hinduism also has one formless God—Brahman—but according to Hinduism, the formless Consciousness takes on various forms to make it easier for followers to relate to them. And all those forms are equally powerful and valid. Hindus are allowed to choose the form of God they relate to most. No one form of God competes with another.

Consider this universal example. Lord Hanuman is an incarnation of Lord Shiva. But the former is also a devotee of Lord Ram who is an avatar of Lord Vishnu. Being a scholar and musician, Hanuman worships Lord Brahma and Goddess Saraswati. Being a warrior, Hanuman is a natural devotee of Goddess Durga. He has been blessed by and received boons from all *devas*, like Indra, Surya, Vayu, Varun, etc. Thus, Hanuman would bless anyone praying to Ram, Vishnu, Lakshmi, Shiva, Brahma, Parvati or Saraswati, and any other god associated with them. He would also shower his grace on anyone who chooses to revere nature. Hanuman would bless even atheists who perform their duties with as much sincerity as Hanuman did.

Hinduism is full of such cross-associations which make all forms of gods equal in stature; and the worship of none of them is compulsory. Therefore, there is decentralization of Divine power in Hinduism—Hence, no one cult or institution can dictate to 1.16 billion Hindus whom to worship and which God is the greatest.

Scriptures: The instructions of all Hindu gods can be summarized in one word—Dharm, or promoting universal good by being courageous, loving and fair. Dharm is a decision taken within the context of each unique situation; it is not a one-formula-for-all commandment. For instance, Lakshman and Bharat leaving the comforts of the royal palace in solidarity with their elder brother Ram is regarded as Dharm. On the other hand, Vibhishan abandoning his elder brothers and even being responsible for their defeat to protect the larger good of the world is also regarded as Dharm.

Hindu scriptures also insist that the entire Creation is a manifestation of one formless God. Thus, every being is as divine as the Paramatma, or God himself. The purpose of all life is to realize this truth and attain Moksh.

Hinduism is totally above petty judgement. One of the highest prayers in Hinduism is *'samasta lokah sukhino bhavantu'*—let all beings in all the worlds be happy.

In fact, as mentioned earlier, by saying that all names and all forms are personifications of the same Brahman or God, Hindus acknowledge that Allah, Tao or Ahura Mazda are as valid names for God as Krishna, Shiva, Shakti, Devi, etc.

Hinduism does have the concept of heaven and hell but these are not absolute spaces of eternal misery or everlasting pleasure. The principal law of Hinduism is the law of karma which states that people's miseries are the outcomes of wrong deeds committed in the past—even in their previous lifetimes— and their joys are the outcomes of their good deeds. Thus, by choosing to do the right thing in their present lives, they can redeem themselves from the wrongs of previous lives. This chance of self-redemption is given endlessly till the soul purifies itself and learns that it is God, regardless of whether such learning takes a hundred or even hundred million lifetimes. The law of karma gives every Hindu the power and choice to write his/her own destiny.

Priests: No priest has the authority to compel a Hindu to worship one god over another.

Rites and Rituals: Over time, Hindus have modified these. For instance, burning a corpse using firewood has been replaced by cremating in an incinerator to protect the environment and save trees. Today, eco-friendly Ganesh idols are preferred for Ganesh Chaturthi.

A Hindu is free to follow any other faith—or no faith at all—without losing his/her status as a Hindu. It simply does not matter.

From all this, it is clear that Hinduism sets Hindus free by giving them the power to choose and decide for themselves how they want to live life. Hence, Hinduism offers no scope whatsoever for 15.1 per cent of the world's population to be controlled in any way. Perhaps, that is why Hinduism is under attack.

How Is Sanatan Attacked?

Hinduism is attacked by using its universal values against Hindus themselves. So, Hindus are asked to refrain from lighting crackers during Diwali in the interest of the environment, beseeched to overlook targeted violence, and forgive those who are not even contrite for the atrocities they have committed on Hindus for the sake of communal harmony. And Hindus accept all such manipulation as noble advice. One does not need to resort to counter-violence or aggression in order to fend off such attacks. All Hindus need to do is understand and respect their culture. These attacks will become futile automatically.

We must not forget that we are blessed to be born into such an open-minded, vibrant faith. But great privileges come with greater responsibility. It is worrisome that over time, we have started taking our freedom so much for granted that we have come to the point of disrespecting our own culture and values. We are so absorbed in our free lives that we do not even consider it our duty to protect and further this great culture. Our open-mindedness has become a disguise for our wilful ignorance and indifference.

It is our duty to stand together as followers of this glorious philosophy which allows each person to pick their own path and pave their own journey in ways that only promote world peace and universal well-being. Thus, if humankind has to survive, Sanatan values must be upheld. By saving the Hindu way of life, we save freedom, tolerance and humanity

34

Is it Necessary to Wear One's Cultural Symbols?

dharmo rakshati rakshitah

[Dharm protects those who protect Dharm.]

—*Manu Smriti* 8:15

The dynamics of brand advertising and marketing may provide an understanding of the importance of cultural identity for a civilization. But before we plunge into cultural identity it is important to examine whether the culture one chooses to embody has any impact at all on the way people live life.

To begin with, what matters is the person we choose to become. Being a fair, compassionate, loving, courageous human being forms the core of human life, and is a common denominator in all cultures. However, does that imply that people can discount their cultural identity completely?

How Culture Impacts Thinking and Behaviour

The world over, Sanatanis are among the most law-abiding and trustworthy citizens, and very accommodating, sincere and successful as a community as well.

Bharat has seen a wave of feminism and woman empowerment, because it understands the hypocrisy of undermining women while worshipping *devi*s (Refer to Chapter

19: 'What Was the Status of Women in Ancient Bharat?').

Until just a few decades back there was a very blatant cultural belief that said, 'the white man must rule', whereas Bharat has always believed in *'vasudhaiva kutumbakam'*. Hence, while the West destroyed their colonies culturally and economically, Bharat had the world's foremost and largest universities that educated both men and women from all over the world free of cost.

The dogmatic approach of some cultures required great philosophers, thinkers and scientists like Pythagoras, Copernicus, Galileo and others to fear for their lives, such that they had to form secret societies just because their scientific discoveries were disagreeable to established dogma (See also, Chapter 22: 'Does Science Have its Origins in Sanatan Dharm?'). Vanquished by radical rulers, great civilizations like Persia, Mesopotamia and others were reduced to unrecognizable rubbles of their glorious past. Even today, religious radicals use the fruits of scienctific development to wreak havoc in the world rather than promote welfare and harmony.

What it Means to Have a Cultural Identity

Cultural identity has two aspects: How it defines who we are and who we choose to become. According to Hindu philosophy the four goals of human life are the following in this specific order:

a. *Dharm* (Righteousness)
b. *Arth* (Wealth)
c. *Kaam* (Desires)
d. *Moksh* (Liberation)

This shows us that earning money is not a crime if it is done by fair, i.e. Dharmic means; the desire for a happy life is not wrong as long as the wealth used to fulfilling one's desires has been earned through fair, i.e. Dharmic means; and that one's desires do not undermine the happiness of others, i.e. they are Dharmic.

The culmination of such a Dharmic life will always be Moksh.

Worshipping Goddess Saraswati is recognizing the importance of continuous learning, knowledge and art in life.

Worshipping instruments and machines on festive occasions like Dusshera or Vishwakarma Diwas is not only recognizing the importance of technology, but also being reminded of how to use it in ways that promote personal and social well-being. Additionally, recognizing the importance of technology means being grateful for the gifts of knowledge, science and innovation.

Sanatanis worship not only the idols of Saraswati and Vishwakarma, but books and machines too. What does this say about Sanatan culture? That knowledge, skill, creativity and invention are essential aspects of life. Hence, the entities presiding over these aspects are revered as gods and *not* the other way round!

An understanding of the *varna* system reveals that it is our duty to take up a profession that we love because that helps us make the greatest contribution to society and harmoniously connect with our inherent God-self.

When goddesses like Adi Shakti, Kali, Durga, Saraswati, Lakshmi are worshipped, the importance of feminine energy in a civilization and the need to maintain equality and balance between the masculine and feminine aspects of our personalities are underscored. Thus, Lord Shiva can shed tears and Goddess Durga can fight a war!

Equality between a man and woman, or the lack of it, and the significance of various relationships as illustrated by the

Ramayan, Mahabharat and Purans, help people understand the qualities that make for a happy marriage and harmonious family, and by extension, a joyous and prosperous society.

Ravan had to be eliminated for the atrocities he committed and for the way he treated women, in spite of being a scholar in all forms of knowledge and unsurpassed in wealth. This proclaims that Dharm reigns supreme.

The lesson to be learnt from the story of Lord Ram—who gave up his rightful kingdom for his father and waged a war against evil—is that war and violence must be avoided at all costs unless as a last resort for the general good. Violence for any other reason—likes and dislikes, cultural or religious beliefs, among others—has no place in civilized society.

The 'Virat Roop' of Krishna demonstrates that there is only one Universal Absolute who is the source and goal of all that there is. Therefore, everything in the universe is a form of that Absolute, proving love, fairness and compassion to be the only righteous means to lead life.

Sanatan Dharm views society and other cultural systems from the prism of social well-being and justice, not from the perspective of likes, dislikes, attires, beliefs, food or traditions. The underlying message is: accept the good in all, correct the bad in yourself, and reject the bad of others.

Understanding what a Shivling symbolizes is realizing that there is existence beyond what one can consciously perceive. Hence, materialism is not the be-all and end-all of life. This gives people the strength to face the vagaries of life and the courage to take a stand for what is considered right for the greater good of all (See also, Chapter 17: 'What Exactly Is the Shivling?').

Most Sanatan scriptures are in the form of questions and answers, highlighting the importance of asking questions, analysing, reflecting, counter-questioning and arriving at personal conclusions. These scriptures encourage scientific enquiry and open-minded temperament. Questioning even the greatest of gods is allowed in Sanatan Dharm.

Lord Shiva's family—Parvati, Ganesh, Kartikeya—is an ideal of how people with different personalities, preferences and abilities can live together harmoniously, loving and celebrating each other's differences. No wonder Bharat is one of the greatest upholders of family as an institution in the world.

The very culture of Sanatan has the thirst for knowledge, evolution and global harmony built into it through prayers like '*asatoma sadgamaya*' (May I go from ignorance to Truth), '*samasta loka sukhino bhavantu*' (Let all beings in all worlds be happy), and many others that expand one's consciousness from the individual to the universal level. Our culture teaches us to live by these prayers. Hence, for example, we have replaced cremation by wood to cremation in an incinerator to protect trees, and have extended Raksha Bandhan to friends, even men tying Rakhis to women who have supported them.

That is why Sanatan Culture is eternal because positive change and evolution is built into it by design.

These are some examples of how cultural identity defines the thinking, attitude and behaviour of individuals in society.

How Culture Helps Protect Liberty and Sovereignty

Wars only kill individuals, but degrading their cultural symbols destroy their civilizations, subduing them into intellectual slavery for generations to come; a feat which a physical war could never accomplish!

In Bharat, when the British did away with Sanskrit and demonized Brahmins, Bharatiyas were left with no scientific or logical framework to their culture. Suddenly:

- English became the language of the 'educated'.

- *Dhoti* became 'uncouth' and coat, trousers and tie became 'gentlemanly'.
- Eating with hands became 'unhygienic' and eating with spoons and forks was 'civilized'.
- Sitting on the floor was a sign of 'destitution' whereas the dining table became a symbol of 'refinement'.
- Ayurveda, neem, tulsi, *haldi*, became 'quackery', and petrochemicals became medicine.
- *Pandit*s and *rishi*s promoted superstitions while clerics promoted 'spirituality'.
- Ram, Krishna, Shiva, Devi and the entire Sanatan culture became 'mythology' while gods of other religions became saviours!

Of course, amidst such sweeping changes, it was easy to forget that *dhoti*-clad Bharatiyas contributed 25 per cent of the world GDP before the British looted them and hermitage-residing *rishi*s had already made many important scientific discoveries for which the West took credit. Soon enough, generations of young Bharatiyas were aping the West, seeking their education and approval, and teaching the same to their subsequent generations even after Independence (See also, Chapter 22: 'Does Science Find its Origins in Sanatan Dharm?').

Conclusion

Cultural symbols are not some prisons of intellectual fanaticism. Rather, they are reminders of who we are and the values we choose to live by, as being born to a culture is to inherit the values, achievements, and lessons learnt and imparted by our ancestors.

Consider culture as the subliminal positioning of a brand, such that the *way of life* espoused by Sanatan Dharm is symbolically communicated through colours, icons, symbols, attires, adornments, beliefs, cuisines and social norms.

Gods like Brahma, Vishnu or Shiva do not exhort Sanatanis to wear a *tilak* on the forehead, visit temples, perform *puja*s or dress in traditional attire. It is us who need to attach ourselves to our cultural symbols as reminders of what we stand for. If we don't embrace them, who will?

As those blessed to be born in Sanatan Dharm, it is up to us whether we want to survive and thrive as one of the world's most successful, open-minded, artistic, scientific and spiritual civilizations, or become hopelessly lost in our own shadow! Embracing our cultural symbols is a very effective way to ensure that we stay on course.

35

Is Sanatan 'Itihas' History or Fantasy?

ko addha veda ka iha pra vocat
kuta ajata kuta iyam visrstih
arvag deva asya visarjanena
atha ko veda yata ababhuva

[Who really knows? Who can speak here?
From where this creation has arisen,
And whether the gods have created it,
Or whether they themselves were created by it.
Who really knows from where it came?]

—'Nasadiya Sukta' (Rigveda 10:129.6)

The British replaced the word *itihas*, traditionally used by Bharatiyas for the events in the Ramayan, Mahabharat and Purans, with the word 'mythology', surreptitiously changing historical fact into myth. Even today, generations of Hindus wonder whether the Ramayan and Mahabharat actually happened or are mere fantastical tales to amuse and entertain society with a fictional culture (See also, Chapter 22: 'Does Science Have its Origins in Sanatan Dharm?'). But why would a scientific and logical culture build its edifice on the shaky foundations of nothing but myth?

Documentary Evidence

The principle Sanatan scriptures comprise:

1. *Four Vedas:* Thousands of verses, including instructions on subjects like grammar, etymology, literary rhythm and phonetics.
2. *Four Upavedas:* Thousands of verses on subjects like medicine, astronomy, economics, martial arts, architecture, engineering, music, dance, drama and art.
3. *108 Upanishads:* Thousands of verses on the science and philosophy of existence, and on empirical science like fetal development in the Garbha Upanishad.
4. *18 Purans:* 81,000 verses in the Skanda Puran, 55,000 verses in the Padma Puran and many more verses in other Purans. Besides history, the Purans also deal in great detail with empirical subjects like engineering, toxicology, physics, cosmology, medicine, child conception, development and birth, geography and structure of Earth, etc.
5. *Mahabharat:* 100,000 verses.
6. *Ramayan:* 24,000 verses.
7. *Siddhant*s: Thousands of verses.
8. *Agama*s: 213 verses.
9. *Bhagvad Gita:* 700 verses.
10. *Six Darshans:* Hundreds of verses.

Add to this vast body of literature, thousands of *bhasya*s (commentaries) based on the Vedas and the Upanishads, written by hundreds of *rishi*s on subjects as diverse as *advaita, dvaita, vishista advaita,* grammar, mathematics, astronomy, physics, chemistry, engineering, technology, cosmology, logic, politics and medicine, including those written by Adi Shankaracharya, Bhaskaracharya, Kautilya, Pingalacharya, Madhavacharya, Maharishi Agastya, Brahmarishi Vishwamitra (who composed the 'Gayatri Mantra') (See section titled 'Experiment on the

Gayatri Mantra' in Chapter 23: 'What Are Yagyas?'), Maharishi Markandeya (who composed the 'Maha Mritunjaya Mantra'), and many renowned scientists.

Many of the aforementioned *rishi*s were also contemporaries of Lord Ram in the Ramayan, of Krishna and the Pandavs in the Mahabharat, and are also mentioned in the Purans in times much before the Ramayan and the Mahabharat.

For instance, *Agastya Samhita*[1], written by Maharishi Agastya, an important associate of Lord Ram in the Ramayana, has practical experiments in physics which have also been proven to work in American labs. Brahmarishi Vishwamitra taught Lord Ram the use of many super-destructive *astra*s.[2] Maharishi Markandeya had met the Pandavs during their exile.[3]

Many parts of the Ramayan, Mahabharat and the Purans have predictions about the future, i.e. life in Kali Yug—the age we are currently living in—and they are indeed true.[4] This begs the question if the future mentioned in the past is true, then why wouldn't the past itself be true? (See section titled 'Four Yugs' in Chapter 38: 'Basic Concepts of Sanatan Dharm')

Often, the same episodes are mentioned in the Ramayan, documented by Maharishi Valmiki in the Treta Yug, and in the Purans and the Mahabharat documented by Maharishi Ved Vyas in the Dwapar Yug.

The 'Uttar Kand' of the Ramayan is one such example. Lord Ram tells Lakshman of an episode which happened long after the events of the Ramayan—King Nriga is cursed by a *rishi* who pronounces that he will be released from the curse by Lord Vishnu, appearing in his Krishna avatar.[5] This, when the Ramayan happened at least 15,000 years before the Mahabharat and the advent of Krishna. Hanuman meeting Bhim in the Mahabharat is another such example.[6]

On the battlefield of Kurukshetra, Lord Krishna delivers the sermon of the Bhagvad Gita to Arjun in the presence of others, the battle itself being the result of all the events mentioned in the Mahabharat leading up to the war. Today, the Bhagvad Gita is recognized the world over as a science, philosophy and *way of life*, remaining just as pertinent for humanity as it was for Arjun 5,000 years ago.

Cities and Sites

Writing a timeless tale is one thing, while carving its awe-inspiring characters and events into colossal edifices across the country, is another matter altogether. Bharat is strewn with temples and monuments that commemorate the spot where a particular event in the Ramayan, Mahabharat or Purans took place. One such temple is deep in the Himalayas, about 30 km from Gauri Kund, the base of Kedarnath, at a height of 18,000 feet, where Shiv and Parvati are believed to have been married. A relatively unknown temple even today, it is considered auspicious for married couples to take the traditional seven *phera*s around the sacred fire here. Kedarnath Temple was built by the Pandavs during their 13-year exile to the forests. Even today, this temple has sculptures of all the five Pandavs and Draupadi in the exterior hall. Besides, episodes from the Ramayan, Mahabharat and Purans have been carved in thousands of temples all over Bharat and across the world. The temples themselves are architectural, engineering and artistic marvels which continue to defy modern science.

The Skanda Puran mentions the history of Kedarnath, Badrinath and other important pilgrimage centres of Bharat that exist even today

Both the Mahabharat and Bhagavat Puran mention that towards the end of Lord Krishna's life, Dwarka was submerged by a tsunami. Deccan College, Pune, the Department of Archaeology, Government of Gujarat and Marine Archaeology

Centre of the National Institute of Oceanography discovered the city of Dwarka submerged in the Arabian Sea during a series of excavations from 1963 to 1990. Ayodhya still exists and so does the family descended from Lord Ram's 'Raghuvansha' lineage.

Satellite images have shown a cobbled path between Rameshwaram and Sri Lanka, now partially submerged under the sea. In Sri Lanka, Ashok Vatika, the garden where Ravan had held Sita captive, still exists. Likewise, in Nepal, remains of Videha, the kingdom of Emperor Janak, Sita's father, also exists.

Many cities and empires mentioned in the Ramayan and the Mahabharat—Ayodhya, Kashi, Magadh, Chedi, Pataliputra, Prayag, Kashmir, Rameshwaram, Kaikeya and Kairana, Mathura, Vrindavan, the entire route from Ayodhya to Sri Lanka, etc.—still exist in Bharat, or at least existed while its modern history was being recorded. In the 'Ayodhya Kand' of the Valmiki Ramayan, Dasharath describes his empire to include Bengal (Vanga), Rajasthan (Matsya), Kashi, Tamil Nadu (Dravid), Saurashtra and Deccan (Dakshinapath).

The Mahabharat mentions silks from China, horses from Arabia, and countries like Egypt, Greece, etc. as kings from these places came bearing gifts for Yudhishthir on the occasion of his *rajasuya yagya*.[7]

Almost 40 generations of Lord Ram's ancestors, Lord Krishna's ancestors and those of the Pandavs and Kauravs have been documented in great detail in the Ramayan, Mahabharat and Purans.

Culture

Not only is Sanatan *itihas* documened in great detail, it has also consistently defined Bharat's vibrant culture, art, festivals, philosophy and values for millennia.

Dance: Bharat is home to some of the most sophisticated and rich classical dance forms in the world. They depict events or scenes from the Ramayan, Mahabharat or Purans. No matter how different the dance forms are, and how a particular scene is choreographed, the story remains the same.

Theatrical presentations in Bharat follow the *navarasa*s—the nine cardinal emotions defined in the *Natya Shastra* which was taught to Bharat Muni by Lord Shiva. These nine emotions are:

1. *Shringar:* Beauty, romance, passion, devotion
2. *Hasya:* Humour
3. *Karuna:* Love, concern, compassion
4. *Raudra:* Anger
5. *Veer:* Valour
6. *Bhayanak:* Horrifying
7. *Bibhatsya:* Disgust
8. *Adbhut:* Fantastical, extraordinary
9. *Shant:* Calmness

The *Natya Shastra* also elaborates on every aspect of stagecraft, including the different types of protagonists, antagonists, costumes, expressions, postures, use of colours, etc.

Festivals: Festivals in Bharat largely celebrate events from the Ramayan, Mahabharat and Purans. Among these:

1. Dusshera celebrates the day Ravan was vanquished by Lord Ram. According to the Devi Puran, it also celebrates the day Goddess Durga slaughtered the demon Mahishasur.
2. Gokul Ashtami celebrates the day Lord Krishna was born, as mentioned in the Bhagavat Puran.
3. Holi celebrates the day Prahlad was saved from the blazing flames by Lord Vishnu, according to the Vishnu Puran.

4. Diwali celebrates the day Lord Ram returned to Ayodhya after 14 years in exile and the day when Goddess Lakshmi emerged from the ocean after the 'Samudra Manthan'.
5. Onam celebrates the day King Bali is believed to return to Earth from the netherworlds to meet his subjects after being sent to the netherworlds by Vaman—the fifth avatar of Vishnu—according to the Vishnu Puran and other texts.
6. Ganesh Chaturthi celebrates the birth of Lord Ganesh according to the Ganesh Puran and Shiva Puran.

Specific Dates: That all these festivals are celebrated on particular dates which changes according to the *tithi*—astronomical calculation of the Sanatan *panchang* (almanac)—confirms that these events happened on specific dates as calculated by planetary positions in various constellations at that particular point in time. We do not have specific dates for the events according to the Gregorian calendar simply because it did not exist when these events were documented. But, modern science can now use these planetary positions, clearly mentioned in the Valmiki Ramayan, Ved Vyas Mahabharat and Purans, to arrive at the exact date of the events according to the Gregorian calendar.

36

Why Do Hindus Often Name Their Children after Gods?

The name should be easy to pronounce, should not suggest any harsh acts, should be pleasing to the ear and should convey some blessing...

—Griha Sutras

Hindu texts proclaim four progressive *mahavakyas* (supreme declarations). Starting with a general enquiry into the nature of existence and the universe, the seeker realizes that everything is a manifestation of God. Hence the first *mahavakya:*

1. *Prajnanam Brahma:* God is Truth or the Supreme Consciousness (Aitareya Upanishad of the Rig Veda).

    The logical inference is that the same God that manifests as the Universe must be within the seeker as well.

This leads to the second *mahavakya:*

2. *Ayam Atma Brahma:* The same God is within me (Mandukya Upanishad of the Atharva Veda).

    To understand and establish a relationship with God, the mind now ascribes certain supernatural forms to Him/Her. The seeker reveres that form and develops an affinity with it. The seeker's enquiry leads Him/Her to the wise who try to awaken him/her to the fact that he/she is the Truth, i.e. the essence of that form of God.

That leads to the third *mahavakya:*

3. *Tat Tvam Asi:* Thou art that (Chandogya Upanishad of the Sama Veda).

   The aspirant continues to contemplate the form until one day, no form is necessary. The aspirant realizes that he/she is not just a part of God, but rather he/she *is* God—that is the state of *samadhi*, Moksh or Enlightenment.

This leads to the final *mahavakya:*

4. *Aham Brahmasmi:* I am God (Brihadaranyaka Upanishad of Yajur Veda).

These *mahavakya*s signify the essence and purpose of all existence, and require deep understanding and contemplation to experience. The ancient *rishi*s compiled four Vedas, 108 Upanishads, 18 Purans, six Vedangas, six Darshans, three philosophies of Vedanta, and so many other texts only to arrive at and illustrate the Ultimate Truth—*aham brahmasmi:* I am God!

Comprehension of the *mahavakya*s was not restricted to the intellectual elite of Hindu society. The Truth that everything in Creation is God was woven into the very fabric of life. The simplest manifestation of that was Hindus calling themselves, their children, their homes by the names of their various gods—Shiva, Ram, Krishna, Narayan, Vishnu, Durga, Lakshmi, Saraswati, Surya, etc.

The tendency to name humans after gods is quite prevalent among Sanatanis. Naming themselves after their revered gods and goddesses was never an act of blasphemy but rather a reminder that the same Divine Energy that created the universe, took on the multifarious, innumerable forms of all gods and of all Creation around humans.

Thus, the idea of naming themselves after gods was not to make gods appear pedestrian but rather to elevate human beings and remind them that no matter what duties they *must* perform to keep the world running, their ultimate goal in life was to discover and experience their innate Divinity, to become one with the God within.

Not only did this simple tradition remind humans of their purpose to experience the Truth, it also showed them the path to achieve this high purpose through the values that the names themselves evoked in the human psyche. The name 'Ram' instantly brings to mind the qualities of compassion, the purest filial affection and sacrifice for the highest good; the name 'Shiva' inspires meditativeness, non-materialism and the understanding of Divine power; the name 'Saraswati' induces a deep appreciation of the higher aspects of life through creative arts and the pursuit of all kinds of knowledge. No wonder then, that ancient Bharat was a joyous society of the rich and the fulfilled, whether in terms of family ties, culture, economics, science, technology or spirituality.

The tradition of naming themselves, their animals, and their homes after their revered gods also gave the world a very potent legacy—the legacy of tolerance that all humans ought to practice today.

Since all forms and all names are God's, it follows that Tao, Ahura Mazda, Jehova and any others, are as valid names for God as Shiva, Brahma, Durga, Narayan. The formless Brahman is the same as the formless Allah or Gabriel's God, and is as Divine as the beloved, elephant-headed Ganesh or Ram or Hanuman.

Sanatan culture is replete with conventions which appear to be simple and innocent but have deeply impacted the consciousness of people not just in Bharat but in the entire world. These modest practices, including worship of nature in all her forms—rivers, trees, crops, the sun and the moon, and the festivals associated with them—have manifested as values of universal love, environmental consciousness, gratitude, truth, peace, harmony, compassion and fairness. The following tenets sum them up well:

1. *Ekam Sat Viprah Bahuda Vadanti:* Truth is one but the wise call it by different names (Rig Veda).
2. *Lokah Samasta Sukhino Bhavantu:* Let all beings (and non-beings) in all the worlds be happy (ancient inscriptions).
3. *Vasudhaiva Kutumbakam:* The world is one family (Maha Upanishad).

37

Did the British Give Bharatiyas the Idea of One India?

...jambudweepe, bharatvarshe...

[...on the super-island/continent of Jambu,
in the land of Bharat...]

As prescribed by Sanatan scriptures across Bharat, every puja begins with '*...jambudweepe, bharatvarshe...*', and is followed by the name of the state, city, *gotra*, *kalpa*, *yug* and date on which it is being conducted, along with the name of the person conducting the puja. This practice indicates that the word 'Bharatvarsha' existed millennia before the invasionss.

Cultural Identity and Unity

Temples: Kedarnath in the north, Rameshwaram in the south, Ujjain and Kashi in Central India and many other Sanatani temples across Bharat are abodes of Lord Shiva; Dwarka in Gujarat, Mathura in Uttar Pradesh and Jagannath Puri in Orissa, among many others, are abodes of Lord Krishna; Martand Temple in Kashmir and Konark Temple in Orissa are abodes of the Sun God.

Carvings on temples across Bharat depicting the same gods and goddesses, and incidents mentioned in the Ramayan, Mahabharat and the Purans affirm of cultural unity that made Bharat one cohesive nation, despite different provinces being ruled by different kings and dynasties.

Scriptures: The Vedas, Purans and various other *shastra*s have been the backbone of Bharatiya social, spiritual, economic, scientific and intellectual thought. These too exist across Bharat.

Throughout Bharat, the 'Rudram' of the Yajur Veda has 11 *anuvak*s and verse 11 of Chapter 3 of the Bhagvad Gita has the same! The same scriptures with the exact same verses provide Bharat its cultural cohesion.

Music and Dance: Bharat is home to some of the most diverse, complex, elegant and sophisticated dance forms in the world. The incidents from the Ramayan, Mahabharat and the Purans depicted in these dance forms across Bharat are the same, irrespective of the dance form or the choreography of the individual piece.

Political Identity

In ancient Bharat, different provinces/kingdoms were led by one Supreme Emperor called the 'Chakravarti Samrat'— Emperor Ikshvaku, Emperor Yayati, Emperor Sagar, Lord Ram, Emperor Bharat, Emperor Yudhishthir. All other kings across Bharat were vassals of such an emperor. The *rajasuya yagya* and *ashwamedh yagya* were conducted by kings who had fulfilled certain conditions to establish supremacy, these rituals were accepted by kingdoms across Bharat.

The word 'Bharatavarsha', pertaining to the Asian subcontinent, exists even in our epics. It is possible that Bharat of the ancient times was much larger than our present map; it certainly included Afghanistan, Nepal, Sri Lanka and Bhutan while remnants of Sanatan culture from thousands of years ago have been found all over the world. Kings from Arabia, Greece, Egypt are mentioned in the Mahabharat who came for

Yudhisthir's *rajasuya yagya* (See also, Chapter 35: 'Is Sanatan Itihas History or Fantasy?').

Conclusion

The idea that it was the British who created a united India is absurd. Sanantan culture and Bharatavarsha as one national, cultural identity have existed and been documented for millennia.

SECTION III

BASICS

38

Basic Concepts of Sanatan Dharm

*Dharm is that which supports
Order in the Universe.*

—Various Sanskrit texts

Sanatan Dharm is a vast ocean of knowledge. Based on an individual's predisposition, one might find it worthy of lifetimes of research. At the same time, it can be summed up in just a few sentences:

> The Truth of existence is that you and all of Creation are nothing but God.
>
> The purpose of existence is to realize this Truth.
>
> Understanding that the karmas you perform for others will come back to you because there are no 'others' and it is all *you,* paves the path to realization.

For a proper perspective on why Sanatan Dharm is so named, and what it means to be a Hindu, it is important to understand some of its basic concepts.

Aum

Aum is one of the predominant features of Sanatan, and it has many manifestations in life. *Aum* is believed to be the first vibration of Creation. Visualize an empty, silent room. Then someone, somewhere plays a musical note—just one note that resounds across the room. Suddenly the silence is replaced by ripples of sound energy. That is *aum*—the first ripple of sound energy, the voice of the Creator, the sound of Consciousness (See the section 'Aum and the Big Bang' in Chapter 22: 'Does Science Have its Origins in Sanatan Dharma?').

Aum is also a sound that can be chanted to match any musical note because it is one vibration just as every musical note is an individual, separate vibration. So, just as a tune is nothing but a combination of several individual music notes, Creation is a combination of the vibrations of *aum*.

Three Syllables

Though *aum* is pronounced as 'om', it has three syllables—A-U-M (अ, ऊ and म्) This has many connotations:

a. *History or Itihas*
   - अ stands for Brahma, the Creator
   - ऊ stands for Vishnu, the Protector
   - म् stands for Shiva (Maheshwar), the Destroyer

b. *Language*

   The sound A (अ) is chanted from the navel and slowly brought up to the base of the throat. The first consonants of Sanskrit, Hindi, Marathi—ka, kha, ga, gha—are articulated in this region.

   The sound U (ऊ) is then taken from the base of the throat to the lips. The next set of consonants—cha, chha, ja, jha, na—are articulated in this region.

   The sound M (म्) is allowed to reverberate over the lips, the region of the next set of consonants—pa, pha, ba, bha, ma.

   The last set of consonants—ya, ra, la, va, sha—fall within the above-mentioned regions. No sound falls outside the auditory region which is activated by the chanting of *aum*.

   Aum is therefore the root of language, and hence, of all communication, cognition and ideation.

c. *Four States of Consciousness*

If an aspirant chants *aum* as mentioned above, they will experience a growing sense of peace, a progressive calmness which signifies the following states of Consciousness:

- When one closes one's eyes and begins chanting 'A' from the navel to the base of the throat, one is in a *jagrit avastha*—awake or in a state of consciousness.
- As *aum* progresses to 'U' from the base of the throat to the lips, the calmness is akin to *swapna avastha*—a dream-like state.
- And when 'M' reverberates on the lips, the state of consciousness is *sushupti* or deep sleep when one loses awareness of even dreams.
- Finally, there is silence, a state which is beyond, which connects to the Universal Consciousness. This state is the *turiya avastha*.

Regular practice of *aum* gives an aspirant the following benefits:

- Trains the mind to connect with the Universal Consciousness.
- Establishes harmony between the right brain and the left brain.
- Leads to flashes of intuition, like stumbling upon the password to the server and gaining access to all the files on it.

That is how ancient *rishi*s were able to predict the future, make scientific discoveries without the use of instruments, invent machines and also transcend space and time.

To give another example—at sea level, one can see only so far. But as one moves higher to reach a birds' eye view, the field of view expands to include multiple locations. And from space, a satellite can see entire continents and planets. Chanting *aum* is akin to moving higher into the plane of Consciousness such that one becomes more aware of the workings of the universe.

Relationship between Man, God and the Universe

As stated earlier, God or Consciousness is like the ocean, and the aspirant is a drop in it. The body is the vessel that receives the drop which takes the shape of that vessel for as long as it needs to. Therefore, human beings are *not* the body; they are the energy, the being, the *atma*—the essence of God living inside the body. This is the truth of existence.

Maya (Illusion)

Sanatan philosophy says that the reason we cannot experience ourselves as Cosmic Consciousness or God is because we are consumed by a focus on the external world brought alive by the perceptions of our five senses—hearing, sight, smell, taste and touch. This is *maya*. It conceals the 'nature of reality' from us.

The concept of *maya* can be best understood through the analogy of a screen and movie. The screen is like Brahman. It exists before the movie is played, throughout the movie and even after the movie stops. The screen remains unaffected, whether there is an earthquake or an explosion in the movie, whether the movie has moments of sadness or joy. Yet, the movie is brought to our perception only because the screen manifests it.

The movie is the sensory universe or *maya*—nothing but fleeting images that come and go on the eternal screen of the Brahman. We are so absorbed by the emotions and perceptions created by the movie that we forget it is all just a transient illusion.

Spirituality is to first understand that life—with all its drama—is *maya* and the Truth lies unaffected beyond it. After this, the aspirant seeks to transcend *maya* through spiritual practices.

Different Levels of Existence

Sanatan Dharm talks about all creatures having different layers of existence.

Three Bodies: The outermost layer is the *sthul sharir* (gross body)—the skin, bones, flesh, muscles and blood. Next is the *sukshma sharir* (subtle body)—the focal centres of the body in the processes of respiration, excretion, circulation, etc. as well as the mental and emotional aspects of a being. And the final layer is the *karan sharir* (energy body)—the energy that makes the maintenance of the flesh and blood possible along with all their mutual processes. That energy is what all living beings really are—the *atma* or the soul.

This is evident in the fact that though the body may exist corporeally even after the energy stops activating bodily processes, it is declared dead.

According to the laws of physics, energy can only be converted, never destroyed. So is the case with all beings. As energy, all beings inhabit different bodies in different lifetimes till they achieve 'Moksh'—the purpose of existence. Thereafter, no being need be born again; it can exist as pure energy.

Five Sheaths of Existence: Sanatan Dharm defines the various dimensions in which a being exists:

1. *Annamaya Kosh:* Body
2. *Pranamaya Kosh:* Breath
3. *Manomaya Kosh:* Mind
4. *Vignyanamaya Kosh:* Intellect
5. *Anandamaya Kosh:* Bliss

As humans, we have all experienced each of these as separate spaces of existence. Often, while the body is still, the mind is flitting from one thought to another, from one feeling to another, thus oscillating between the first three *kosha*s. From here, we enter the fourth *kosh* where the intellect makes decisions. It chooses to act on some thoughts and feelings and ignore others, so as to allow us to enter the fifth *kosh* of bliss and fulfilment.

In people's day-to-day life, they keep coming back from the fifth *kosh* to the first four. However, the state of Moksh is when they no longer have to pass from one *kosh* to another, and exist in a permanent state of bliss, regardless of the stresses in life.

The biographies of Sanatani saints like Gyaneshwar, Tukaram, Janabai, Sakubai, Thyagaraj, Surdas, among others, clearly illustrate that they reached this state of bliss in spite of problems in their personal lives.

Five Prans: Pran is the channelization of energy through various physical and mental processes. The five types of *prans* in the human system as mentioned earlier are *pran, apan, saman, udan* and *vyan*. (See also, Chapter 22: 'Does Science Have its Origins in Sanatan Dharma?')

Daily Duties of a Sanatani

The *shastras* have laid down the *pancha yagya*—five things Sanatanis must perform each day of their lives.

1. *Pitra Yagya:* Express gratitude to ancestors and pray for them, look after parents and other elders in the family. We still carry the DNA of our ancestors. Praying to or for them is also praying for our own selves.
2. *Brahma Yagya:* Read spiritual, i.e. good, positive, elevating literature.
3. *Dev Yagya:* Express gratitude and pray to the five primary *devatas*, i.e. to the fundamental elements of Creation:

    - Space (Indra)
    - Wind (Vayu)

- Fire (Agni)
- Water (Varun)
- Earth (Prithvi)

Additionally, taking care of the environment, and following a balanced diet and lifestyle help perform this *yagya*.
4. *Bhut Yagya:* Offer food and water to plants, animals and birds, not harm any creature and help those in need.
5. *Atithi Yagya:* Treat a guest with utmost dignity and respect.

Five Mothers

The mother is revered in every religion, but in Sanatan Dharma a human being is believed to have five mothers, and must revere them all:

1. *Deha Mata* (Biological Mother): For she gave birth to our body
2. *Gow Mata* (Cow): For she provided the milk which sustained and strengthened the body
3. *Bhu Mata* (Earth): For she provided shelter and food
4. *Desh Mata* (Country): For she offered protection, rights, culture and the opportunity to elevate ourselves and serve humanity
5. *Veda Mata* (Heritage): For she gave us the aim and purpose of life, and illuminated the path to its attainment

Three Paths

Sanatan has three paths for self-realization. An individual is free to choose any one or a combination of multiple paths based on their personality and temperament.

1. *Gyan Marg* (Path of Knowledge): This path is for those who have the temperament to study, contemplate and

intellectualize. The followers of the *gyan marg* study the scriptures, meditate on their meaning and apply its understanding to life till they experience the Truth that 'God and I are one'. Most *rishi*s were followers of this path.

2. *Bhakti Marg* (Path of Devotion): This path is for those who are driven by emotions and can thus emotionally connect with God. The follower of the *bhakti marg* loves God and hence sees God in every speck of Creation, and *experiences* the Truth that 'God and I are One'. Saints like Meerabai, Surdas, Thyagaraj, Namdeo and Eknath were followers of this path.

3. *Karma Marg* (Path of Action): This path is for those who are neither intellectual nor emotional. They are practical and dynamic. The followers of this path can connect with God best through service. Hence, serving God and society are the best ways for them to realize the Truth, 'God and I are One.' Hanuman and Arjun were followers of this path.

Four Yugs

Sanatan defines time in cycles of *yug*s (See also, Chapter 22: 'Does Science Have its Origins in Sanatan Dharm?'). A *yug* is like an era lasting for a specific number of years. The form, strength, nature of human beings, beneficial aspects of natural phenomena, general sense of values and the recognition of what is right or wrong declined from the Satya Yug to Kali Yug as human beings and the world become increasingly chaotic, weak, selfish and joyless.

The differences in the environment, character of individuals and their ways of life in different *yug*s has been elucidated in many Purans as well as the epics. Given below is what Lord Hanuman told Bhim[1] and Rishi Markandeya told the Pandavs about the impact of a *yug* on human life in the 'Van Parva' of the Ved Vyas Mahabharat.[2]

Basic Concepts of Sanatan Dharm

Yug	Satya/Krita	Treta	Duvapar	Kali
Degree of Dharm in personal and social life	Approx. 100 per cent. There was only good and right. People were sensitive to each other and no one hurt or cheated another knowingly.	Approx. 75 per cent. Good and bad, right and wrong had clear boundaries.	Approx. 50 per cent. Good and bad, right and wrong were more intertwined.	Approx. 25 per cent. People have lost all understanding of good, bad, right and wrong.
Duration	4,800 *daiva* years	3,600 *daiva* years	2,400 *daiva* years	1,200 *daiva* years
Physical attributes of human beings	Height—31 feet; lifespan—(approx.) 100,000 years	Height—21 feet; lifespan—(approx.) 10,000 years	Height—10 feet; lifespan—(approx.) 1,000 years	Height—less than 7 feet; lifespan—(approx.) 100 years or less
Power of beings	People were perfectly attuned to their Divinity and hence, could accomplish everything by mere will.	Slightly digressed from their innate Divinity, people needed will, *mantras* and effort to accomplish what they wanted.	People were more attuned to the world than with their Divinity. Hence, they needed will, *mantras* and much more effort to accomplish what they wanted.	Devoid of almost all personal power and completely out of touch with their Divinity, people have to depend mostly on effort alone and man-made gross technology, but are still not able to accomplish what they want. In fact, people even fear starvation.

Yug	Satya/Krita	Treta	Dwapar	Kali
Yagyas	No rituals like *yagyas* were needed.	*Yagyas* began during this *yug* and people performed *yagyas*, *tapasyas* and charity as offerings to God.	*Yagyas*, charity and taking God's name continued, but there was widespread corruption in society.	Neither *yagya* nor *tapasya*, nor true charity exists in this *yuga*. Any rites that do exist are taken up only hypocritically in complete ignorance of their purpose, or significance.
Vedas	The Vedas were one single body of knowledge and not classified. Everyone was adept in the Vedas.	Most people adhered to the knowledge in the Vedas.	The Vedas were classified into four branches. Not everyone was adept in the Vedas. Many did not know the Vedas at all.	People forget the Vedas. The so-called experts of the Vedas malign them and have no inkling of their meaning or import.
Vices	None of the vices—lust, arrogance, hatred, jealousy, greed, attachment, laziness, worry, anger, gossip and fear—	Vices like arrogance, worry and anger started seeping into society but in general, most people were *sattvic*. They had high moral standards, and happily fulfilled their duties.	Vices like lust, arrogance, hatred, jealousy, greed, attachment, laziness, worry, anger, gossip and fear existed, and people became *rajasic*.	All kinds of vices exist at their worst. People are mostly *tamasic*. Materialism rules and people knowingly inflict pain on each other for selfish gains.

Yug	Satya/Krita	Treta	Dwapar	Kali
	existed. Everyone was *sattvic* in nature and considered selflessness as the ultimate value, and Enlightenment or Moksh as the ultimate goal of life.			Success comes to those who follow Adharm while the righteous suffer. Children murder their parents and vice versa. Brothers steal from each other. Even people with high moral standards fall prey to vices like falsehood, greed and manipulation. People become so ruthless that they even loot the destitute, the widowed and the disabled. Human beings stop trusting each other.

Yug	Satya/Krita	Treta	Dwapar	Kali
				Marriages break and people abandon their families to stay in foreign lands. They repeatedly attack the righteous, steal their wealth and even molest their women. World leaders become corrupt and instead of protecting their subjects, they exploit and loot them. Fools become powerful and drive the world into chaos. Trees yield little fruit and fields yield little crop. There is widespread deforestation and people do not feel the pain of nature.

Yug	Satya/Krita	Treta	Dwapar	Kali
Religion	Every person believed in one God—the Parabrahma. Experiencing God was the only objective of every person's life. Everyone followed Sanatan Dharm.	There was awareness of different gods and goddesses, who were worshipped for specific gains. *Yagyas* and ritual practices happened, but they were performed by pure-souled priests with pure-intentions and were effective and powerful.	Selfishness and impurity began seeping into religious rituals. Many were conducted out of jealousy and false competition.	Religious practices are only a sham designed to fool and manipulate. Pseudo-intellectuals are devoid of all wisdom and use warped logic to justify criminal activities committed in the name of religion.
Varnas	People of all four *varnas* were happy, accomplished, scholarly, dutiful and sincere. They loved their work and performed it, with excellence, as an offering to God. They only relied on the Vedas for guidance.	Most people were occupied in professions that they loved and were passionate about. Hence, there was sincerity and excellence.	People began to interfere in other *varnas*, and took up occupations more out of greed and arrogance rather than their own calling.	People ignore their natural calling and do not take up occupations according to their *varna*, i.e. they take up occupations which are against their basic nature, personality, talents and passion. Education is so debased that it renders students unskilled, materialistic and foolish. Hence, sincerity, joy and excellence are replaced by decadence and corruption.

Yug	Satya/Krita	Treta	Dwapar	Kali
Disease and natural disasters	Neither disease nor natural disasters existed in this *yug*.	Diseases and natural disasters were almost negligible.	Many diseases and natural disasters occured regularly.	People live in constant fear of newer diseases. Not only are they physically unhealthy, even mental disorders are widespread. Human lifespan is drastically reduced. Natural disasters, including inadequate rainfall, storms, floods, extreme and unpredictable weather and climatic conditions plague the earth constantly.

While it may be difficult to believe history from the previous *yug*s, none can deny that whatever has been said about Kali Yug in the Mahabharat is indeed the reality that humans are living today.

There are many other concepts in Sanatan Dharm and several layers to what has been mentioned in this chapter. If the reader found this chapter and book interesting, I would urge them to conduct their own research into Sanatan civilization, and see for themselves what a vibrant legacy it is to own, follow and enrich.

Jai Bharat
Jai Shri Ram
Aum Namah Shivaya

Glossary

Acharya: A respected teacher or spiritual guide in Hinduism, Buddhism and Jainism, responsible for imparting wisdom and guiding others on their spiritual path.

Adharm: The opposite of Dharm, referring to actions or behaviours that are immoral, unjust, or contrary to the natural and cosmic order.

Adharmic: Describing something or someone that goes against Dharm, representing unrighteousness, chaos or immorality.

Adi Shakti: The primordial, Divine Feminine energy in Hinduism, often personified as Goddess Durga or Parvati, representing the source of creation and cosmic power.

Agni: The Vedic god of fire, symbolizing both the physical element and the Divine force that facilitates offerings and rituals in Hinduism.

Agnihotra: A Vedic fire ritual performed at sunrise and sunset, meant to purify the environment and align practitioners with the cosmic order.

Agnipariksha: A trial by fire, symbolizing a test of purity, resolve, or virtue, erroneously associated in the Ramayan with Sita's ordeal.

Agnipravesh: The act of entering fire, symbolizing a spiritual or physical trial, often representing courage, purification or steadfastness.

Akashvani: A divine or celestial voice, often seen as an announcement from the heavens; also refers to All India Radio in modern usage.

Akshay Patra: A mythical vessel that provides endless food, symbolizing Divine abundance and the ability to provide for all needs without end.

Anadi: Referring to something that has no beginning; something that is eternal, or without origin; often used to describe the Divine or the cosmos.

Ananta: Meaning infinite or endless; often used to describe the eternal nature of the Divine, such as Ananta-Shesh, the serpent upon which Lord Vishnu rests.

Angaraj: A term used for the 'king of the *angars*', referring to fire or a fiery deity, symbolizing power and energy; also used to refer to Karn after he was made the king of Anga by Duryodhan.

Anshavatar: A partial incarnation or divine manifestation, where a deity takes a smaller form or aspect to fulfil a specific purpose.

Anushthan: A term for a religious or spiritual practice, ritual or observance, often performed with specific rules and intentions.

Anuvak: A verse or section in Vedic texts, typically referring to short passages or portions that are recited in rituals or prayers.

Arth: One of the four aims of human life in Hinduism, representing wealth, prosperity and material well-being, often in balance with Dharm.

Ashtami: The eighth day of a lunar fortnight, often observed with fasting or worship, especially dedicated to Goddess Durga or Lord Krishna.

Ashtapadi: Refers to a type of devotional poem or song with eight stanzas, often associated with the *Geet Govinda* by Jayadev.

Astra: A divine weapon or celestial missile, often associated with gods or heroes, possessing extraordinary powers.

Asur: In Vedic literature, a powerful being often considered an antagonist to the gods, representing evil or chaos in contrast to the *dev*s (gods).

Atma Nivedanam: The act of completely surrendering one's soul to the Divine will, a concept found in devotional practices.

Atma: The soul or self, considered the eternal, unchanging essence of an individual, synonymous with consciousness or spirit.

Aum: A sacred sound and spiritual symbol in Hinduism, representing the ultimate reality, the universe, and the Divine essence.

Avastha: A state or condition of being, often referring to the different mental or physical states an individual experiences, such as wakefulness, dreaming and deep sleep.

Ayurveda: A traditional system of medicine in India focused on balancing the body, mind and spirit through diet, herbs and lifestyle practices.

Bhakt: A devotee or follower, someone who expresses deep love and devotion towards a deity, particularly in the context of *bhakti* (devotion).

Bhakti: The path of devotion to a personal god, emphasizing love, surrender and deep emotional connection with the Divine.

Bheda: Difference or distinction, often used in the context of Vedanta to describe the apparent duality between the individual soul (*atma*) and the Supreme Consciousness (Brahman).

Bhiksha: Alms or food given to a monk or holy person, typically in a ritualistic or charitable context.

Bhumi Nirupana: A term referring to the act of measuring, assessing, or describing the land or earth, often in sacred contexts.

Bilva Patra: The leaves of the *bael* tree, considered sacred in Hinduism, especially for worship of Lord Shiva.

Brahma Peetham: The seat or throne of Brahma, symbolizing the highest place of creation or spiritual authority.

Brahman: The ultimate, formless and infinite reality or Cosmic Consciousness in Hindu philosophy, transcending all phenomena and divisions.

Brahmarishi: A revered sage who has attained the highest spiritual knowledge and insight, often credited with the creation of sacred texts.

Brahmastra: A powerful, divine weapon, said to be capable of destroying the world, invoked through *mantra*s by sages or gods.

Brahmavadini: A woman who possesses profound spiritual knowledge, especially one who studies or teaches the ultimate Truth (Brahman).

Brahmin: One of the *varna*s in Hindu society pursuing intellectual tasks like teaching, research, philosophy, religious rites and preserving sacred knowledge.

Chakra: Energy centres within the body, often visualized as spinning wheels, associated with spiritual and physical health in yogic traditions.

Chakravarti: A universal ruler or emperor who rules over all the territories, often depicted as a just and righteous monarch.

Chhaya: Shadow or reflection; in spiritual terms, it can represent an illusion or something ephemeral.

Daanveer: A person known for their generosity, particularly one who donates or gives alms selflessly, often regarded as heroic for their charity.

Dama: Self-control or restraint, particularly over one's senses or mind, considered a key practice in spiritual development; also, in statecraft, the practice of creating factions in the enemy camp.

Danav: A race of demons, often in opposition to the gods (*dev*s), symbolizing unrighteousness.

Danda: A staff or rod, symbolizing authority or punishment; in a spiritual context, it can also represent discipline and justice; in statecraft it means creating dire consequences for the enemy.

Darshan: The act of seeing a deity or holy person, believed to bring blessings or spiritual benefits; a philosophical or spiritual view or perspective, especially in the context of different schools of Hindu thought, such as Vedanta or Sankhya.

Dev: A god or celestial being in Hinduism, often associated with specific natural forces or cosmic functions.

Devata: A deity or divine being, often invoked in rituals and worship, representing specific qualities or elements of nature. *Dev* and *devata* are often used interchangeably

Devi: The female counterpart of a *dev* or *devata*

Dharm: Righteousness, duty, or moral law in Hinduism, representing the ethical foundation of life and one's responsibilities in the world.

Dharmic: Referring to actions, behaviours, or practices that are in accordance with Dharm, emphasizing righteousness and moral duty.

Dharmraj: The king or ruler who rules with perfect righteousness and justice, often associated with Yudhishthir, the eldest Pandav.

Dharmyuddh: A righteous war fought not for personal ambition but for the establishment of righteousness. The Kurukshetra war in the Mahabharat is called a *dharmyuddh* from the point of view of the Pandavs.

Dhruv: A young prince mentioned in the Vishnu Puran, who, after performing intense penance, is granted a place in the sky as the star Polaris, symbolizing steadfastness and devotion.

Divya Drishti: Divine vision or spiritual insight; the ability to see beyond the material world into higher truths; also, the ability to see across vast distances, into various dimensions.

Gan: A group of attendants or followers, often associated with Lord Shiva.

Gandharv: Celestial musicians or beings, known for their musical skills and role in the Divine court. They are also the attendants of various gods.

Gop: A cowherd, particularly associated with the childhood and youth of Lord Krishna, who lived in the rural regions and took care of cattle, symbolizing simplicity and devotion.

Gopi: A female devotee or cowherd girl, particularly associated with Lord Krishna, known for their deep love and devotion to him.

Gopuram: A monumental, elaborately decorated entrance tower of a Hindu temple, especially found in South India.

Gun: The three fundamental qualities (*sattva*, *rajas*, tamas) that govern the mind and nature, representing goodness, passion and ignorance, respectively.

Guru Dakshina: A traditional offering or gift given by a student to their *guru* (teacher) as a token of gratitude for the knowledge imparted.

Gurukul: A traditional educational system in ancient India where students lived and learned under the guidance of a *guru*, typically in a secluded environment.

Haldi: Turmeric, a spice commonly used in Hindu rituals, ceremonies and traditional medicine, symbolizing purity and auspiciousness.

Havan: A Vedic fire ritual or sacrifice, involving offerings to the fire to invoke divine blessings and purify the environment.

Itihas: A genre of ancient Indian literature that includes epic narratives like the Ramayan and Mahabharat, and parts of the Purans.

Jap: The recitation or chanting of sacred *mantra*s, often repeated in meditation to focus the mind and invoke divine presence.

Jivatma: The individual soul or consciousness, which is considered eternal and a part of the Supreme Soul (Brahman).

Jyotish: The study of light in Hinduism—though often associated with astrology—used for understanding celestial influences on human life and guiding decisions.

Kaam: Desire, passion, or love, one of the four goals of life (Purusharthas) in Hinduism, associated with fulfilment of all types of desires which are supposed to be Dharmic.

Kaal/Kala: Time or the eternal aspect of the cosmos; can also refer to a specific art form, talent or skill in the context of creative endeavours.

Kali Yug/Kalyug: The fourth and final age in the Hindu cyclical timeline of *yug*s, characterized by decline in righteousness, morality and truth.

Kalpa: A long period of time, often used in Hindu cosmology to refer to one cycle of creation, preservation, and destruction of the universe.

Kavach: A protective armour or charm, often used in rituals or worn to safeguard the wearer from harm or negative influences.

Kinnar: A celestial being or musician in Hinduism and Buddhism known for their artistic skills, often depicted as part-human and part-animal.

Kuldevata: A family deity or ancestral god worshipped by a particular family or clan, believed to protect and bless the family.

Kuldevi: The female counterpart of *kuldevata*, a goddess worshipped by a family or lineage for protection and blessings.

Kundal: A type of earring, often associated with Divine or royal figures, symbolizing beauty and ornamentation in Hindu culture.

Kundali: The astrological birth chart that represents the position of celestial bodies at the time of a person's birth, used to interpret fate and personality.

Latagraha: A green house or a place shaded by vines on a latticework; a bower; an arbour.

Leela: The divine play or cosmic drama, representing the actions or manifestations of a deity, especially the playful, creative acts of Lord Krishna.

Lingam: A symbolic representation of Lord Shiva, often in the form of a cylindrical or abstract form, used in worship and rituals.

Lok: A realm or world, often referring to different planes of existence in Hindu cosmology, such as Swarg (heaven), Bhu Lok (Earth), etc.

Mahabhut: The five great elements (earth, water, fire, air, and ether) that constitute the material universe in Hindu and Buddhist philosophy.

Mandapam: A pavilion or hall, especially in temples or during religious ceremonies, used for rituals, worship or gatherings.

Maryada Purushottam: A title for Lord Ram, meaning 'The Perfect Man' or 'The Upholder of Limits', signifying his exemplary adherence to Dharm.

Maya: The illusion or Divine power that creates the appearance of the material world, concealing the true, unchanging reality (Brahman).

Moksh: Liberation from the cycle of birth, death and rebirth (*samsar*), achieved through self-realization and union with the Divine.

Mridanga: A traditional Indian drum, often used in religious and classical music, especially in South Indian temples.

Muni: A sage or ascetic, particularly one who practises meditation and deep spiritual contemplation in Hinduism.

Nad Brahma: The concept that the universe is made of sound, and that sound (*nad*) is a manifestation of the Divine (Brahman).

Nad Brahman: The belief that sound is the essence of the cosmos, with the Divine expressing itself through sound.

Nad Shabd: The primordial sound, believed to be the essence of creation, often associated with the cosmic vibration or sound of the universe.

Nag: A divine or semi-divine being, often depicted as a serpent, associated with water and fertility, and revered in Hinduism and Buddhisim

Naivedya: Offerings of food or other items presented to deities during worship, considered sacred and often distributed among devotees later.

Nakshatra: A constellation or lunar mansion in Vedic astrology, believed to influence a person's characteristics and destiny based on their birth.

Nataraj: A form of Lord Shiva, depicted as the cosmic dancer, symbolizing the creation, preservation, and destruction of the universe.

Navarasa: The nine fundamental emotions (such as love, anger, fear, etc.) expressed in Indian art and drama, used to evoke a wide range of feelings.

Nayak: The protagonist or hero in classical Indian drama or literature, often embodying qualities of valour, wisdom and righteousness.

Nirvana: The ultimate state of liberation and peace, achieved by extinguishing desire and the ego, commonly associated with Buddhism and certain Hindu philosophies.

Niyog: An ancient practice in Hinduism where a man could appoint another to father a child in case he was childless, usually under specific conditions.

Paap: Sin or immoral action, referring to deeds that go against Dharm and ethical principles, leading to negative karmic consequences.

Pancha Mahabhut: The five great elements (earth, water, fire, air, and ether) that form the physical universe in Hindu and Buddhist cosmology.

Panchang: A Hindu calendar system, which includes the five key elements: *tithi* (lunar day), *vaar* (day of the week), *nakshatra* (lunar mansion), yoga (specific time period), and *karana* (subdivision of a *tithi*).

Pankti: A verse or stanza in Indian classical music or poetry, usually referring to a rhythmic or melodic line.

Paramatma: The Supreme Soul, representing the Divine Consciousness that pervades all existence.
Pathshala: A traditional school or place of learning, particularly for religious or spiritual education in ancient India.
Patni: A wife or female partner in Hindu tradition, signifying a key role in the family unit.
Prakriti: Nature or the material world, the physical and mental environment that interacts with consciousness, consisting of the three guns (*sattva, rajas, tamas*).
Pralaya Kal: The period of dissolution or destruction in Hindu cosmology, where the universe goes through a phase of rest before renewal.
Pran: Vital life force or energy that flows through all living beings, sustaining life and health in Hindu philosophy and yogic practices.
Prasad: A sacred offering, often food, given to devotees after being blessed by the deity, considered to be imbued with divine grace.
Punya: Meritorious or virtuous deeds that accumulate good karma, leading to spiritual advancement or favourable circumstances in life.
Purandhar: A title for Lord Vishnu, often associated with his role as the remover of obstacles and the protector of the universe.
Purohit: A priest, especially one who performs religious ceremonies, rituals, and sacrifices for a family or community.
Purusha: The cosmic being or consciousness in Hindu philosophy, often associated with the universal spirit or self.
Purushartha: The four goals of human life in Hinduism—Dharm (duty), Arth (prosperity), Kaam (desires) and Moksh (liberation).
Raghuvansha: The royal dynasty of the Ramayan, descended from King Raghu, often regarded as a lineage of righteous kings, including Lord Rama.

Raja: A king or ruler, typically one who governs a kingdom with authority and responsibility.

Rajas: One of the three *gun*s (qualities) in Hindu philosophy, representing passion, activity and desire.

Rajasuya: A Vedic sacrifice performed by a king to establish their supremacy and authority,

Rajdharm: The moral and ethical duties and responsibilities of a king or ruler, guiding them in ruling justly.

Rakshas: A demon or evil being in Hindu mythology, often depicted as adversaries of gods and humans, possessing supernatural powers.

Ramrajya: The ideal rule of Lord Ram, symbolizing justice, righteousness, peace and the welfare of all people.

Ras Leela: A Divine dance, especially associated with Lord Krishna and the Gopis (cowherd girls), symbolizing Divine love and devotion.

Reta: Semen or seed, often used in a spiritual context to refer to the vital essence of life.

Rishi: A sage or seer, particularly one who has realized Divine knowledge through meditation and spiritual practices.

Rudraksha: A seed from the fruit of the Rudraksha tree, believed to have sacred significance and used in prayer beads in Hinduism.

Sadhana: A spiritual practice or discipline aimed at attaining a higher state of consciousness or enlightenment.

Sama: One of the four Vedas (Sama Veda) focused on chants and melodies for religious rituals and ceremonies; in statecraft, it is the practice of forging strategic alliances.

Samadhi: The ultimate state of meditation, where the practitioner merges with the Divine, achieving union with the self or the universe.

Samayojaka: A person or thing that harmonizes or unites, often referring to someone who brings things together or balances.

Samrat: An emperor, or supreme ruler, often associated with vast, unified territories or an expansive kingdom.
Samudra Manthan: The churning of the ocean by the gods and demons to obtain the nectar of immortality.
Sanskriti: Culture or civilization, representing the customs, practices, arts, and intellectual achievements of a society.
Sanyasi: A renunciant or ascetic who has given up worldly attachments to pursue spiritual enlightenment.
Satchitananda: The state of existence, consciousness, and bliss, representing the ultimate reality in Hindu philosophy.
Sattvic: One of the three *gun*s (qualities), representing purity, goodness and harmony, associated with balanced and virtuous behaviour.
Satya: Truth or reality, often considered a key virtue in Hindu philosophy, signifying honesty and the pursuit of truth.
Shabd Brahman/Nad Brahman: The concept that sound, particularly sacred sound or vibration (like *aum*), is the essence of the Divine or the ultimate reality.
Shakti: Divine feminine energy or power, often personified as goddesses like Durga, Lakshmi or Saraswati, symbolizing creation, preservation and destruction.
Shastra: A scripture, treatise or body of knowledge, particularly relating to religious, ethical, or philosophical teachings.
Shastrartha: A debate or discourse based on sacred texts or scriptures, often focused on the interpretation and understanding of religious principles.
Shivling: A symbolic representation of Lord Shiva, often depicted as a cylindrical or abstract shape, worshipped in temples.
Shlok: A verse, particularly in Sanskrit, often used in Hindu scriptures like the Bhagvad Gita, typically set to meter and rhythm.
Shudra: The fourth *varna* (social class) in traditional Hindu

society, typically associated with the service-oriented professions like doctors, engineers, artists and workers.

Siddha: A perfected being or sage who has achieved spiritual or mystical power, often through intense meditation or ascetic practices.

Siddhi: Supernatural or spiritual powers acquired through meditation, austerities, or the grace of God, often associated with advanced *yogi*s.

Sudarshan Chakra: A spinning, disk-like weapon of Lord Vishnu, symbolizing protection, destruction of evil and Divine power.

Supari: Betel nut, often used in religious rituals, offerings, or as a chewable item in cultural practices.

Sushupti: The state of deep, dreamless sleep in Hindu philosophy, considered one of the states of consciousness.

Sutaputra: The son of a charioteer, *suta* is also a community among the Vaishyas and the Shudras.

Swarg: Heaven, the abode of gods and the place of eternal pleasure in Hinduism.

Swayambhu: Self-manifested, referring to something that appears or is created naturally without human intervention, like a deity or sacred object.

Swayamvar: A traditional practice where a woman chooses her husband from among suitors, typically through a challenge or contest.

Tamas: One of the three *gun*s (qualities), representing darkness, ignorance and inertia in Hindu philosophy.

Tapasvi: A person engaged in intense spiritual austerities or penance, often for self-purification or gaining spiritual powers.

Tapasya: Spiritual discipline or penance undertaken for attaining divine favour, knowledge or power.

Tithi: A lunar day in the Hindu calendar, used to determine the timing of rituals and festivals.

Trikal Darshi: A seer who has the ability to perceive the past, present and future.

Trishul: The trident, a weapon often associated with Lord Shiva, symbolizing his power over creation, protection, and destruction.

Tulsi: A sacred plant in Hinduism, revered for its medicinal and spiritual properties.

Upaveda: A branch of knowledge that complements the four Vedas, dealing with subjects like medicine, architecture and military science.

Vaimanika: Pertaining to aircraft or flying machines, often mentioned in ancient texts describing celestial vehicles.

Vanar: A monkey or ape, often used to refer to the warrior-like species of monkeys in the Ramayan.

Varna: The system of occupational classifications in Hindu society, consisting of four main groups: Brahmin, Kshatriya, Vaishya and Shudra.

Vedi: An altar or platform used for performing *yagya*s (sacrificial rites) in Hindu rituals.

Veena: A classical Indian musical instrument, typically associated with the goddess Saraswati and played during devotional practices.

Viman: An aircraft, often mentioned in ancient texts and scriptures, used by gods and kings.

Virat Roop: The universal, cosmic form of God, particularly the manifestation of Lord Vishnu or Krishna in their all-encompassing form.

Vishnu Peetham: A sacred seat or place associated with Lord Vishnu, often symbolizing his Divine authority or throne; also, the top of the pedestal holding the Shivling.

Vrata: A religious vow or observance undertaken for spiritual growth, blessings, or in honour of a deity.

Yagya Kund: A fire pit or altar where the *yagya* (Vedic sacrifice) is performed.

Yagya: A Vedic fire sacrifice performed to appease gods, purify the environment, or seek blessings.

Yagyashala: A dedicated space or hall for conducting *yagya*s or sacred fire rituals.

Yagyavedi: The altar or sacred platform specifically meant for performing the yagya.

Yajman: The sponsor or the person who arranges and offers sacrifices in a yagya.

Yaksha: A nature spirit or demi-god, often associated with wealth and prosperity in Hindu, Buddhist and Jain traditions.

Yamraj: The god of death, responsible for overseeing the souls of the departed and the process of reincarnation.

Yogi: A practitioner of yoga, someone who seeks spiritual growth, self-realization and union with the Divine.

Yojana: A traditional measurement of distance, approximately equal to 12 kilometres.

Yoni: The symbol of the feminine divine, representing the goddess Shakti, often depicted as a sacred, geometric form.

Yug Dharm: The moral and spiritual duties that are relevant and appropriate for the specific age or yug in Hinduism.

Yug: An era or age in Hindu cosmology, each yug has distinct characteristics, with four major yugs forming a complete cycle.

References

Chapter 01: Why Did Lord Ram Abandon Mother Sita?

1. Sharma, Jankinath (trans.), 'Bal Kanda: Canto 4, Verse 1–3', *Srimad Valmiki-Ramayana (with Sanskrit Text and Translation into English): Part-I, Revised Edition*, Gita Press, Gorakhpur, 2022, p. 77.
2. Sharma, Jankinath (trans.), 'Uttar Kanda: Canto 43, Verse 13 and 20', *Srimad Valmiki-Ramayana (with Sanskrit Text and Translation into English): Part-II Revised Edition*, Gita Press, Gorakhpur, 2022, p. 996, 997
3. ——'Uttar Kanda: Canto 43, Verses 16–18', pp. 996–997.
4. ——'Uttar Kanda: Canto 43, Verse 19', p. 997.
5. Sharma, Jankinath (trans.), 'Ayodhya Kanda: Canto 19, Verses 24, 33, 36, 37, 40', *Srimad Valmiki-Ramayana (with Sanskrit Text and Translation into English): Part-I, Revised Edition*, Gita Press, Gorakhpur, 2022, pp. 365–366.
6. Sharma, Jankinath (trans.), 'Uttar Kanda: Canto 44, Verses 15–17', *Srimad Valmiki-Ramayana (with Sanskrit Text and Translation into English): Part-II, Revised Edition*, Gita Press, Gorakhpur, 2022, p. 998.
7. ——'Uttar Kanda: Canto 45, Verses 14–15', p. 1000.
8. ——'Uttar Kanda: Canto 45, Verses 8–19', p. 1000.
9. ——'Uttar Kanda: Canto 91, Verse 25; Canto 99, Verse 8', pp. 1098 and 1113.
10. ——'Uttar Kanda: Canto 91, Verse 25; Canto 99, Verse 8', pp. 1098 and 1113.
11. ——'Uttar Kanda: Canto 93, Verses 1, 5–10'. pp. 1100–1101.
12. ——'Uttar Kanda: Canto 96, Verses 12–14', p. 1107.
13. ——'Uttar Kanda: Canto 95, Verses 1–2', pp. 1104–1105.
14. ——'Uttar Kanda: Canto 96, Verses 3–6', p. 1105.
15. ——'Uttar Kanda: Canto 97, Verses 13–16', p. 1109.
16. ——'Uttar Kanda: Canto 97, Verses 17–18', p. 1109.
17. ——'Uttar Kanda: Canto 97, Verse 19', p. 1109.
18. ——'Uttar Kanda: Canto 97, Verse 20'. p. 1109.
19. Sharma, Jankinath (trans.), 'Ayodhya Kanda: Canto 27, Verses 1–3', *Srimad Valmiki-Ramayana (with Sanskrit Text and Translation into English): Part-I, Revised Edition*, Gita Press, Gorakhpur, 2022, p. 398; Also 'Canto 29, Verses 9, 13–14, 18', pp. 403–404.
20. ——'Ayodhya Kanda: Canto 27, Verse 10', p. 399.
21. ——'Ayodhya Kanda: Canto 30, Verses 3–5', pp. 405–406

22. Sharma, Jankinath (trans.), 'Aranya Kanda: Canto 6, Verses 22–25', *Srimad Valmiki-Ramayana (with Sanskrit Text and Translation into English): Part-I, Revised Edition*, Gita Press, Gorakhpur, 2022, p. 729.
23. ——'Aranya Kanda: Canto 9, Verses 9–33', pp. 733–735.
24. ——'Aranya Kanda: Canto 10, Verses 1–22', pp. 736–737.
25. ——'Aranya Kanda: Canto 45, Verses 5–9, 23–28'. pp. 833–834.
26. Sharma, Jankinath (trans.), 'Sundar Kanda: Canto 37, Verses 45–68', *Srimad Valmiki-Ramayana (with Sanskrit Text and Translation into English): Part-II, Revised Edition*, Gita Press, Gorakhpur, 2022, pp. 174–176.
27. Sharma, Jankinath (trans.), 'Uttar Kanda: Canto 48, Verses 10–19', *Srimad Valmiki-Ramayana (with Sanskrit Text and Translation into English): Part-II, Revised Edition*, Gita Press, Gorakhpur, 2022, p. 1006.

Chapter 02: Why Did The Pandavs Cheat in the Kurukshetra War?

1. Shastri Pandey, Pt. Ramnarayandutt (trans.), 'Sambhav Parva: Chapter 100, Verse 103', *Mahabharata (Volume I): Adi Parva and Sabha Parva*, Gita Press, Gorakhpur, 2016, p. 756.
2. ——'Aranya Parva: Chapter 7, Verses 14–24', pp. 91–92.
3. ——'Aranya Parva: Chapter 10, Verses 28–36', pp. 102–104.
4. Shastri Pandey, Pt. Ramnarayandutt (trans.), 'Bheeshma Vadha Parva: Chapter 59, Verses 72–105', *Mahabharata (Volume III): Udyog Parva and Bheeshma Parva*, Gita Press, Gorakhpur, 2016, pp. 1836–1843.

Chapter 03: Ram or Ravan: Who was the Better Man?

1. Sharma, Jankinath (trans.), 'Bal Kanda: Canto 16, Verse 7 ', *Srimad Valmiki-Ramayana (with Sanskrit Text and Translation into English): Part-I, Revised Edition*, Gita Press, Gorakhpur, 2022, p. 115; Also 'Aranya Kanda: Canto 32, Verses 12–14', p. 799
2. Sharma, Jankinath (trans.), 'Uttar Kanda: Canto 24, Verses 1–24', *Srimad Valmiki-Ramayana (with Sanskrit Text and Translation into English): Part-II, Revised Edition*, Gita Press, Gorakhpur, 2022, pp. 923–925.
3. Sharma, Jankinath (trans.), 'Aranya Kanda: Canto 38, Verse 30', *Srimad Valmiki-Ramayana (with Sanskrit Text and Translation into English): Part-I, Revised Edition,* Gita Press, Gorakhpur, 2022, p. 815.
4. Sharma, Jankinath (trans.), 'Uttar Kanda: Canto 26, Verses 39–57', *Srimad Valmiki-Ramayana (with Sanskrit Text and Translation into English): Part-II, Revised Edition,* Gita Press, Gorakhpur, 2022, pp. 934–935.
5. Ibid.

6. Sharma, Jankinath (trans.), 'Yuddha Kanda: Canto 13, Verse 12', *Srimad Valmiki-Ramayana (with Sanskrit Text and Translation into English): Part-II, Revised Edition,* Gita Press, Gorakhpur, 2022, p. 334.
7. ——'Yuddha Kanda: Canto 13, Verse 13–15', Ibid.
8. ——'Yuddha Kanda: Canto 13, Verses 1–5', pp. 333–334.
9. ——'Yuddha Kanda: Canto 13, Verses 11–15', pp. 334–335.
10. Sharma, Jankinath (trans.), 'Uttar Kanda: Canto 24, Verses 27–39', *Srimad Valmiki-Ramayana (with Sanskrit Text and Translation into English): Part-II, Revised Edition,* Gita Press, Gorakhpur, 2022, pp. 925–926.
11. Sharma, Jankinath (trans.), 'Aranya Kanda: Canto 45, Verses 19–24', *Srimad Valmiki-Ramayana (with Sanskrit Text and Translation into English): Part-I, Revised Edition,* Gita Press, Gorakhpur, 2022, p. 834; Also 'Canto 46, Verses 26–31', p. 838.
12. Sharma, Jankinath (trans.), 'Yuddha Kanda: Canto 31, Verses 6–45', *Srimad Valmiki-Ramayana (with Sanskrit Text and Translation into English): Part-II, Revised Edition,* Gita Press, Gorakhpur, 2022, pp. 401–404.
13. Sharma, Jankinath (trans.), 'Aranya Kanda: Canto 33, Verses 1–23', *Srimad Valmiki-Ramayana (with Sanskrit Text and Translation into English): Part-I, Revised Edition,* Gita Press, Gorakhpur, 2022, pp. 800–802.
14. Ibid.
15. ——'Aranya Kanda: Canto 32, Verses 12–22', pp. 799–800.
16. Sharma, Jankinath (trans.), 'Bal Kanda: Canto 15, Verses 5–34', *Srimad Valmiki-Ramayana (with Sanskrit Text and Translation into English): Part-I, Revised Edition,* Gita Press, Gorakhpur, 2022, pp. 111–114.
17. Sharma, Jankinath (trans.), 'Uttar Kanda: Canto 10, Verses 19–20', *Srimad Valmiki-Ramayana (with Sanskrit Text and Translation into English): Part-II, Revised Edition,* Gita Press, Gorakhpur, 2022, p. 877.
18. Sharma, Jankinath (trans.), 'Aranya Kanda: Canto 17, Verse 5', *Srimad Valmiki-Ramayana (with Sanskrit Text and Translation into English): Part-I, Revised Edition,* Gita Press, Gorakhpur, 2022, p. 759.
19. Ibid; Also, 'Canto 17, Verses 24–29', p. 760.
20. ——'Aranya Kanda: Canto 18, Verses 6–7', p. 761.
21. ——'Aranya Kanda: Canto 18, Verses 2–5', p. 761.
22. ——'Aranya Kanda: Canto 18, Verse 9', p. 761.
23. ——'Aranya Kanda: Canto 18, Verses 15–17', p. 762.
24. ——'Aranya Kanda: Canto 18, Verses 18–21', p. 762.
25. ——'Aranya Kanda: Canto 34, Verses 21–23', p. 804.
26. ——'Aranya Kanda: Canto 34, Verses 15–20', p. 804.
27. ——'Aranya Kanda: Canto 34, Verses 22–26', pp. 804–805.
28. Sharma, Jankinath (trans.), 'Uttar Kanda: Canto 16, Verses 34–44', *Srimad*

Valmiki-Ramayana (with Sanskrit Text and Translation into English): Part-II, Revised Edition, Gita Press, Gorakhpur, 2022, pp. 897–898.
29. Ibid.

Chapter 04: How Could the All-Knowing Shiva Not Recognize His Own Son?

1. Veda Vyasa, 'Ganpati Khand: Chapter 12', *Brahma-Vaivarta Purana*, Gita Press, Gorakhpur, 2018, pp. 345–347.
2. Khemka, Radheyshyam (ed.), 'Rudra Samhita: Kumar Khanda, Chapter 13, Verses 5–9', *Shiva Mahapurana: Part I*, Gita Press, Gorakhpur, 2019, pp. 787–788.
3. Shastri Pandey, Pt. Ramnarayandutt (trans.), 'Markandeysamasya Parva: Chapter 188', *Mahabharata (Volume II): Van Parva and Virat Parva*, Gita Press, Gorakhpur, 2016, pp. 1282–1300.
4. Khemka, Radheyshyam (ed.), 'Rudra Samhita: Kumar Khanda, Chapter 13, Verses 10–14', *Shiva Mahapurana: Part I*, Gita Press, Gorakhpur, 2019, p. 788.
5. ——'Rudra Samhita: Kumar Khanda, Chapter 13', pp. 788–790; Also 'Chapter 15', pp. 796–801.
6. ——'Rudra Samhita: Kumar Khanda, Chapter 13, Verses 16–30', pp. 788–789.
7. ——'Rudra Samhita: Kumar Khanda, Chapter 13, Verses 31–37', pp. 788–790.
8. ——'Rudra Samhita: Kumar Khanda, Chapter 13, Verses 31–39', pp. 788–790.
9. ——'Rudra Samhita: Kumar Khanda, Chapter 14, Verses 2–8', pp. 790–791.
10. ——'Rudra Samhita: Kumar Khanda, Chapter 14, Verses 9–11', p. 791.
11. ——'Rudra Samhita: Kumar Khanda, Chapter 14, Verses 12–14, 25–26, 57–59', pp. 791, 792–793, 795.
12. ——'Rudra Samhita: Kumar Khanda, Chapter 15, Verses 21–22', p. 797.
13. ——'Rudra Samhita: Kumar Khanda, Chapter 15, Verses 27–29', p. 798.
14. ——'Rudra Samhita: Kumar Khanda, Chapter 15, Verses 30–33', p. 798.
15. ——'Rudra Samhita: Kumar Khanda, Chapter 15, Verses 34–53', pp. 798–799.
16. ——'Rudra Samhita: Kumar Khanda, Chapter 15, Verses 54–72', pp. 800–801; Also 'Chapter 16, Verses 23–24', p. 803.
17. ——'Rudra Samhita: Kumar Khanda, Chapter 14, Verses 33–45', pp. 793–794.
18. ——'Rudra Samhita: Kumar Khanda, Chapter 15, Verses 44–53', p. 799.
19. ——'Rudra Samhita: Kumar Khanda, Chapter 16, Verses 20–33', pp. 803–804.
20. ——'Rudra Samhita: Kumar Khanda, Chapter 16, Verses 33–37', p. 804.
21. ——'Rudra Samhita: Kumar Khanda, Chapter 17, Verses 4–18', pp. 804–805.
22. ——'Rudra Samhita: Kumar Khanda, Chapter 17, Verses 30–41', pp. 806–807.
23. ——'Rudra Samhita: Kumar Khanda, Chapter 17, Verses 42–43', p. 807.

24. ——'Rudra Samhita: Kumar Khanda, Chapter 17, Verses 46–47', p. 808.
25. ——'Rudra Samhita: Kumar Khanda, Chapter 17, Verses 48–49', pp. 808–809.
26. ——'Rudra Samhita: Kumar Khanda, Chapter 17, Verses 52–55', p. 808.
27. ——'Rudra Sanhita: Kumar Khanda, Chapter 15, Verses 69–72', p. 801.
28. ——'Rudra Samhita: Kumar Khanda, Chapter 18, Verses 20–24', p. 810.
29. ——'Rudra Samhita: Kumar Khanda, Chapter 17, Verse 59', p. 809.
30. ——'Rudra Samhita: Kumar Khanda, Chapter 18, Verses 13–14', p. 810.
31. ——'Rudra Samhita: Kumar Khanda, Chapter 18, Verses 18–19', p. 810.
32. ——'Rudra Samhita: Kumar Khanda, Chapter 15, Verses 22–24', p. 797.
33. ——'Rudra Samhita: Kumar Khanda, Chapter 14, Verse 63'; Also, 'Chapter 15, Verses 22–24', p. 797.
34. ——'Rudra Samhita: Kumar Khanda, Chapter 18, Verses 18–19', p. 810

Chapter 05: Why Did Mother Sita Undergo the Demeaning Agnipariksha?

1. Sharma, Jankinath (trans.), 'Yuddha Kanda, Canto 114, Verse 7', *Srimad Valmiki-Ramayana (with Sanskrit Text and Translation into English): Part-II, Revised Edition*, Gita Press, Gorakhpur, 2022, p. 785.
2. Ibid., p. 786.
3. ——'Yuddha Kanda, Canto 115, Verse 11', p. 789.
4. ——'Yuddha Kanda, Canto 115, Verse 17', p. 789.
5. ——'Yuddha Kanda, Canto 115, Verse 18', p. 789.
6. ——'Yuddha Kanda, Canto 116, Verse 4', p. 790.
7. ——'Yuddha Kanda, Canto 116, Verses 5–16', pp. 791–792.
8. ——'Yuddha Kanda, Canto 116, Verse 15', p. 791.
9. ——'Yuddha Kanda, Canto 116, Verses 5 and 9', p. 791.
10. ——'Yuddha Kanda, Canto 116, Verses 17–18', p. 792.
11. ——'Yuddha Kanda, Canto 116, Verse 20', p. 792.
12. ——'Yuddha Kanda, Canto 116, Verse 21', p. 792.
13. ——'Yuddha Kanda, Canto 116, Verses 30–36', p. 793.
14. ——'Yuddha Kanda, Canto 116, Verse 33, 36', p. 793; Also 'Canto 117, Verse 1–4', p. 794.
15. ——'Yuddha Kanda, Canto 116, Verse 29', p. 793.
16. ——'Yuddha Kanda, Canto 117, Verse 1', p. 794.
17. ——'Yuddha Kanda, Canto 116, Verses 25–28', pp. 792–793.
18. ——'Yuddha Kanda, Canto 117, Verses 6 and 9', p. 794.
19. ——'Yuddha Kanda, Canto 118, Verse 1', p. 797.
20. ——'Yuddha Kanda, Canto 118, Verse 10', p. 798.
21. ——'Yuddha Kanda, Canto 118, Verses 15–20', pp. 798–799.
22. ——'Yuddha Kanda, Canto 116, Verses 26–36', pp. 792–793.

23. Sharma, Jankinath (trans.), 'Ayodhya Kanda, Canto 19, Verses 1–40', *Srimad Valmiki-Ramayana (with Sanskrit Text and Translation into English): Part-I, Revised Edition*, Gita Press, Gorakhpur, 2022, pp. 363–366.
24. Sharma, Jankinath (trans.), 'Bal Kanda; Canto 49, Verses 16–17', *Srimad Valmiki-Ramayana (with Sanskrit Text and Translation into English): Part-I, Revised Edition*, Gita Press, Gorakhpur, 2022, p. 208.
25. ———'Bal Kanda; Canto 48, Verses 19–21', p. 205.
26. Sharma, Jankinath (trans.), 'Kishkinda Kanda, Canto 18, Verses 19–26', *Srimad Valmiki-Ramayana (with Sanskrit Text and Translation into English): Part-I, Revised Edition*, Gita Press, Gorakhpur, 2022, pp. 998–999.
27. Sharma, Jankinath (trans.), 'Sundar Kanda, Canto 18–26', *Srimad Valmiki-Ramayana (with Sanskrit Text and Translation into English): Part-II, Revised Edition*, Gita Press, Gorakhpur, 2022, pp. 107–134.
28. ———'Sundar Kanda, Canto 22, Verses 20–21', p. 120.
29. ———'Sundar Kanda, Canto 37, Verse 64', p. 175.
30. ———'Sundar Kanda, Canto 36, Verses 17–18', p. 167.
31. Sharma, Jankinath (trans.), 'Yuddha Kanda, Canto 118, Verses 12–22', *Srimad Valmiki-Ramayana (with Sanskrit Text and Translation into English): Part-II, Revised Edition*, Gita Press, Gorakhpur, 2022, pp. 798–799.
32. ———'Yuddha Kanda, Canto 117, Verses 13–32', pp. 795–797.
33. Tulsidas, 'Aranya Kanda, Canto 23, Verses 1–2', *Shri Ramcharitamanas: A Romanized Edition with English Translation*, Editorial Team (trans.), Gita Press, Gorakhpur, 2024, pp. 668–669; Also, Veda Vyasa, 'Prakriti Khanda, Canto 14, 29–36', *Brahma-Vaivarta Purana*, pp. 165–170, pp. 236–270.
34. Sharma, Jankinath (trans.), 'Bal Kanda, Canto 15, Verse 28', *Srimad Valmiki-Ramayana (with Sanskrit Text and Translation into English): Part-I, Revised Edition*, Gita Press, Gorakhpur, 2022, p. 113.
35. Sharma, Jankinath (trans.), 'Bal Kanda, Canto 4, Verse 7', *Srimad Valmiki-Ramayana (with Sanskrit Text and Translation into English): Part-I, Revised Edition*, Gita Press, Gorakhpur, 2022, p. 77.

Chapter 06: What was Krishna's Ras-Leela?

1. Swami Mukundananda, 'Bhagavad Gita: Chapter 11, Verse 5', *Bhagavad Gita: The Song of God*, https://tinyurl.com/3fxvkyss. Accessed on 6 March 2025.
2. Subramaniam, Kamala (trans.), 'Chapter 186: Nanda Rescued from Varuna'; 'Chapter 187: Krishna and the Gopis'; 'Chapter 188: The Search for their Lost Love'; Chapter 189: Discourse on Love'; 'Chapter 190: Rasa Krida', *Srimad Bhagavatam*, Bharatiya Vidya Bhavan, Mumbai, 2017, pp. 557–568;

Also 'Chapter 199: Akrura, The Cruel!', pp. 588–591; 'Chapter 208: Uddhava Sent to Brindavan', pp. 616–619 and 'Chapter 209: Uddhava Comforts the Gopis', *Srimad Bhagavatam*, Bharatiya Vidya Bhavan, Mumbai, 2017, pp. 620–624.
3. Veda Vyasa, 'Brahma Khanda: Chapter 5', *Brahma-Vaivarta Purana*, Gita Press, Gorakhpur, 2018, pp. 33–36; Also 'Prakriti Khanda: Chapters 2 and 3', pp. 112–120, 'Shrikrishnajanam Khanda: Chapter 1', pp. 416–417.

Chapter 07: Was Vibhishan Right in Abandoning His Brother?

1. Sharma, Jankinath (trans.), 'Yuddha Kanda, Canto 12, Verses 27–34', *Srimad Valmiki-Ramayana (with Sanskrit Text and Translation into English): Part-II, Revised Edition*, Gita Press, Gorakhpur, 2022, p. 332.
2. Sharma, Jankinath (trans.), 'Uttar Kanda, Canto 10, Verses 1–49', *Srimad Valmiki-Ramayana (with Sanskrit Text and Translation into English): Part-II, Revised Edition*, Gita Press, Gorakhpur, 2022, pp. 876–879.
3. ——'Uttar Kanda, Canto 10, Verses 30–32', p. 878.
4. ——'Uttar Kanda, Canto 10, Verses 34–36', p. 878.
5. ——'Uttar Kanda, Canto 10, Verses 15–16', p. 877.
6. ——'Uttar Kanda, Canto 10, Verse 17', p. 877.
7. ——'Uttar Kanda, Canto 10, Verses 19–20', p. 877.
8. ——'Uttar Kanda, Canto 11, Verses 33–34', p. 882.
9. ——'Uttar Kanda, Canto 13, Verses 12–40', pp. 887–889.
10. Sharma, Jankinath (trans.), 'Bal Kanda, Canto 15, Verses 5–34', *Srimad Valmiki-Ramayana (with Sanskrit Text and Translation into English): Part-I, Revised Edition*, Gita Press, Gorakhpur, 2022, pp. 111–114.
11. Sharma, Jankinath (trans.), 'Yuddha Kanda, Canto 9, Verses 7–22', *Srimad Valmiki-Ramayana (with Sanskrit Text and Translation into English): Part-II, Revised Edition*, Gita Press, Gorakhpur, 2022, pp. 321–322; Also, 'Canto 10, Verses 1–2', p. 323; 'Canto 9, Verse 22', p. 322; 'Cantos 15–16', pp. 339–343.
12. ——'Yuddha Kanda, Canto 63, Verses 1–22, 35–40, and 31–58', 2022, pp. 537–542.

Chapter 08: Duryodhan or Yudhisthir: Who was the Real Villain?

1. Shastri Pandey, Pt. Ramnarayandutt (trans.), 'Sambhav Parva, Chapter 114, Verses 26–40', *Mahabharata (Volume I): Adi Parva and Sabha Parva*, Gita Press, Gorakhpur, 2016, pp. 830–831; Also, 'Sambhav Parva, Chapter 127, Verses 5–9', pp. 918–919.

2. ——'Sambhav Parva, Chapter 127, Verses 25-57', pp. 921-926; Also, 'Sambhav Parva, Chapter 128. Verses, 33-41', pp. 933-934.
3. ——'Sambhav Parva, Chapter 137, Verses 1-77', pp. 1000-1010.
4. Shastri Pandey, Pt. Ramnarayandutt (trans.), 'Jatugraha Parva, Chapter 140, Verses 1-2, 20-21', *Mahabharata (Volume I): Adi Parva and Sabha Parva,* Gita Press, Gorakhpur, 2016, p. 1033, pp. 1035-1036; Also, 'Chapter 141, Verses 14-15', pp. 1041-1042.
5. ——'Jatugraha Parva, Chapter 140, Verses 14-15', p. 1035.
6. Shastri Pandey, Pt. Ramnarayandutt (trans.), 'Viduragamanarajyalambha Parva, Chapter 200, Verses 1-20', *Mahabharata (Volume I): Adi Parva and Sabha Parva,* Gita Press, Gorakhpur, 2016, pp. 1399-1401.
7. ——'Viduragamanarajyalambha Parva, Chapter 206, Verses 26-28', p. 1437.
8. Shastri Pandey, Pt. Ramnarayandutt (trans.), 'Dyuta Parva, Chapter 49, Verse 36', *Mahabharata (Volume I): Adi Parva and Sabha Parva,* Gita Press, Gorakhpur, 2016, p. 2043; Also, 'Chapter 49, Verses 45-46', p. 2045; 'Chapter 50, Verse 19', p. 2050; 'Chapter 51, Verses 1-35', pp. 2057-2062; 'Chapter 52, Verses 1-49'; pp. 2063-2069; 'Chapter 53, Verses 1-26', pp. 2070-2073.
9. ——'Dyuta Parva, Chapter 49, Verses 45-46', p. 2045; Also 'Chapter 54, Verses 1-11', pp. 2074-2076; 'Chapter 55, Verses 20-21', p. 2080.
10. Shastri Pandey, Pt. Ramnarayandutt (trans.), 'Sambhav Parva, Chapter 122, Verses 8-9', *Mahabharata (Volume I): Adi Parva and Sabha Parva,* Gita Press, Gorakhpur, 2016, p. 874.
11. ——'Sambhav Parva, Chapter 128, Verses 41-42', p. 934.
12. Shastri Pandey, Pt. Ramnarayandutt (trans.), 'Jatugraha Parva, Chapter 140, Verses 23-29', *Mahabharata (Volume I): Adi Parva and Sabha Parva,* Gita Press, Gorakhpur, 2016, pp. 1036-1037.
13. Shastri Pandey, Pt. Ramnarayandutt (trans.), 'Sambhav Parva, Chapter 137, Verses 1-77', *Mahabharata (Volume I): Adi Parva and Sabha Parva,* Pt. Ram Narayan Dutt Shastri Pandey 'Ram' (trans.), Gita Press, Gorakhpur, 2016, pp. 1000-1010.
14. Shastri Pandey, Pt. Ramnarayandutt (trans.), 'Swayamvar Parva, Chapter 190, Verses 3-16', *Mahabharata (Volume I): Adi Parva and Sabha Parva,* Gita Press, Gorakhpur, 2016, pp. 1329-1332.
15. Shastri Pandey, Pt. Ramnarayandutt (trans.), 'Khandavdaha Parva, Chapter 221, Verses 2-13', *Mahabharata (Volume I): Adi Parva and Sabha Parva,* Gita Press, Gorakhpur, 2016, pp. 1530-1532; Also 'Rajasuya Parva, Chapter 33, Verses 1-8', pp. 1839-1840.
16. Shastri Pandey, Pt. Ramnarayandutt (trans.), 'Lokpalsabhakhyan Parva, Chapter 12, Verses 23-28', *Mahabharata (Volume I): Adi Parva and Sabha Parva,* Gita Press, Gorakhpur, 2016, pp. 1686-1687; Also, 'Rajsuya Arambha Parva, Chapters 13-15', pp. 1689-1713.

17. Shastri Pandey, Pt. Ramnarayandutt (trans.), 'Dyuta Parva, Chapter 50, Verse 22', *Mahabharata (Volume I): Adi Parva and Sabha Parva*, Pt. Ram Narayan Dutt Shastri Pandey 'Ram' (trans.), Gita Press, Gorakhpur, 2016, p. 2051.
18. ——'Dyuta Parva, Chapter 46, Verses 7-12', p. 2023.
19. ——'Dyuta Parva, Chapter 46, Verses 23-31', pp. 2025-2026.
20. ——'Dyuta Parva, Chapter 58, Verses 8-18, 20-21', pp. 2089-2096.
21. ——'Dyuta Parva, Chapter 59, Verses 1-6, 10-13', pp. 2099-2100.
22. ——'Dyuta Parva, Chapter 59, Verse 20-21', p. 2102.
23. Ibid; Also, 'Chapter 49, Verses 37-40', p. 2044; 'Chapter 58, Verse 13', p. 2091.
24. ——'Dyuta Parva, Chapter 65, Verses 29-32', pp. 2130-2131.
25. ——'Dyuta Parva, Chapter 65, Verses 40-42', p. 2132; Also 'Chapter 71, Verse 7', p. 2177.
26. Shastri Pandey, Pt. Ramnarayandutt (trans.), 'Draupadiharana Parva, Chapters 269-270', pp. 1790-1802; 'Chapter 271, Verse 43', p. 1808; 'Jayadrathvimokshan Parva, Chapter 272, Verses 15-22', p. 1814, *Mahabharata (Volume II): Van Parva and Virat Parva*, Gita Press, Gorakhpur, 2016, pp. 1798-1801, 1808-1815.
27. Shastri Pandey, Pt. Ramnarayandutt (trans.), 'Dyuta Parva, Chapter 71, Verse 22', *Mahabharata (Volume I): Adi Parva and Sabha Parva*, Gita Press, Gorakhpur, 2016, p. 2180.
28. ——'Dyuta Parva, Chapter 71, Verses 27-36', pp. 2182-2184; Also, 'Chapter 73, Verse 2', p. 2188.
29. Shastri Pandey, Pt. Ramnarayandutt (trans.), 'Anudyuta Parva, Chapter 74, Verses 1-27', *Mahabharata (Volume I): Adi Parva and Sabha Parva*, Gita Press, Gorakhpur, 2016, pp. 2191-2203.
30. Shastri Pandey, Pt. Ramnarayandutt (trans.), 'Aranya Parva, Chapter 7, Verses 5-13', *Mahabharata (Volume II): Van Parva and Virat Parva*, Gita Press, Gorakhpur, 2016, pp. 89-91.
31. ——'Aranya Parva, Chapter 7, Verses 14-24', pp. 91-92.
32. ——'Aranya Parva, Chapter 10, Verses 28-36', pp. 102-104.
33. Shastri Pandey, Pt. Ramnarayandutt (trans.), 'Ghoshayatra Parva, Chapter 237, Verses 14-22', *Mahabharata (Volume II): Van Parva and Virat Parva*, Gita Press, Gorakhpur, 2016, pp. 1628-1629; Also, 'Chapter 238, Verses 1-24', pp. 1630-1633.
34. ——'Ghoshayatra Parva, Chapter 243, Verses 1-22', pp. 1654-1659.
35. Shastri Pandey, Pt. Ramnarayandutt (trans.), 'Draupadiharana Parva, Chapter 262, Verses 18-28', *Mahabharata (Volume II): Van Parva and Virat Parva*, Gita Press, Gorakhpur, 2016, pp. 1755-1756.

36. Shastri Pandey, Pt. Ramnarayandutt (trans.), 'Arjunabhigaman Parva, Chapter 36, Verses 9–20', *Mahabharata (Volume II): Van Parva and Virat Parva*, Gita Press, Gorakhpur, 2016, pp. 278–279.
37. Shastri Pandey, Pt. Ramnarayandutt (trans.), 'Bhagwadgyan Parva, Chapter 128, Verses 1–50', *Mahabharata (Volume III): Udyog Parva and Bheeshma Parva*, Gita Press, Gorakhpur, 2016, pp. 829–835.
38. Shastri Pandey, Pt. Ramnarayandutt (trans.), 'Aranya Parva, Chapter 1, Verses 12–32', *Mahabharata (Volume II): Van Parva and Virat Parva*, Gita Press, Gorakhpur, 2016, pp. 212–213, pp. 30–34.
39. ——'Aranya Parva, Chapter 1, Verses 33–38', p. 34.
40. ——'Aranya Parva, Chapter 3, Verses 1–74', pp. 50–69.
41. Shastri Pandey, Pt. Ramnarayandutt (trans.), 'Arjunabhigaman Parva, Chapter 27, Verses 37–40', 'Chapter 33, Verses 6–13', 'Chapter 33, Verses 43–44', *Mahabharata (Volume II): Van Parva and Virat Parva*, Gita Press, Gorakhpur, 2016, pp. 212–213, pp. 252–253, p. 258; Also, 'Nalopakhyan Parva, Chapter 52, Verses 8–14 and Verses 30–40', pp. 378–379 and pp. 381–382.
42. Shastri Pandey, Pt. Ramnarayandutt (trans.), 'Teerthyatra Parva, Chapter 144, Verses 10–13', *Mahabharata (Volume II): Van Parva and Virat Parva*, Gita Press, Gorakhpur, 2016, pp. 976–977.
43. ——'Teerthyatra Parva, Chapter 120, Verses 1–30', pp. 834–840.
44. Shastri Pandey, Pt. Ramnarayandutt (trans.), 'Arjunabhigaman Parva, Chapter 36, Verses 8–20', *Mahabharata (Volume II): Van Parva and Virat Parva*, Gita Press, Gorakhpur, 2016, pp. 278–279.
45. Shastri Pandey, Pt. Ramnarayandutt (trans.), 'Nalopakhyan Parva, Chapter 79, Verses 20–21', *Mahabharata (Volume II): Van Parva and Virat Parva*, Gita Press, Gorakhpur, 2016, pp. 555–556.
46. Shastri Pandey, Pt. Ramnarayandutt (trans.), 'Ghoshayatra Parva, Chapter 243, Verses 1–22', *Mahabharata (Volume II): Van Parvaand Virat Parv*, Gita Press, Gorakhpur, 2016, pp. 1654–1659.
47. Shastri Pandey, Pt. Ramnarayandutt (trans.), 'Aranya Parva, Chapter 314, Verses 1–29', *Mahabharata (Volume II): Van Parva and Virat Parva*, Gita Press, Gorakhpur, 2016, pp. 2109–2113.

Chapter 09: Why is the Bungling Indra King of the Gods?

1. Sharma, Jankinath (trans.), 'Bal Kanda, Canto 48, Verses 16–18', *Srimad Valmiki-Ramayana (with Sanskrit Text and Translation into English): Part-I, Revised Edition*, Gita Press, Gorakhpur, 2022, pp. 204–205.
2. Shastri Pandey, Pt. Ramnarayandutt (trans.), 'Kundalharana Parva, Chapter

310, Verse 4', *Mahabharata (Volume II): Van Parva and Virat Parva*, Gita Press, Gorakhpur, 2016, p. 2066.
3. Subramaniam, Kamala (trans.), 'Chapter 182: Not Indra, But Govardhana!', *Srimad Bhagavatam*, Bharatiya Vidya Bhavan, Mumbai, 2017, pp. 457–465.
4. Sharma, Jankinath (trans.), 'Uttar Kanda, Canto 56, Verse 28', *Srimad Valmiki-Ramayana (with Sanskrit Text and Translation into English): Part-II, Revised Edition*, Gita Press, Gorakhpur, 2022, p. 1022.
5. Sharma, Jankinath (trans.), 'Bal Kanda', *Srimad Valmiki-Ramayana (with Sanskrit Text and Translation into English): Part-I, Revised Edition*, Gita Press, Gorakhpur, 2022, p. 205.
6. Ibid.

Chapter 10: Why is Dev Rishi Narad So Respected and Adored?

1. Shastri Pandey, Pt. Ramnarayandutt (trans.), 'Lokpalsabhakyan Parva, Chapter 5, Verses 16–129', *Mahabharata (Volume I): Adi Parva and Sabha Parva*, Gita Press, Gorakhpur, 2016, pp. 1629–1648.
2. ——'Lokpalsabhakyan Parva, Chapter 5, Verses 1–12', pp. 1627–1628.
3. Ibid.

Chapter 11: Was Karn a Victim of the Caste System?

1. Shastri Pandey, Pt. Ramnarayandutt (trans.), 'Sambhav Parva, Chapter 131, Verses 11 and 12', *Mahabharata (Volume I): Adi Parva and Sabha Parva*, Gita Press, Gorakhpur, 2016, p. 958.
2. Shastri Pandey, Pt. Ramnarayandutt (trans.), 'Kundalharana Parva, Chapter 309, Verses 16–20', *Mahabharata (Volume II): Van Parva and Virat Parva*, Gita Press, Gorakhpur, 2016, p. 2064.
3. Shastri Pandey, Pt. Ramnarayandutt (trans.),, 'Sambhav Parva, Chapter 135, Verses 1–12', *Mahabharata (Volume I): Adi Parva and Sabha Parva*, Gita Press, Gorakhpur, 2016, pp. 988–989.
4. Shastri Pandey, Pt. Ramnarayandutt (trans.), 'Sambhav Parva, Chapter 135, Verses 13–41', *Mahabharata (Volume I): Adi Parva and Sabha Parva*, Gita Press, Gorakhpur, 2016, pp. 989–994.
5. Shastri Pandey, Pt. Ramnarayandutt (trans.), 'Kundalharana Parva, Chapter 309, Verses 13–16', *Mahabharata (Volume II): Van Parva and Virat Parva*, Gita Press, Gorakhpur, 2016, pp. 2063–2064.
6. Shastri Pandey, Pt. Ramnarayandutt (trans.), 'Sambhav Parva, Chapter 136, Verses 8–19, 22', *Mahabharata (Volume I): Adi Parva and Sabha Parva*, Gita Press, Gorakhpur, 2016, pp. 997–998; Also, p. 999.

7. ———'Sambhav Parva, Chapter 136, Verse 19', p. 998.
8. Shastri Pandey, Pt. Ramnarayandutt (trans.), 'Swayamvar Parva, Chapter 185, Verses 1–4', *Mahabharata (Volume I): Adi Parva and Sabha Parva*, Gita Press, Gorakhpur, 2016, p. 1300.
9. ———'Swayamvar Parva, Chapter 184, Verse 27', p. 1296; Also, 'Chapter 186, Verses 9–10', pp. 1304–1305.
10. ———'Swayamvar Parva, Chapters 187–189', pp. 1310–1328.
11. Shastri Pandey, Pt. Ramnarayandutt (trans.), 'Arjunabhigaman Parva, Chapter 36, Verses 18–20', *Mahabharata (Volume II): Van Parva and Virat Parva*, Gita Press, Gorakhpur, 2016, p. 279.
12. Shastri Pandey, Pt. Ramnarayandutt (trans.), 'Arghabhiharan Parva, Chapter 37, Verses 15–16', *Mahabharata (Volume I): Adi Parva and Sabha Parva*, Gita Press, Gorakhpur, 2016, p. 1864.
13. Shastri Pandey, Pt. Ramnarayandutt (trans.), 'Jatugraha Parva, Chapter 140, Verses 1–2, 20–21 ', *Mahabharata (Volume I): Adi Parva and Sabha Parva*, Gita Press, Gorakhpur, 2016, pp. 1033 and 1035.
14. Shastri Pandey, Pt. Ramnarayandutt (trans.), 'Dyuta Parva, Chapter 67, Verse 44–45', *Mahabharata (Volume I): Adi Parva and Sabha Parva*, Gita Press, Gorakhpur, 2016, p. 2148; Also, 'Chapter 68, Verses 27–33', pp. 2156–2157.
15. ———'Dyuta Parva, Chapter 68, Verses 36–38', p. 2157.

Chapter 12: How Could Hanuman Swallow the Sun?

1. Yogi Madhavacharya (ed.), 'Chapter 3: Vibhuti Pada', *Yoga Sutras of Patanjali*, Michael Beloved, Guyana, 2007, pp. 36–54.
1. Sastry, Subbaraya, 'Chapter 6: Atha Jaatyadhikaranam: Varieties of Vimaanas', *Maharishi Bharadwaaja's Vyamaanika-Shaastra or Science of Aeronautics*, G.R. Joyser (trans.), Coronation Press, Mysore, 1973, pp. 85–87.
2. Sharma, Jankinath (trans.), 'Bal Kanda, Canto 17, Verses 3–4', *Srimad Valmiki-Ramayana (with Sanskrit Text and Translation into English): Part-I, Revised Edition*, Gita Press, Gorakhpur, 2022, pp.117–118.
3. ———'Bal Kanda, Canto 17, Verses 16–17', pp. 118–119.

Chapter 13: Was It Fair for Ahilya to be Cursed?

1. Sharma, Jankinath (trans.), 'Bal Kanda, Canto 48, Verse 19', *Srimad Valmiki-Ramayana (with Sanskrit Text and Translation into English): Part-I, Revised Edition*, Gita Press, Gorakhpur, 2022, p. 205.

2. ———'Bal Kanda, Canto 48, Verses 20–21', p. 205.
3. ———'Bal Kanda, Canto 48, Verses 21–22', p. 205.
4. ———'Bal Kanda, Canto 48, Verse 27', p. 205.
5. ———'Bal Kanda, Canto 48, Verse 32', p. 206.
6. Shastri Pandey, Pt. Ramnarayandutt (trans.), 'Sambhav Parva, Chapter 83, Verse 31', *Mahabharata (Volume I): Adi Parva and Sabha Parva*, Gita Press, Gorakhpur, 2016, p. 629.
7. Veda Vyasaa, 'Ganpati Khand: Chapter 12', *Brahma-Vaivarta Purana*, Gita Press, Gorakhpur, 2018, pp. 342–345.
8. Sharma, Jankinath (trans.) 'Bal Kanda, Canto 48, Verses 29-30', *Srimad Valmiki-Ramayana (with Sanskrit Text and Translation into English): Part-I, Revised Edition*, Gita Press, Gorakhpur, 2022, p. 206.
9. ———'Bal Kanda, Canto 49, Verse 2', p. 206.
10. ———'Bal Kanda, Canto 49, Verses 16–17', p. 208.
11. ———'Bal Kanda, Canto 49, Verses 19–20', *Srimad Valmiki-Ramayana (with Sanskrit Text and Translation into English): Part-I, Revised Edition*, p. 208.
12. ———'Bal Kanda, Canto 48, Verses 20–21', p. 205.

Chapter 14: Was it Misogynistic for Draupadi to Have Five Husbands?

1. Shastri Pandey, Pt. Ramnarayandutt (trans.), 'Chaitrarth Parva, Chapter 166, Verses 45–46', *Mahabharata (Volume I): Adi Parva and Sabha Parva*, Gita Press, Gorakhpur, 2016, pp. 1184–1185.
2. ———'Chaitrarth Parva, Chapter 166, Verse 47', p. 1185.
3. ———'Chaitrarth Parva, Chapter 166, Verses 48–49', p. 1185.
4. ———'Chaitrarth Parva, Chapter 166, Verses 50', p. 1185; Also p. 1190.
5. ———'Chaitrarth Parva, Chapter 168, Verses 15–16', pp. 1196–1197; Also p. 1190.
6. ———'Chaitrarth Parva, Chapter 168, Verses 1–14', pp. 1194–1196.
7. Shastri Pandey, Pt. Ramnarayandutt (trans.), 'Swayamvar Parva, Chapter 186, Verse 23', *Mahabharata (Volume I): Adi Parva and Sabha Parva*, Gita Press, Gorakhpur, 2016, p. 1307.
8. ———'Swayamvar Parva, Chapter 190, Verse 2', *Mahabharata (Volume I): Adi Parva and Sabha Parva*, p. 1329.
9. ———'Swayamvar Parva, Chapter 190, Verse 3–16', pp. 1329–1332.
10. Shastri Pandey, Pt. Ramnarayandutt (trans.), 'Vaivahika Parva, Chapter 195, Verse 14', *Mahabharata (Volume I): Adi Parva and Sabha Parva*, Gita Press, Gorakhpur, 2016, p. 1362.
11. ———'Vaivahika Parva, Chapter 195, Verses 15', pp. 1362–1363.
12. ———'Vaivahika Parva, Chapter 195, Verses 1–12', pp. 1360–1362.

13. ——'Vaivahika Parva, Chapter 196, Verses 1–53', pp. 1365–1378.
14. ——'Vaivahika Parva, Chapter 196, Verses 27–36', pp. 1373–1375.
15. ——'Vaivahika Parva, Chapter 196, Verses 37–41', p. 1375–1376.
16. Shastri Pandey, Pt. Ramnarayandutt (trans.), 'Viduragmanrajyalambha Parva, Chapter 211, Verses 28–29', *Mahabharata (Volume I): Adi Parva and Sabha Parva*, Gita Press, Gorakhpur, 2016, p. 1473.
17. Shastri Pandey, Pt. Ramnarayandutt (trans.), 'Arjunvanvas Parva, Chapter 212, Verses 1–35', *Mahabharata (Volume I): Adi Parva and Sabha Parva*, Gita Press, Gorakhpur, 2016, pp. 1475–1480.

Chapter 15: Why Does Sanatan Dharm Have So Many Gods and Goddesses? How to Know Which One to Worship?

1. Mahajan, Ishan, 'Do Hindus Really Have 33 Crore Gods?', *Medium*, 14 Aug 2022. https://tinyurl.com/432h5ctj. Accessed 6 March 2025.
2. Swami Tathagatananda, 'Hinduism Emphasizes The Supreme Importance Of Spiritual Life', *Vedanta Society of New York*. https://tinyurl.com/2mkkxrr3. Accessed 6 March, 2025.

Chapter 16: Why Do Sanatan Gods Behave Like Humans?

1. Sathya Sai, 'Chapter VIII', *Spirituality and Science: The Turn of the Tide in Scientific Thought, Revised Second Edition*, Sathya Sai Publications, Puttaparthi, 1995, p. 103.

Chapter 17: What Is The Shivling?

1. Veda Vyasa, 'Vishveshwar Samhita: Chapter 9, Verses 36–43', *Shiva Mahapurana: Part I*, Radheyshyam Khemka (ed.), Gita Press, Gorakhpur, 2019, pp. 72–73.
2. Swami Mukundananda, 'Bhagavad Gita: Chapter 9, Verses 7–8', *Bhagavad Gita: The Song of God*, https://tinyurl.com/39u2khwc. Accessed on 6 March 2025.
3. Sri Mookambika Temple, https://tinyurl.com/2n7y6cnb. Accessed on 6 March 2025.
4. Sri Swami Sivananda, *Lord Shiva and His Worship*, Divine Life Society, Rishikesh, 2008, pp. 111–116.
5. Khemka, Radheyshyam (ed.), 'Vishveshwar Samhita: Chapter 9, Verses 36–43', *Shiva Mahapurana: Part I*, Gita Press, Gorakhpur, 2019, pp. 72–73.

Chapter 19: What was the Status of Women in Ancient Bharat?

1. Shastri Pandey, Pt. Ramnarayandutt (trans.), 'Sambhav Parva, Chapter 122, Verses 76-78', *Mahabharata (Volume I): Adi Parva and Sabha Parva*, Gita Press, Gorakhpur, 2016, pp. 885-886.
2. Cole, Owen W. and V.P. Kanitkar, 'Chapter 8: Scriptures', *Hinduism: An Introduction*, Teach Yourself, London, 2010, pp. 210-220.
3. Shastri Pandey, Pt. Ramnarayandutt (trans.), 'Pandavpravesh Parva, Chapter 11, Verse 10', *Mahabharata (Volume II): Van Parva and Virat Parva*, Gita Press, Gorakhpur, 2016, p. 2189.
4. Subramaniam, Kamala (trans.), 'Chapter 203: The Great Bow is Broken', *Srimad Bhagavatam*, Bharatiya Vidya Bhavan, Mumbai, 2017, p. 600.
5. Sharma, Jankinath (trans.), 'Ayodhya Kanda, Canto 9, Verses 15-16', *Srimad Valmiki-Ramayana (with Sanskrit Text and Translation into English): Part-I, Revised Edition*, Gita Press, Gorakhpur, 2022, p. 92; Also, 'Canto 11, Verses 18-19', p. 97.
6. Sharma, Jankinath (trans.), 'Kishkinda Kanda, Canto 16, Verse 12', *Srimad Valmiki-Ramayana (with Sanskrit Text and Translation into English): Part-I, Revised Edition*, Gita Press, Gorakhpur, 2022, p. 969; Also, 'Canto 15, Verses 1-31', pp. 985-987.
7. Sharma, Jankinath (trans.), 'Sundar Kanda, Canto 36, Verses 17-18', *Srimad Valmiki-Ramayana (with Sanskrit Text and Translation into English): Part-II, Revised Edition*, Gita Press, Gorakhpur, 2022, p. 167.
8. Shastri Pandey, Pt. Ramnarayandutt (trans.), 'Sambhav Parva, Chapter 125, Verses 5-13', *Mahabharata (Volume I): Adi Parva and Sabha Parva*, Gita Press, Gorakhpur, 2016, pp. 918-920.
9. Veda Vyasa, 'Prakriti Khand: Chapter 14, Verses 5-6', *Brahma-Vaivarta Purana*, Gita Press, Gorakhpur, 2018, pp. 167-168.
10. Sharma, Jankinath (trans.), 'Ayodhya Kanda, Canto 117, Verses 9-12', *Srimad Valmiki-Ramayana (with Sanskrit Text and Translation into English): Part-I, Revised Edition*, Gita Press, Gorakhpur, 2022, p. 704.
11. Shastri Pandey, Pt. Ramnarayandutt (trans.), 'Ambopakhyana Parva, Chapter 178, Verses 1-95', *Mahabharata (Volume III): Udyog Parva and Bheeshma Parva*, Gita Press, Gorakhpur, 2016, pp. 1129-1141.
12. Sharma, Jankinath (trans.), 'Uttar Kanda, Canto 27, Verses 28-34', *Srimad Valmiki-Ramayana (with Sanskrit Text and Translation into English): Part-II, Revised Edition*, Gita Press, Gorakhpur, 2022, p. 901.
13. Veda Vyasa, 'Prakriti Khand: Chapter 14, Verses 16-21', *Brahma-Vaivarta Purana*, Gita Press, Gorakhpur, 2018, pp. 167-168.
14. Shastri Pandey, Pt. Ramnarayandutt (trans.), 'Kichakvadha Parva, Chapter

16', *Mahabharata (Volume II): Van Parva and Virat* Parva, Gita Press, Gorakhpur, 2016, pp. 2225–2246.
15. Sharma, Jankinath (trans.), 'Ayodhya Kanda, Canto 19, Verse 13', *Srimad Valmiki-Ramayana (with Sanskrit Text and Translation into English): Part-I, Revised Edition*, Gita Press, Gorakhpur, 2022, p. 404.
16. Sharma, Jankinath (trans.), 'Bal Kanda, Canto 48, Verse 19–21', *Srimad Valmiki-Ramayana (with Sanskrit Text and Translation into English): Part-I, Revised Edition*, Gita Press, Gorakhpur, 2022, p. 205.
17. Khemka, Radheyshyam (ed.), 'Kumar Khanda: Chapter 15, Verses 36-66; Chapter 16, Verses 2–8', *Shiva Mahapurana: Part I*, Gita Press, Gorakhpur, 2019, pp. 901–903.
18. Chakraborty, Angsuman, '12 Notable Female Indian Gurus', *Medium*, 21 February 2017, https://tinyurl.com/2xry6huu. Accessed on 6 March 2025.
19. Sharma, Jankinath (trans.), 'Ayodhya Kanda, Canto 37, Verses 23–25', *Srimad Valmiki-Ramayana (with Sanskrit Text and Translation into English): Part-I, Revised Edition*, Gita Press, Gorakhpur, 2022, p. 435
20. Shastri Pandey, Pt. Ramnarayandutt (trans.), 'Sambhav Parva, Chapter 102, Verses 1–26', *Mahabharata (Volume I): Adi Parva and Sabha Parva*, Gita Press, Gorakhpur, 2016, pp. 771–774; Also, 'Chapter 103, Verses 1–10', pp. 775–776.
21. Shastri Pandey, Pt. Ramnarayandutt (trans.), 'Kundalharan Parva, Chapter 305, Verse 7', *Mahabharata (Volume II): Van Parva and Virat Parva*, Gita Press, Gorakhpur, 2016, p. 2045.
22. Shastri Pandey, Pt. Ramnarayandutt (trans.), 'Pandavpravesh Parva, Chapter 3, Verses 18–21', *Mahabharata (Volume II): Van Parva and Virat Parva*, Gita Press, Gorakhpur, 2016, p. 2136.
23. Shastri Pandey, Pt. Ramnarayandutt (trans.), 'Dyuta Parva, Chapter 65, Verses 36–37', *Mahabharata (Volume I): Adi Parva and Sabha Parva*, Gita Press, Gorakhpur, 2016, p. 2131.
24. Shastri Pandey, Pt. Ramnarayandutt (trans.), 'Arjunvanvas Parva, Chapter 213, Verses 17-36', *Mahabharata (Volume I): Adi Parva and Sabha Parva*, Gita Press, Gorakhpur, 2016, pp.1481–1485.
25. Shastri Pandey, Pt. Ramnarayandutt (trans.), 'Hidimba Parva', *Mahabharata (Volume I): Adi Parva and Sabha Parva*, Gita Press, Gorakhpur, 2016, p. 1096; Also 'Chapter 153, Verses 5–9', pp. 1108–1109, and 'Chapter 154, Verses 1–56', pp. 1115–1128.
26. Shastri Pandey, Pt. Ramnarayandutt (trans.), 'Swayamvar Parva, Chapter 186, Verse 23', *Mahabharata (Volume I): Adi Parva and Sabha Parva*, Gita Press, Gorakhpur, 2016, p. 1307.
27. Shastri Pandey, Pt. Ramnarayandutt (trans.), 'Sambhav Parva, Chapter 83,

Verses 32–34', *Mahabharata (Volume I): Adi Parva and Sabha Parva*, Gita Press, Gorakhpur, 2016, p. 630.

28. Subramaniam, Kamala (ed.), 'Chapter 239: Usha's Dream', *Srimad Bhagavatam*, Mumbai, 2017, pp. 700–703.
29. ——'Chapter 220: Rukmini Sends a Messenger'; 'Chapter 221: Dwarka, the Rose-Red City'; 'Chapter 222: Rukmini's Message', pp. 651–659.
30. Shastri Pandey, Pt. Ramnarayandutt (trans.), 'Pativratamahatmya Parva, Chapter 293, Verses 32–33', *Mahabharata (Volume II): Van Parva and Virat Parva*, Gita Press, Gorakhpur, 2016, pp. 1967–1968; Also 'Chapter 293, Verses 39–41', p. 1969.
31. Shastri Pandey, Pt. Ramnarayandutt (trans.), 'Sambhav Parva, Chapter 83, Verses 32–34', *Mahabharata (Volume I): Adi Parva and Sabha Parva*, Gita Press, Gorakhpur, 2016, p. 630.
32. Gita Press, 'Brahmaparva: Chapter 7: Description of the Three Sources of Wealth and Women, and the Mutual Behaviour Between Men and Women', Gorakhpur, 2018, p. 34.
33. ——'Brahmaparva: Chapter 6: Explanation of Marriage-Related Principles, Characteristics of a Marriageable Maiden, Eight Types of Marriage, and the Description of Brahmavarta, Aryavarta, and Other Prominent Regions', p. 33.
34. Shastri Pandey, Pt. Ramnarayandutt (trans.), 'Teerthayatra Parva, Chapter 144, Verse 17', *Mahabharata (Volume II): Van Parva and Virat Parva*, Gita Press, Gorakhpur, 2016, p. 978.
35. Shastri Pandey, Pt. Ramnarayandutt (trans.), 'Dyuta Parva, Chapter 65, Verses 40–44', *Mahabharata (Volume I): Adi Parva and Sabha Parva*, Gita Press, Gorakhpur, 2016, pp. 2132–2133.
36. Shastri Pandey, Pt. Ramnarayandutt (trans.), 'Nalopakhyan Parva, Chapter 57, Verses 30–40', *Mahabharata (Volume II): Van Parva and Virat* Parva, Gita Press, Gorakhpur, 2016, pp. 412–414.
37. Gita Press, 'Brahmaparva: Chapter 6: Explanation of Marriage-Related Principles, Characteristics of a Marriageable Maiden, Eight Types of Marriage, and the Description of Brahmavarta, Aryavarta, and Other Prominent Regions', *Bhavishya Purana*, Gorakhpur, 2018, p. 33.
38. Sharma, Jankinath (trans.), 'Uttar Kanda, Canto 24, Verses 1–26', *Srimad Valmiki-Ramayana (with Sanskrit Text and Translation into English): Part-II, Revised Edition*, Gita Press, Gorakhpur, 2022, pp. 923–925; Also 'Bala Kanda, Canto 15, Verses 8–26', *Srimad Valmiki-Ramayana (with Sanskrit Text and Translation into English): Part-I, Revised Edition,* pp. 112–113.
39. Sharma, Jankinath (trans.), 'Aranya Kanda, Canto 38, Verse 30', *Srimad Valmiki-Ramayana (with Sanskrit Text and Translation into English): Part-I, Revised Edition*, Gita Press, Gorakhpur, 2022, p. 815.

40. Shastri Pandey, Pt. Ramnarayandutt (trans.), 'Arjunbhigaman Parva, Chapter 12, Verses 128-129', *Mahabharata (Volume II): Van Parva and Virat Parva*, Gita Press, Gorakhpur, 2016, pp. 135-136.
41. Shastri Pandey, Pt. Ramnarayandutt (trans.), 'Indralokabhigaman Parva, Chapter 45, Verses 1-16', *Mahabharata (Volume II): Van Parva and Virat Parva*, Gita Press, Gorakhpur, 2016, pp. 340-342.
42. Sharma, Jankinath (trans.), 'Yuddha Kanda, Canto 13, Verses 11-14', *Srimad Valmiki-Ramayana (with Sanskrit Text and Translation into English): Part-II, Revised Edition*, Gita Press, Gorakhpur, 2022, pp. 334-335.
43. Shastri Pandey, Pt. Ramnarayandutt (trans.), 'Sambhav Parva, Chapter 119, Verses 32-36', *Mahabharata (Volume I): Adi Parva and Sabha Parva*, Gita Press, Gorakhpur, 2016, pp. 859-860.
44. Sharma, Jankinath (trans.), 'Bala Kanda, 11, Verses 2-3', *Srimad Valmiki-Ramayana (with Sanskrit Text and Translation into English): Part-I, Revised Edition*, Gita Press, Gorakhpur, 2022, p. 96.
45. Shastri Pandey, Pt. Ramnarayandutt (trans.), 'Kundalharan Parva, Chapter 303, Verses 20-25', *Mahabharata (Volume II): Van Parva and Virat Parva*, Gita Press, Gorakhpur, 2016, pp. 2037-2038.
46. Shastri Pandey, Pt. Ramnarayandutt (trans.), 'Chaitrarath Parva, Chapter 166, Verse 47-50, and 54-54', *Mahabharata (Volume I): Adi Parva and Sabha Parva*, Gita Press, Gorakhpur, 2016, p. 1185 and 1186.
47. Shastri Pandey, Pt. Ramnarayandutt (trans.), 'Pativratamahatmya Parva, Chapter 293, Verses 15-20', *Mahabharata (Volume II): Van Parva and Virat Parva*, Gita Press, Gorakhpur, 2016, pp. 1965-1966.
48. Olivelle, Patrick, 'Dharmasutras', *Dharmasutras: The Law Codes of Ancient India*. Oxford University Press, Oxford, 1999, pp. 43-58.
49. Centre for Indic Studies, 'Was Sati a Religious Obligation?', *YouTube*, 13 November 2019, https://tinyurl.com/bdwnf6cp. Accessed on 6 March 2025.
50. Jain, Meenakshi, 'Chapter 1: The Backdrop', *Sati, Evangelicals, Baptist Missionaries and the Changing Colonial Discourse*, Aryan Books International, New Delhi, 2016, p. 4.
51. Shastri Pandey, Pt. Ramnarayandutt (trans.), 'Sambhav Parva, Chapter 124, Verses 1-31', *Mahabharata (Volume I): Adi Parva and Sabha Parva*, Gita Press, Gorakhpur, 2016, pp. 895-905.
52. Ibid.
53. Jain, Meenakshi, 'Chapter 10: Missionaries and Sati', *Sati, Evangelicals, Baptist Missionaries and the Changing Colonial Discourse*, Aryan Books International, New Delhi, 2016, p. 188; Also, 'Chapter 11: Abolition of Sati', p. 208 and 'Chapter 2: Sati as Described in Foreign Accounts', pp. 25-43.
54. Ibid., p.3.

55. Sharma, Jankinath (trans.), 'Bala Kanda, Canto 26, Verses 21–22', *Srimad Valmiki-Ramayana (with Sanskrit Text and Translation into English): Part-I, Revised Edition*, Gita Press, Gorakhpur, 2022, p. 145.
56. ——'Bal Kanda, Canto 25, Verse 21', p. 142.
57. Ibid.
58. ——'Bal Kanda, Canto 25, Verses 20–21', p. 142.

Chapter 20: What was the Caste System in Ancient Bharat?

1. Malhotra, Rajiv, 'Chapter 4: Distortions About Caste', *Varna, Jati, Caste: A Primer on Indian Social Structures*, Occam, Delhi, 2023, pp. 46–70.
2. Roopak, M. Sai, 'Rigveda, Purusha-Suktam, Verses 1 and 2', *Veda Pushpanjali*, Sri Sathya Sai Research Centre, Puttapurthi, 2003, pp. 114–115.
3. Ibid. pp. 108–111.
4. Swami Mukundananda, 'Bhagavad Gita: Chapter 18, Verse 41', *Bhagavad Gita: The Song of God*, https://tinyurl.com/2s3vfz7d. Accessed on 6 March 2025.
5. ——'Bhagavad Gita: Chapter 18, Verse 42'——
6. ——'Bhagavad Gita: Chapter 18, Verse 43'——
7. ——'Bhagavad Gita: Chapter 18, Verse 44'——
8. Ibid.
9. ——'Bhagavad Gita: Chapter 18, Verse 45,'——
10. ——'Bhagavad Gita: Chapter 18, Verse 46'——
11. ——'Bhagavad Gita: Chapter 9, Verse 32'——
12. Mookerji, Radha Kumud, 'Chapter 11: Industrial and Vocational Education', *Ancient Indian Education: Brahmanical and Buddhist*, Motilal Banarsidass, Delhi, 2011, pp. 345–346.
13. Adi Shankara's commentary on Brahma Sutras (34–38): Refuses the right of practicing Vedas by Shudras, but his *Manisa Pancakam* salutes a Chandala: 'chandalo astu sa tu dvijostu...' ('May he be a Brahman or a Profaner, salute him [who has right knowledge about the Absolute...]'); *Valmiki Ramayana*, 'Aranya Kanda', https://tinyurl.com/4n35mket. Accessed on 6 March 2025.
14. Sharma, Jankinath (trans.), 'Bala Kanda, Canto 9, Verse 1', *Srimad Valmiki-Ramayana (with Sanskrit Text and Translation into English): Part-I, Revised Edition*, Gita Press, Gorakhpur, 2022, p. 91.
15. ——'Bal Kanda, Canto 6, Verses 15–17', p. 84.
16. Sharma, Jankinath (trans.), 'Ayodhya Kanda, Canto 50, Verses 33–50', *Srimad Valmiki-Ramayana (with Sanskrit Text and Translation into English): Part-I, Revised Edition*, Gita Press, Gorakhpur, 2022, pp. 476–480; Also, 'Chapters 51–52', pp. 478–480, and 'Chapters 84–87', pp. 593–603.

17. Sharma, Jankinath (trans.), 'Bala Kanda, Canto 51, Verses 17–20', *Srimad Valmiki-Ramayana (with Sanskrit Text and Translation into English): Part-I, Revised Edition*, Gita Press, Gorakhpur, 2022, pp. 212–213.
18. Shastri, J.L. and G.B. Bhatt (eds.), 'Nagar Khanda: Chapter 124, Creation of Mukhara Tirtha', *The Skanda Purana: Part XVII*, Motilal Banarsidass, Delhi, 1958, pp. 506–513.
19. Sharma, Jankinath (trans.), 'Aranyaka Kanda, Chapter 74, Verses 1–35 ', *Srimad Valmiki-Ramayana (with Sanskrit Text and Translation into English): Part-I, Revised Edition*, Gita Press, Gorakhpur, 2022, pp. 923–926.
20. Sharma, Jankinath (trans.), 'Bal Kanda, Canto 13, Verses 13–15', *Srimad Valmiki-Ramayana (with Sanskrit Text and Translation into English): Part-I, Revised Edition*, Gita Press, Gorakhpur, 2022, p. 102.
21. ——'Bal Kanda, Canto 13, Verses 13–16', p. 102.
22. Sharma, Jankinath (trans.), 'Uttar Kanda, Canto 9, Verses 1–33', *Srimad Valmiki-Ramayana (with Sanskrit Text and Translation into English): Part-II, Revised Edition*, Gita Press, Gorakhpur, 2022, pp. 872–874.
23. Shastri Pandey, Pt. Ramnarayandutt (trans.), 'Lokpalsabhakyan Parva, Chapter 5, Verse 18', *Mahabharata (Volume I): Adi Parva and Sabha Parva*, Gita Press, Gorakhpur, 2016, p. 1631.
24. Shastri Pandey, Pt. Ramnarayandutt (trans.), 'Dyuta Parva, Chapters 50–56', *Mahabharata (Volume I): Adi Parva and Sabha Parva*, Gita Press, Gorakhpur, 2016, pp. 2048–2085.
25. Shastri Pandey, Pt. Ramnarayandutt (trans.), 'Anudyuta Parva, Chapter 81, Verses 1–39', *Mahabharata (Volume I): Adi Parva and Sabha Parva*, Gita Press, Gorakhpur, 2016, pp. 2247–2252.
26. Shastri Pandey, Pt. Ramnarayandutt (trans.), 'Sambhav Parva, Chapter 114, Verse 1', *Mahabharata (Volume I): Adi Parva and Sabha Parva*, Gita Press, Gorakhpur, 2016, p. 826.
27. ——'Sambhav Parva, Chapter 100, Verses 48–54', *Mahabharata (Volume I): Adi Parva and Sabha Parva*, Gita Press, Gorakhpur, 2016, pp. 743–744.
28. ——'Sambhav Parva, Chapter 104, Verses 12–14', *Mahabharata (Volume I): Adi Parva and Sabha Parva*, Gita Press, Gorakhpur, 2016, p. 777.
29. Sadhu Bhadredas, 'The Chāndogya Upanishad Simple Conversations on Highly Spiritual Matters (Part 4)', *BAPS Swaminarayan Sanstha*, https://tinyurl.com/yyaexzad. Accessed on 6 March 2025.

Chapter 22: Does Science Have Its Origins In Sanatan?

1. Prasad, Rama, 'Chapter II: Evolution', *Nature's Finer Forces*, The Theosophical Publishing Society, London, 1907, p. 13

2. Nolte, David D., 'A Short History of Multiple Dimensions', *Galileo Unbound*, 8 March 2023. https://tinyurl.com/2pbx6fkr. Accessed on 6 March 2025.
3. Petersen, W., 'How Formal Concept Lattices Solve a Problem of Ancient Linguistics', *Conceptual Structures: Common Semantics for Sharing Knowledge*, F. Dau, M.L. Mugnier and G. Stumme (eds.), *Lecture Notes in Computer Science*, Vol. 3596, Springer, 2005, pp. 292–305.
4. Petersen, W., 'A Mathematical Analysis of Pāṇini's Śivasūtras', *Journal of Logic, Language and Information*, Vol. 13, 2004, pp. 471–489.
5. Bloomfield, Leonard, 'Chapter 10: The Study of Language', *An Introduction to the Study of Language*, Henry Holt and Company, New York, 1914, pp. 307–319; Also, Project Shivoham, 'The Untold Story of Sanskrit: A Film on Research about Sanskrit and Computing', *YouTube*, 11 March 2021, https://tinyurl.com/4k5d4u3z. Accessed on 6 March 2025.
6. Project Shivoham, 'The Real Story of Sanskrit and Computing', *YouTube*, 31 May 2021, https://tinyurl.com/bdze8xch. Accessed on 6 March 2025.
7. Ibid.
8. Ibid.
9. Project Shivoham, 'The Untold Story of Sanskrit: A Film on Research about Sanskrit and Computing', 11 March 2021, *YouTube*, https://tinyurl.com/4k5d4u3z. Accessed on 6 March 2025.
10. Fibonacci, 'Introduction', *Fibonacci's Liber Abaci: A Translation into Modern English of Leonardo Pisano's Book of Calculation*, Sigler, L.E. (trans.), Springer, New York, 2002, p. 4.
11. Project Shivoham, 'The Untold Story of Sanskrit: A Film on Research about Sanskrit and Computing', 11 March 2021, *YouTube*, https://tinyurl.com/4k5d4u3z. Accessed on 6 March 2025.
12. Ibid.
13. Project Shivoham, 'The Vedic Biology on Pregnancy, Garbha Upanishad', *YouTube*, 5 January 2022, https://tinyurl.com/mswap8ad. Accessed on 6 March 2025; Deussen, Paul, 'Garbha Upanishad', *Sixty Upanishads of the Veda: Volume II*, V.M. Bedekar and G.B. Palsule (trans.), Motilal Banarsidass, Delhi, 1997, pp. 639–640.
14. Lipton, Bruce H., 'Introduction', *The Biology of Belief, Unleashing the Power of Consciousness, Matter and Miracles*, Elite Books, Santa Rosa, CA, 2005, p. 27.
15. Yogi Paramhansa, 'Chapter 35: The Christlike Life of Lahiri Mahasaya', *Autobiography of a Yogi*, Jaico, Bombay, 1958, p. 329; Srinivasan, Dr Amrutur V., 'Chapter 19: The Six Schools of Thought: The Darshanas', *Hinduism for Dummies*, Wiley Publishing, Inc. Hooken, NJ, 2011, pp. 298–299; Project Sivoham, 'The Atomic Theory in Ancient India; A Film on Vaiseshika

Sutras', *YouTube*, 27 August 2021, https://tinyurl.com/sztjapxw. Accessed on 6 March 2025.
16. Project Shivoham, 'The Untold Story of Ayurvedam: Part I', *YouTube*, 16 April 2021, https://tinyurl.com/4eemy4ff. Accessed on 6 March 2025.
17. Sathya Sai, 'Chapter VIII', *Spirituality and Science: The Turn of the Tide in Scientific Thought, Revised Second Edition*, Sathya Sai Publications, Puttaparthi, 1995, pp. 84–85.
18. Ibid., pp. 42–43.
19. Project Shivoham, 'Dhanurvedam: A Documentary on Ancient Indian Warfare', *YouTube*, 1 January 2021, https://tinyurl.com/5n7zef44. Accessed on 6 March 2025; Also, *Spirituality and Science*, p. 155.
20. 'O.A. Vijayan, the eminent Indian journalist has reflected in *The Illustrated Weekly of India*, that the Soviet scholar Dr A.A. Gorbovsky said in his article with heading *Ancient India may have had N-arms*, in *The Statesman*, with dateline Moscow, Sept. 8, 1986.' *Valmiki Ramayana*, 'Book I: Bala Kanda— The Youth', https://tinyurl.com/bdhyyms9. Accessed on 6 March 2025.
21. *Indian Vedas*, 'Darshan Shastras: An Introduction', https://tinyurl.com/mr2kn4u4. Accessed on 6 March 2025; *Spirituality and Science*, p. 45.
22. Srinivasan, *Hinduism for Dummies*, pp. 294–297.
23. Sastry, Subbaraya 'First Chapter', *Maharishi Bharadwaja's Vyamaanika Shastra or Science of Aeronautics*, G.R. Joyser (trans.), Coronation Press, Mysore, 1973, pp. 2–4.
24. Shastri Pandey, Pt. Ramnarayandutt (trans.), 'Swayamvar Parva, Chapter 186, Verse 6', *Mahabharata (Volume I): Adi Parva and Sabha Parva*, Gita Press, Gorakhpur, 2016, pp. 1304.
25. Sharma, Jankinath (trans.), 'Yuddha Kanda, Canto 117, Verses 1–4', *Srimad Valmiki-Ramayana (with Sanskrit Text and Translation into English): Part-I, Revised Edition*, Gita Press, Gorakhpur, 2022, p. 794.
26. Subramaniam, Kamala (trans.), 'Chapter 252: Bhakti–A Definition', *Srimad Bhagavatam*, Bharatiya Vidya Bhavan, Mumbai, 2017, pp. 330–333.
27. *History TV*, 'Ancient Aliens: Vimana Model Aircraft Experiment, Season 12, Episode 11', *YouTube*, 5 October 2018, https://tinyurl.com/4whyehy9. Accessed on 6 March 2025.
28. The Epic Channel, 'Sage Bharadwaja - Vimana Shastra', *YouTube*, 8 December 2022, https://tinyurl.com/5fdhxnj5. Accessed on 6 March 2025.
29. Johnson, Mary Ann, 'On the Aviation Trail in the Wright Brothers' West Side Neighborhood in Dayton, Ohio', *Following in the Footsteps of the Wright Brothers: Their Sites and Stories*, Wright State University, 28 September 2001, Paper 3, https://tinyurl.com/3znpz5nv. Accessed on 6 March 2025.
30. Project Shivoham, 'The Ancient Knowledge of Vruksha Ayurvedam',

YouTube, 9 October 2021, https://tinyurl.com/dewkt4ky. Accessed on 6 March 2025; Srikanth, Narayanam, Devesh Tewari, and Anupam Mangal, 'The Science of Plant Life (Vriksha Ayurveda) in Archaic Literature: An Insight on Botanical, Agricultural, and Horticultural Aspects of Ancient India', *World Journal of Pharmacy and Pharmaceutical Sciences*, Vol. 4, 2015, pp. 388–404.

31. Pennisi, Elizabeth, 'Plants Communicate Distress Using their own Kind of Nervous System', *Science.org*, 13 September, 2018, https://tinyurl.com/6tnx5jb2. Accessed on 6 March 2025.
32. Srikanth, Narayanam, Devesh Tewari, and Anupam Mangal, 'The Science of Plant Life (Vriksha Ayurveda) in Archaic Literature: An Insight on Botanical, Agricultural, and Horticultural Aspects of Ancient India', *World Journal of Pharmacy and Pharmaceutical Sciences*, Vol. 4, 2015, pp. 388–404.
33. Sathya Sai, *Spirituality and Science: The Turn of the Tide in Scientific Thought*, Revised Second Edition, Sathya Sai Publications, Puttaparthi, 1995, p. 56.
34. Ibid., pp. 137–38.
35. Joshi, Pt. Mahadevshastri (ed.), *Bharatiya Sanskritik Kosha (Volume 11)*, p. 179.
36. Swami Mukundananda, 'Bhagavad Gita: Chapter 10, Verse 7', Bhagavad Gita: The Song of God, https://tinyurl.com/39u2khwc. Accessed on 6 March 2025.
37. Sathya Sai, *Spirituality and Science: The Turn of the Tide in Scientific Thought*, Revised Second Edition, Sathya Sai Publications, Puttaparthi, 1995, p. 58.
38. Ibid.
39. Ibid.
40. Ibid., p. 62.
41. Ibid., p. 63.
42. Yogi Paramhansa, 'Chapter 8: India's Greatest Scientist, Sir J.C. Bose', *Autobiography of a Yogi*, Jaico, Bombay, 1958, pp. 66–67.
43. Sathya Sai, *Spirituality and Science: The Turn of the Tide in Scientific Thought*, Revised Second Edition, Sathya Sai Publications, Puttaparthi, 1995, p. 68.
44. 'Aum Ityetaaksharam Brahma: Aksharam Paramo Naadaha. Shabda Bramheti Kathyate – Yogashikha Upanishad.' Ibid., p. 64.
45. Ibid., p. 82.
46. Swami Mukundananda, 'Bhagavad Gita: Chapter 11, Verse 11', *Bhagavad Gita: The Song of God*, https://tinyurl.com/2k6xtzkf. Accessed on 6 March 2025.
47. Sathya Sai, *Spirituality and Science: The Turn of the Tide in Scientific Thought*, Revised Second Edition, Sathya Sai Publications, Puttaparthi, 1995, p. 82.
48. Ibid., p. 58.

49. Capra, Fritjof, *The New Vision of Reality: A Synthesis of Eastern Wisdom and Western Science*, Bhartiya Vidya Bhawan, Mumbai, 1983, pp. 139-140.
50. Coomaraswamy, Ananda, 'The Dance of Shiva', *The Dance of Shiva: Fourteen Essays*, The Sunwise Turn Inc., New York, 1918, p. 66.
51. Sai, Sathya, *Spirituality and Science: The Turn of the Tide in Scientific Thought*, Revised Second Edition, Sathya Sai Publications, Puttaparthi, 1995, pp. 62-63
52. Sacred Texts, 'Introduction to Baudhayana', https://tinyurl.com/mr2prezp. Accessed on 6 March 2025.
53. WION, 'Gravitas Plus: 75 Years Since Independence, Time for India to Reclaim its Heritage', *YouTube*, 29 January 2022, https://tinyurl.com/4u2f3jcy. Accessed on 6 March 2025; Agarrwaal, Krishna Neha, *Magnificent Bharat*, 2021, ebook, p. 15.
54. Pandey, G.S., 'Divisions of Time and Measuring Instruments of Varaḥmihira', *Ancient Indian Leaps into Mathematics*, B. Yadav and M. Mohan (ed.), Birkhäuser, 2009, p. 80.
55. Hayashi, Takao, 'Brahmagupta', *Britannica*, https://tinyurl.com/bdm7974v. Accessed on 6 March 2025.
56. Editors (Encyclopaedia Britannica), 'Bhaskara II', *Britannica*, https://tinyurl.com/jz7rs9f3. Accessed on 6 March 2025.
57. Hayashi, Takao, 'Mahavira', *Britannica*, https://tinyurl.com/yvtzat4u. Accessed on 6 March 2025.
58. Editors (Encyclopaedia Britannica), 'Varahamira', *Britannica*, https://tinyurl.com/bdzzzz4x. Accessed on 6 March 2025.
59. Agarrwaal, Krishna Neha. *Magnificent Bharat*, 2021, ebook, p. 43.
60. Kansupada, K.B. and Joseph W. Sassani, 'Sushruta: The Father of Indian Surgery and Ophthalmology', *Documenta Ophthalmologica*, Vol. 93, 2007, pp. 159-167.
61. WION, 'Gravitas Plus: 75 Years Since Independence, Time for India to Reclaim its Heritage', *YouTube*, 29 January 2022, https://tinyurl.com/4u2f3jcy. Accessed on 6 March 2025.
62. Allahabadia, Ranveer, 'Indian Archaeologist Anica Mann On Ancient Indian History & Tantra', *YouTube*, https://tinyurl.com/2y8ftzt9. Accessed on 6 March 2025.
63. Robert Emerson, (November 4, 1903 - February 4, 1959) was an American scientist noted for his discovery that plants have two distinct photosynthetic reaction centres; Yogi Paramhansa, 'Chapter 8: India's Greatest Scientist, Sir J.C. Bose', *Autobiography of a Yogi*, Jaico, Bombay, 1958, p. 66.
64. Srikanth, Narayanam, Devesh Tewari, and Anupam Mangal, 'The Science of Plant Life (Vriksha Ayurveda) in Archaic Literature: An Insight on Botanical, Agricultural, and Horticultural Aspects of Ancient India,' *World*

Journal of Pharmacy and Pharmaceutical Sciences, Vol. 4, 2015, pp. 388–404.
65. Jain, Meenakshi, 'Chapter 3: Early British Appreciation of Indian Civilization', *Sati, Evangelicals, Baptist Missionaries and the Changing Colonial Discourse*, Aryan Books International, New Delhi, 2016, pp. 58–59.
66. Ibid., p. 51.
67. Ibid., p. 61.
68. Sathya Sai, *Spirituality and Science: The Turn of the Tide in Scientific Thought, Revised Second Edition*, Sathya Sai Publications, Puttaparthi, 1995, p. 21.
69. Yogi Paramhansa, 'Chapter 35: The Christlike Life of Lahiri Mahasaya', *Autobiography of a Yogi*, Jaico, Bombay, 1958, p. 330.

Chapter 23: What are Yagyas?

1. Roopak, M. Sai, *Veda Pushpanjali: Volume I*, Sri Sathya Sai Research Centre, Puttapurthi, 2003, pp. 78–83; Also, *Veda Pushpanjali: Volume II*, p. 18.
2. Swami Mukundananda, 'Bhagavad Gita: Chapter 10, Verse 35', *Bhagavad Gita: The Song of God*, https://tinyurl.com/mrxt2pja. Accessed on 6 March 2025.
3. All in 1, 'Scientific Study on Chanting Gayatri Mantra', *YouTube*, 29 February 2020, https://tinyurl.com/yxr43x2z. Accessed on 6 March 2025.
4. Acharya, Pt. Shriram Sharma, 'Gayatri Upanishad', *Super Science of Gayatri*, Satya Narayan Pandya (trans.), Yugantar Chetna Press, Haridwar, 2000, pp. 112–117.
5. Shastri Pandey, Pt. Ramnarayandutt, 'Arjunabhigaman Parva, Chapter 36, Verses 36–41', *Mahabharata (Volume II): Van Parva and Virat Parva*, Gita Press, Gorakhpur, 2016, pp. 281–282.
6. Swami Mukundananda, 'Bhagavad Gita: Chapter 4, Verse 24', *Bhagavad Gita: The Song of God*, https://tinyurl.com/2f76s9ef. Accessed on 6 March 2025.

Chapter 24: What Do Rituals in Sanatan Dharm Mean?

1. Swami Mukundananda, 'Bhagavad Gita: Chapter 9, Verse 26', *Bhagavad Gita: The Song of God*, https://tinyurl.com/3daufczp. Accessed on 6 March 2025.

Chapter 26: What Were Prosperity and Society Like in Ancient Bharat?

1. Sharma, Jankinath (trans.), 'Bala Kanda, Canto 5, Verse 5', *Srimad Valmiki-Ramayana (with Sanskrit Text and Translation into English): Part-I, Revised Edition*, Gita Press, Gorakhpur, 2022, p. 81.

2. ——'Bala Kanda, Canto 5, Verse 6', p. 81.
3. ——'Bala Kanda, Canto 5, Verse 7', p. 81.
4. ——'Bala Kanda, Canto 5, Verse 8', p. 81.
5. ——'Bala Kanda, Canto 5, Verse 10', p. 81.
6. ——'Bala Kanda, Canto 5, Verse 12', p. 81.
7. ——'Bala Kanda, Canto 5, Verse 13', p. 81.
8. ——'Bala Kanda, Canto 5, Verse 14', p. 81; Also, 'Canto 6, Verse 28', p. 85.
9. ——'Bala Kanda, Canto 5, Verse 15', pp. 81–82.
10. ——'Bala Kanda, Canto 5, Verse 16', p. 82.
11. ——'Bala Kanda, Canto 5, Verse 17', p. 82.
12. ——'Bala Kanda, Canto 5, Verse 18', p. 82.
13. ——'Bala Kanda, Canto 5, Verse 19', p. 82.
14. ——'Bala Kanda, Canto 5, Verse 20', p. 82.
15. ——'Bala Kanda, Canto 5, Verse 23', p. 82.
16. ——'Bala Kanda, Canto 6, Verse 9', p. 83.
17. ——'Bala Kanda, Canto 6, Verse 10', p. 83.
18. ——'Bala Kanda, Canto 6, Verse 11', p. 83.
19. ——'Bala Kanda, Canto 6, Verses 14–15', p. 84.
20. ——'Bala Kanda, Canto 6, Verse 16', p. 84.
21. ——'Bala Kanda, Canto 6, Verse 17', p. 84.
22. ——'Bala Kanda, Canto 6, Verse 25', p. 85.
23. ——'Bala Kanda, Canto 7, Verse 1', p. 85.
24. ——'Bala Kanda, Canto 7, Verse 2', pp. 85–86.
25. ——'Bala Kanda, Canto 7, Verse 4', p. 86.
26. ——'Bala Kanda, Canto 7, Verses 6–8', pp. 86.
27. ——'Bala Kanda, Canto 7, Verse 10', p. 86.
28. ——'Bala Kanda, Canto 7, Verse 17', p. 87.
29. ——'Bala Kanda, Canto 7, Verse 20', p. 87.
30. Sharma, Jankinath (trans.),'Ayodhya Kanda, Canto 16, Verse 25', *Srimad Valmiki-Ramayana (with Sanskrit Text and Translation into English): Part-I, Revised Edition*, Gita Press, Gorakhpur, 2022, p. 355.
31. ——'Ayodhya Kanda, Canto 16, Verses 27–28', p. 355.
32. ——'Ayodhya Kanda, Canto 16, Verses 29–30', p. 355.
33. ——'Ayodhya Kanda, Canto 16, Verse 34', p. 356.
34. ——'Ayodhya Kanda, Canto 16, Verse 35', p. 356.
35. ——'Ayodhya Kanda, Canto 16, Verse 36', p. 356.
36. ——'Ayodhya Kanda, Canto 16, Verse 44', p. 356.
37. ——'Ayodhya Kanda, Canto 16, Verse 46', p. 356.
38. ——'Ayodhya Kanda, Canto 16, Verse 47', p. 357.
39. ——'Ayodhya Kanda, Canto 17, Verse 5', pp. 357–358.

40. ——'Ayodhya Kanda, Canto 17, Verse 7', p. 358.
41. ——'Ayodhya Kanda, Canto 17, Verse 9', p. 358.
42. Sharma, Jankinath (trans.), 'Kishkinda Kanda, Canto 33, Verse 4', *Srimad Valmiki-Ramayana (with Sanskrit Text and Translation into English): Part-I, Revised Edition*, Gita Press, Gorakhpur, 2022, p. 1064.
43. Ibid.
44. ——'Kishkinda Kanda, Canto 33, Verse 5', p. 1064.
45. ——'Kishkinda Kanda, Canto 33, Verse 6', p. 1064.
46. ——'Kishkinda Kanda, Canto 33, Verse 7', p. 1064.
47. ——'Kishkinda Kanda, Canto 33, Verse 8', p. 1064.
48. ——'Kishkinda Kanda, Canto 33, Verses 9-12', p. 1064.

Chapter 27: Is God Serious and Punishing or Happy and Fun-Loving?

1. Sharma, Jankinath, 'Bala Kanda, Canto 18, Verses 18-19', *Srimad Valmiki-Ramayana (with Sanskrit Text and Translation into English): Part-I, Revised Edition*, Gita Press, Gorakhpur, 2022, p. 122.
2. Sathya Sai, *Spirituality and Science: The Turn of the Tide in Scientific Thought, Revised Second Edition*, Sathya Sai Publications, Puttaparthi, 1995, p. 70.
3. Ibid., p. 117.

Chapter 28: Why do Sanatanis Fast?

1. Swami Mukundananda, 'Bhagavad Gita: Chapter 15, Verse 14', *Bhagavad Gita: The Song of God*, https://tinyurl.com/bdd3w9zt. Accessed on 6 March 2025.

Chapter 35: Is Sanatan 'Itihas' History or Fantasy?

1. Td Tv, 'Sage Agastya mentioned about Dry Electric Battery in his Ancient Text', *YouTube*, 30 January 2017, https://tinyurl.com/mw5w3rxd. Accessed on 6 March 2025.
2. Sharma, Jankinath, 'Aranya Kanda, Cantos 11-13', *Srimad Valmiki-Ramayana (with Sanskrit Text and Translation into English): Part-I, Revised Edition*, pp. 741-747; Also 'Uttar Kanda, Cantos 1-36', pp. 845-974.
3. Shastri Pandey, Pt. Ramnarayandutt (trans.), 'Markandeyasamasya Parva, Chapters 182-232', *Mahabharata (Volume II): Van Parva and Virat Parva*, Gita Press, Gorakhpur, 2016, pp. 1230-1600.
4. Shastri Pandey, Pt. Ramnarayandutt (trans.), 'Teerthyatra Parva, Verses 1-40', *Mahabharata (Volume II): Van Parva and Virat Parva*, Gita Press, Gorakhpur, 2016, pp. 1014-1019.

5. Sharma, Jankinath (trans.), 'Uttar Kanda, Canto 53, Verses 20-22', *Srimad Valmiki-Ramayana (with Sanskrit Text and Translation into English): Part-II, Revised Edition*, Gita Press, Gorakhpur, 2022, p. 1016.
6. Shastri Pandey, Pt. Ramnarayandutt (trans.), 'Teerthyatra Parva, Chapter 146, Verse 65-66', *Mahabharata (Volume II): Van Parva and Virat Parva*, Gita Press, Gorakhpur, 2016, p. 999.
7. Shastri Pandey, Pt. Ramnarayandutt (trans.), 'Dyuta Parva, Chapters 51-53', *Mahabharata (Volume I): Adi Parva and Sabha Parva*, Gita Press, Gorakhpur, 2016, p. 2054-2073.

Chapter 38: Basic Concepts of Sanatan Dharm

1. Shastri Pandey, Pt. Ramnarayandutt (trans.), 'Teerthyatra Parva, Chapter 149', *Mahabharata (Volume II): Van Parva and Virat Parva*, Gita Press, Gorakhpur, 2016, pp. 1014-1019; Also, 'Chapter 150, Verses 10-39', pp. 1022-1026.
2. Ibid.

Bibliography

Texts

Bhavishya Purana, Gita Press, Gorakhpur, 2018,

Fibonacci, 'Introduction', *Fibonacci's Liber Abaci: A Translation into Modern English of Leonardo Pisano's Book of Calculation*, L.E. Sigler (trans.), Springer, New York, 2002.

Khemka, Radheyshyam (ed.), *Shiva Mahapurana: Part I*, Gita Press, Gorakhpur, 2019.

Sharma, Jankinath (trans.), *Srimad Valmiki-Ramayana (with Sanskrit Text and Translation into English): Part-I, Revised Edition*, Gita Press, Gorakhpur, 2022.

Sharma, Jankinath (trans.), *Srimad Valmiki-Ramayana (with Sanskrit Text and Translation into English): Part-II Revised Edition*, Gita Press, Gorakhpur, 2022.

Shastri Pandey, Pt. Ramnarayandutt (trans.), *Mahabharata (Volume I): Adi Parva and Sabha Parva*, Gita Press, Gorakhpur, 2016.

Shastri Pandey, Pt. Ramnarayandutt (trans.), *Mahabharata (Volume II): Van Parva and Virat Parva*, Gita Press, Gorakhpur, 2016.

Shastri Pandey, Pt. Ramnarayandutt (trans.), *Mahabharata (Volume III): Udyog Parva and Bheeshma Parva*, Gita Press, Gorakhpur, 2016.

Sastry, Subbaraya, *Maharishi Bharadwaja's Vyamaanika Shastra or Science of Aeronautics*, G.R. Joyser (trans.), Coronation Press, Mysore, 1973.

Subramaniam, Kamala (trans.), *Srimad Bhagavatam*, Bharatiya Vidya Bhavan, Mumbai, 2017.

Tulsidas, *Shri Ramcharitamanas: A Romanized Edition with English Translation*, Editorial Team (trans.), Gita Press, Gorakhpur, 2024.

Veda Vyasa, *Brahma-Vaivarta Purana*, Gita Press, Gorakhpur, 2018.

Yogi Madhavacharya (ed.), *Yoga Sutras of Patanjali*, Michael Beloved, Guyana, 2007.

Books

Acharya, Pt. Shriram Sharma, 'Gayatri Upanishad', *Super Science of Gayatri*, Satya Narayan Pandya (trans.), Yugantar Chetna Press, Haridwar, 2000.

Agarrwaal, Krishna Neha, *Magnificent Bharat*, 2021, ebook.

Bloomfield, Leonard, *An Introduction to the Study of Language*, Henry Holt and Company, New York, 1914.

Capra, Fritjof, *The New Vision of Reality: A Synthesis of Eastern Wisdom and Western Science*, Bhartiya Vidya Bhawan, Mumbai, 1983.

Cole, Owen W. and V.P. Kanitkar, *Hinduism: An Introduction*, Teach Yourself, London, 2010.

Coomaraswamy, Ananda, 'The Dance of Shiva', *The Dance of Shiva: Fourteen Essays*, The Sunwise Turn Inc., New York, 1918.

Deussen, Paul, *Sixty Upanishads of the Veda: Volume II*, V.M. Bedekar and G.B. Palsule (trans.), Motilal Banarsidass, Delhi, 1997.

Jain, Meenakshi, *Sati, Evangelicals, Baptist Missionaries and the Changing Colonial Discourse*, Aryan Books International, New Delhi, 2016.

Lipton, Bruce H., *The Biology of Belief, Unleashing the Power of Consciousness, Matter and Miracles*, Elite Books, Santa Rosa, CA, 2005.

Malhotra, Rajiv, *Varna, Jati, Caste: A Primer on Indian Social Structures*, Occam, Delhi, 2023.

Olivelle, Patrick, *Dharmasutras: The Law Codes of Ancient India*, Oxford University Press, Oxford, 1999.

Prasad, Rama, *Nature's Finer Forces*, The Theosophical Publishing Society, London, 1907.

Roopak, M. Sai, *Veda Pushpanjali*, Sri Sathya Sai Research Centre, Puttapurthi, 2003.

Sathya Sai, *Spirituality and Science: The Turn of the Tide in Scientific Thought*, Revised Second Edition, Sathya Sai Publications, Puttaparthi, 1995.

Sri Swami Sivananda, *Lord Shiva and His Worship*, Divine Life Society, Rishikesh, 2008.

Srinivasan, Dr. Amrutur V., *Hinduism for Dummies*, Wiley Publishing Inc., Hooken, NJ, 2011.

Yogi Paramhansa, *Autobiography of a Yogi*, Jaico, Bombay, 1958.

Journals

Johnson, Mary Ann. 'On the Aviation Trail in the Wright Brothers' West Side Neighborhood in Dayton, Ohio', *Following in the Footsteps of the Wright Brothers: Their Sites and Stories*, Wright State University, 28 September 2001, Paper 3, https://tinyurl.com/3znpz5nv.

Joshi, Pt. Mahadevshastri, *Bharatiya Sanskritik Kosha (Volume 11)*, Bharatiya Sanskriti Kosha Mandal, 1964.

Kansupada, K.B. and Joseph W. Sassani, 'Sushruta: The father of Indian surgery and ophthalmology', *Documenta Ophthalmologica*, Vol. 93, 2007, 159–167.

Pandey, G.S., 'Divisions of Time and Measuring Instruments of Varaḥmihira', *Ancient Indian Leaps into Mathematics*, B. Yadav and M. Mohan (eds.), Birkhäuser, 2009, p. 80.

Petersen, W., 'A Mathematical Analysis of Pāṇini's Śivasūtras'. *Journal of Logic, Language and Information*, Vol. 13, 2004, pp. 471–489.

Petersen, W., 'How Formal Concept Lattices Solve a Problem of Ancient Linguistics', *Conceptual Structures: Common Semantics for Sharing Knowledge*, F. Dau, M. L. Mugnier and G. Stumme (ed.), Vol. 3596, Springer, 2005, pp. 292–305.

Srikanth, Narayanam, Devesh Tewari and Anupam Mangal, 'The Science of Plant Life (Vriksha Ayurveda) in Archaic Literature: An Insight on Botanical, Agricultural, and Horticultural Aspects of Ancient India', *World Journal of Pharmacy and Pharmaceutical Sciences*, Vol. 4, 2015.

Online Resources

All in 1, 'Scientific Study on Chanting Gayatri Mantra', *YouTube*, 29 February 2020, https://tinyurl.com/yxr43x2z. Accessed on 6 March 2025.

Allahabadia, Ranveer, 'Indian Archaeologist Anica Mann On Ancient Indian History & Tantra' *YouTube*, https://tinyurl.com/2y8ftzt9. Accessed on 6 March 2025.

Britannica, 'Bhaskara II', https://tinyurl.com/jz7rs9f3. Accessed on 6 March 2025.

Britannica, 'Varahamira', https://tinyurl.com/bdzzzz4x. Accessed on 6 March 2025.

Centre for Indic Studies, 'Was Sati a Religious Obligation?', *YouTube*, 13 November 2019, https://tinyurl.com/bdwnf6cp. Accessed on 6 March 2025.

Hayashi, Takao, 'Brahmagupta', *Britannica*, https://tinyurl.com/bdm7974v. Accessed on 6 March 2025.

Hayashi, Takao, 'Mahavira', *Britannica*, https://tinyurl.com/yvtzat4u. Accessed on 6 March 2025.

History TV, 'Ancient Aliens: Vimana Model Aircraft Experiment, Season 12, Episode 11', *YouTube*, https://tinyurl.com/4whyehy9. Accessed on 6 March 2025.

Indian Vedas, 'Darshan Shastras: An Introduction', https://tinyurl.com/mr2kn4u4. Accessed on 6 March 2025.

Mahajan, Ishan, 'Do Hindus Really Have 33 Crore Gods?', *Medium*, 14 August 2022. https://tinyurl.com/432h5ctj. Accessed 6 March 2025.

Nolte, David D., 'A Short History of Multiple Dimensions', *Galileo Unbound*, 8 March 2023, https://tinyurl.com/2pbx6fkr. Accessed on 6 March 2025.

Pennisi, Elizabeth, 'Plants Communicate Distress Using their own Kind of Nervous System', *Science.org*, 13 September, 2018, https://tinyurl.com/6tnx5jb2. Accessed on 6 March 2025.

Project Shivoham, 'Dhanurvedam: A Documentary on Ancient Indian Warfare', *YouTube*, 1 January 2021, https://tinyurl.com/5n7zef44. Accessed on 6 March 2025.

Project Shivoham, 'The Ancient Knowledge of Vruksha Ayurvedam', *YouTube*, 9 October 2021, https://tinyurl.com/dewkt4ky. Accessed on 6 March 2025.

Project Shivoham, 'The Real Story of Sanskrit and Computing', *YouTube*, 31 May 2021, https://tinyurl.com/bdze8xch. Accessed on 6 March 2025.

Project Shivoham, 'The Untold Story of Ayurvedam: Part I', *YouTube*, 16 April 2021, https://tinyurl.com/4eemy4ff. Accessed on 6 March 2025.

Project Shivoham, 'The Untold Story of Sanskrit: A Film on Research about Sanskrit and Computing', *YouTube*, 11 March 2021, https://tinyurl.com/4k5d4u3z. Accessed on 6 March 2025.

Project Shivoham, 'The Vedic Biology on Pregnancy, Garbha Upanishad', *YouTube*, 5 January 2022, https://tinyurl.com/mswap8ad. Accessed on 6 March 2025.

Project Sivoham, 'The Atomic Theory in Ancient India; A Film on Vaiseshika Sutras', *YouTube*, 27 August 2021, https://tinyurl.com/sztjapxw. Accessed on 6 March 2025.

Sacred Texts, 'Introduction to Baudhayana', https://tinyurl.com/mr2prezp. Accessed on 6 March 2025.

Sadhu Bhadredas, 'The Chāndogya Upanishad Simple Conversations on Highly Spiritual Matters (Part 4)', *BAPS Swaminarayan Sanstha*, https://tinyurl.com/yyaexzad. Accessed on 6 March 2025.

Sri Mookambika Temple, https://tinyurl.com/2n7y6cnb. Accessed on 6 March 2025.

Swami Mukundananda, *Bhagavad Gita, The Song of God*, https://tinyurl.com/mtyyephj. Accessed 6 March 2025.

Td Tv, 'Sage Agastya Mentioned About Dry Electric Battery in His Ancient Text', *YouTube*, 30 January 2017, https://tinyurl.com/mw5w3rxd. Accessed on 6 March 2025.

The Epic Channel, 'Sage Bharadwaja - Vimana Shastra', *YouTube*, 8 December 2022, https://tinyurl.com/5fdhxnj5. Accessed on 6 March 2025.

Valmiki Ramayana, 'Aranya Kanda', https://tinyurl.com/4n35mket. Accessed on 6 March 2025.

Valmiki Ramayana, 'Book I: Bal Kanda—The Youth', https://tinyurl.com/bdhyyms9. Accessed on 6 March 2025.

WION, 'Gravitas Plus: 75 Years Since Independence, Time for India to Reclaim its Heritage', *YouTube*, 29 January 2022, https://tinyurl.com/4u2f3jcy. Accessed on 6 March 2025.